THE FUTURE THAT WORKS

BABU
THE FUTURE THAT WORKS

SELECTED WRITINGS OF
A. M. BABU

EDITED BY
SALMA BABU AND AMRIT WILSON

Africa World Press, Inc.

P.O. Box 1892
Trenton, NJ 08607

P.O. Box 48
Asmara, ERITREA

Africa World Press, Inc.

P.O. Box 1892
Trenton, NJ 08607

P.O. Box 48
Asmara, ERITREA

Copyright: © 2002 Salma Babu & Amrit Wilson

First Printing 2002

All rights reserved. No part of this publication may be reproduced, stored in a retrieval system or transmitted in any form or by any means electronic, mechanical, photocopying, recording or otherwise without the prior written permission of the publisher.

Book Design: Jonathan Gullery
Cover Design: Debbie Hird and Ashraful Haque

Library of Congress Cataloging-in-Publication Data

Babu, Abdul Rahman Mohamed.
   The future that works : selected writings of A.M. Babu / edited by Salma Babu and Amrit Wilson.
     p. cm.
   Includes bibliographical references and index.
   ISBN 0-86543-833-1 – ISBN 0-86543-834-X (pbk.)
     1.Tanzania–Politics and government–1964- 2.Tanzania–Economic conditions–1964- 3. Tanzania–Social conditions–1964- I. Babu, Salma. II. Wilson, Amrit, 1941- III. Title.

DT448.2 .B33 2000
967.804–dc21   00-033218

CONTENTS

Acknowledgements

Introduction

1. ECONOMIC POLICIES AND DEVELOPMENT

Postscript to 'How Europe
Underdeveloped Africa' 1971. 3
Open letter to Mugabe, 1980. 10
The Tanzania that might have been 198. 16
Bleak, bleak future for Africa, 1984. 24
From China with lessons for Africa, 1984. 29
The masses are hungry, 1985. 35
Counter Punch, 1985. 40
Basic Needs Approach –
arguing for the sake of argument, 1988. 46
Aid perpetuates dependency, 1994. 51

2. PANAFRICANISM

Speech delivered at 4th
PAFMECA conference, 1958. 59
Patrice Lumumba, 1987. 63
Regional co-operation in Africa, 1987. 67
The visionary Neto, 1988. 73
Challenges ahead for the
new Secretary General of the OAU, 1989. 78
Speech delivered at the
International Conference on Malcolm X, 1990. 84
The OAU – help or hindrance? 1993. 89
Pan Africanism and the New World Order, 1994. 94
Visions of Africa, 1995. 100
A hopeful dawn of
post-colonial initiatives, 1996. 105

3. IMPERIALISM: STRATEGIES OF CONTROL, STRATEGIES OF RESISTANCE

a) Internationalism

Twenty years after the
non-aligned movement, 1981................... 115
Cancun: A postmortem, 1981................... 119
Non-Alignment in the
post-Gulf War era, 1991...................... 123
Third World concern
about 'humanitarian' interventions, 1993.......... 135

b) Africa and the World

After the OAU summit, 1981..................... 138
Crowning of Emperor Mitterand, 1982............ 141
A dialogue between Dr Banda
and Mr de Klerk, 1982....................... 144
Portugal's new empire, 1984.................... 148
The struggle for Africa's mind, 1984.............. 154
Israel's diplomatic offensive 1986................ 159
China and Africa: can we
learn from each other? 1987................... 166
Cultural subversion through education, 1988....... 175
Soviet policy to Africa after Perestroika, 1993....... 179
Gromyko: Political Commisar to President, 1995..... 191

4. DEMOCRACY

Obscenities of Preventive Detention, 1980......... 199
Giving the left a bad name, 1983................ 208
Leader knows best, 1985....................... 215
Uganda's lesson in democracy, 1986.............. 219
The right to demand freedoms, 1992............. 224

The Future that Works vii

5. NATIONAL LIBERATION IN THE ERA OF NEO-COLONIALISM

Eritrea: its present is the remote future
of others, 1985. 231
The future that works, 1985. 239
The shadow of Iran- Apartheid power in the
Black townships, 1985. 243
Who are the good guys in Rwanda? 1994. 246
South Africa—do the fundamentals
remain the same? 1995. 249

6. MARXIST THEORY

Introduction to 'Dar es Salaam Debates on Class,
State & Imperialism', 1982. 255
Letter to Karim Essack, 1982. 276
Ideologies and the Third World—
a response to Ali Mazrui, 1986. 284
A tragedy for socialism, 1995. 291

7. THE AFRICA WE NEED

The New World Disorder -
which way Africa? 1996. 301

8. Key dates in Babu's life 344

9. Sources 346

10. Index 347

ACKNOWLEDGEMENTS

Work on this volume could not have begun, much less been completed, without the help, encouragement, critical advice and support of a number of people. Some of them are Miriam Mohamed, Wangui Wa Goro, Ashura Elmi Duale, our friends at the Eritrean Embassy in London, dee dee Glass, Shaaban Salim, John Fernandes, and Diana Mukuma
 We are grateful to Patrick Wilmott, Sandy Close, Hashil S. Hashil and Hemed Hilal for help in locating Babu's magazine articles; the University of Luton for giving Amrit the time to complete the editing of this book and Kate Duffy for typing parts of the manuscript. We would also like to thank the journals and magazines, some of which sadly have ceased publication, in which Babu's writings appeared - African Concord, Africa Contemporary Record, Africa Events, Africa Now, Africa World Review, East Africa and the Horn, Inqilab, New African, Pacific News Service, Red Pepper, South, Southern Africa Political and Economic Monthly and Third World Book Review.
 We must acknowledge the support of Tarik Babu, Omar Babu and Mohamed Babu who gave us permission to reproduce Babu's writings the copyright for which they hold jointly with Salma.
 Our thanks are also due to our ever-patient publisher Kassahun Checole who stuck with us through all the ups and downs of this project.
 Finally we would like to thank David K.Boadu and Kalpana Wilson for being there for us when we needed them most

THE FUTURE THAT WORKS: AN INTRODUCTION

"I hope you'll make good use of this experience" - this was the inscription which Abdul Rahman Babu wrote when he gave a copy of his book 'African Socialism or Socialist Africa'[1] to a young friend some years ago, and if he had been alive today, no doubt the same thought would have occurred to him about this collection of his writings. Babu was a politician, scholar and writer but above all he was a revolutionary who for nearly forty years was always at the frontline of the struggle against oppression, always seeking to create a progressive politics of the future and living his life through it all with undiminished intensity.

Selecting and editing the creative output of such a life has been daunting, but these writings themselves have continually urged us on with their clarity, and the broad horizons of their optimism; and the many activists and scholars who are eager to see Babu's work in print again have given us encouragement and support. We have been strengthened too by our knowledge that Babu would have wanted this - from time to time he had selected small groups of articles but with typical modesty and the pressure of more urgent work, had not taken them any further towards publication.

Here, we have tried to select those writings which most clearly highlight Babu's ideas. We have included not only his essays and articles, but a few speeches, occasional lecture notes, a letter, one or two satirical articles and chapters from, and introductions to, books - some of which like 'How Europe Underdeveloped Africa'[2] are now classics[3].

This volume of his writings is in six sections, but this is largely in the interests of conventional structure. In fact, much of Babu's work defies categories. What appears under Pan-Africanism is also Marxist; what is under economic policy is also about national liberation; what is about democracy is also about imperialism and this is because in almost everything he wrote there is an underlying dialectic between theoretical analysis and active engagement. Analysis was not for just its own sake but to find a way forward.

For Babu historical materialism was a primary analytical tool. He discusses it at some length in his introduction to the Dar es Salaam debates explaining it with his usual lucidity. In his postscript to 'How Europe Underdeveloped Africa' he again argues for this approach, writing in a characteristic vigorous and down to earth style:

"If by looking into the past we have known the present, to know the future we must look into the past and the present. Our action must be related to our concrete experience and we must not give way to metaphysical hopes and wishes, hoping and wishing that the monster who has been after us throughout our history will some day change into a lamb. He won't."

The aspect of the past to which Babu traced most of Africa's problems was colonialism, particularly the economic and political structures inherited from colonialism. These structures were put in place for the benefit of metropolitan capital and were held in place by repressive laws and policies. Having identified this, the point of course was to change it. In 1967 as Minister of Planning in the Tanzanian government, Babu wrote a series of articles in the country's main daily paper, 'The Nationalist'. Titled 'The Meaning of Self Reliance', and written not under his name but simply as Pressman's Commentary, these seminal essays, which we include in Vol. 2, laid out clearly and succinctly details of the policies needed to transform Tanzania from a country with a colonial economic and political structure, geared to meet the needs of foreign capital, to a country which would meet the needs of its own people.

He was never to implement his plans. His approach brought him into sharp contradiction with President Nyerere's policies of so-called 'African Socialism' which focussed on 'welfarism' neglecting the crucial task of restructuring the colonial economy. In 1972, Babu along with other comrades from the Umma Party of Zanzibar (see below) were arrested on false charges of murdering President Karume of Zanzibar. Though never convicted, Babu remained in prison in Tanzania until 1978, when he was released after an international campaign. Tanzania never followed the policies he had formulated.

However, those early articles formed a core of Babu's thinking on how a country which had experienced colonialism could throw off its shackles. As he wrote in 'The Tanzania That Might Have Been' p 14:

The colonial state... "was not intended to develop the people but to undermine their self-respect so as to make it easier to rule them. ...to transform the state into a real people's state the one we had inherited had to be "smashed" as a first priority. The second priority was to do away with the colonial economy and in its place develop an independent national economy whose first prerequisite was to provide for the basic needs of the people, namely, food, clothing and shelter, and to continually raise their standards.... What all this means in practice is a serious restructuring of the state and economy based on a correct appraisal of the concrete situation in the country."

Babu expanded on this in later writings. Whether in his newspaper articles in Tanzania, his essays in African magazines, or later in authoritative chapters in books, he never shied away from providing a blueprint in simple accessible language for us all to read and understand.

For Babu socialism was first and foremost about transforming the lives of the people and at the heart of that change was production, because this was where neo-colonial exploitation was based -as he wrote in the Introduction to the Dar es Salaam Debates:

"exploitation takes place only at the level of production where new value is created. In our case the developed capitalist countries exploit the surplus value created by the workers in mines, industries, as well as by agricultural workers, ...in much the same way as they exploit "their" workers at home. The cheap labour in neocolonies helps to create a colossal return to the capital so invested. For instance, in developed capitalist countries the average return to capital is about 5% while in our countries it ranges from 40%, to 200% as in gold mining and petroleum. Thus the huge transfer of wealth from the neocolonies to the metropolitan countries takes place through the exploitation of our workers and the looting of our peasants.... exploitation does not take place at the point of exchange because at this level no new value is created - it is only transferred from one party to another. It can take the form of legalized looting or plunder which we call "trade". There can never be equal or unequal exchange between commodities of the subjugator and the subjugated"

In this situation even welfare programmes which in any case the state can ill-afford and which therefore have to be shored up with foreign aid must be seen as merely palliatives; and negotiations with international agencies and representatives of global capital from a position of weakness are also futile. Instead, Babu argued, forcefully and always with an underlying optimism, that Africa must focus on internal causes which are the basis of change, because:

"an economy must have internal material basis for it to develop and then, and only then, can external causes create conditions for such development. ...like an egg, it must have an internal basis before the incubator can turn it into a chicken. No amount of external conditions can transform a stone into a chicken. But we do the opposite. We say once the external conditions are right - for example, the New International Economic Order - then our development will follow irrespective of the internal basis. It is this topsy-turvy way of looking at things that we must combat if we are to utilise our resources to our maximum advantage. No amount of UN resolutions can achieve that for us. The solution is within our own reach."

While discussing this internal basis - the material reality of Africa - he argued that the contradiction between the need to develop productive forces on the one hand, and class struggle on the other, must be clearly understood. In his Open Letter to Prime Minister Mugabe, see p 8 written at the time of Zimbabwe's independence, he urged him to

regard the development of productive forces as top priority, even over that of the relations of production:
"In Maoist terms, development of productive forces in this case becomes the principal aspect of the contradiction with production relations a secondary one..... It cannot be over emphasised that people are our most precious capital and, therefore, they must eat well, be housed and clothed well."
At the same time he emphasised the need for a proportional development of the economy following Mao's Ten Relationships [4] maintaining a balance between heavy industry on the one hand, and light industry and agriculture on the other.

The Chinese revolution was for Babu both an inspiration as well as a subject of intense lifelong critical study. From every visit to China he gained new perspectives and drew new lessons.

His first visit in 1959 was quite early in his political life - only three years after he had returned home to Zanzibar from his studies in London. Zanzibar was then still a British colony but the anti-colonial struggle was gathering momentum. Babu, an enormously popular young leader, was working to reorganise the Zanzibar Nationalist Party, ZNP, building it into the first mass party in Zanzibar. He was thrilled to accept the official invitation to visit China.[5] As he was to write many years later:

"It was an opportunity for me to see this great country and meet its revered leaders..an opportunity for me to deepen my knowledge of the Chinese revolution, especially its theoretical and practical foundations. The meetings with the Chinese leadership and the late night discussions with them on all questions of anti-imperialist struggle were most inspiring and helped to mould my world outlook. I was probably the first anti-colonial fighter from East and Central Africa to have been accorded this opportunity".[6]

The late fifties was also the time when the movement for Pan African Unity was gathering force all over Africa.. Babu joined in it with enthusiasm and energy. Nkrumah's victory in Ghana in 1956 had affected him deeply: "coming as it did", he wrote "after the Chinese Revolution, the Viet Minh victory against the French at Dien Bien Phu and the Algerian Revolution, Nkrumah's victory re-invigorated Africa's liberation struggle... it introduced us in a concrete way to the importance and effectiveness of the 'mass political party' against colonialism".[7]

As a delegate of the Pan African Movement for East and Central Africa he attended the historic All African People's Conference at Accra in December 1958. On the way to Accra the delegation stopped over in Leopoldville (now Kinshasha). In this city overshadowed by Belgian colonialism they had a remarkable chance encounter. They met Patrice Lumumba who till then, because of the machinations of the Belgians, had been completely isolated from all Pan African movements and alliances. In his article on Lumumba, (p 59) Babu tells the story of that meeting and its historic consequences.

In 1962 Zanzibar became nominally independent under a right-wing coalition government still controlled by the British. Repression against trade unionists, youth leaders and other progressive elements intensified. The ZNP meanwhile had polarised into a right- and left-wing. By 1963 it was clear that the left could no longer play an effective role within the party and under the leadership of Babu, a mass revolutionary party, the Umma (People's) Party, was launched, galvanising working class and peasant youth across racial groupings into action.

The Zanzibar Revolution took place in 1964. Essentially it was an uprising led by a number of political forces which the Umma Party was able to partially transform into a revolutionary insurrection. For the U.S., Zanzibar was now the 'Cuba of Africa' from which communism would spread across the continent, and there followed a period of intense CIA activity. Only four months after the Revolution, the U.S. succeeded in engineering a union between Tanganyika and Zanzibar (to form Tanzania) which effectively crushed the progressive potential of the revolution and 'neutralised' Zanzibar.[8]

Babu was offered a post in the Tanzanian cabinet[9] and between 1964 and 1972, he headed various ministries notably Planning and Trade. This was the phase in which he negotiated the construction by China of the historic Tanzania/Zambia Railways (TAZARA)[10].

In China and Africa can we learn from each other, p.. he writes about this project describing the attitude of the Chinese workers on the one hand and the attitude of the Tanzanian authorities on the other. He also discusses briefly an underlying theme which illuminated much of his politics- the relationship between nationalism and socialism:
"China's socialist revolution was an extension of its own national liberation struggle and consequently there was a very thin dividing line between her nationalism and socialism. This dual loyalty to the two great movements of the period enabled the Chinese to share more intimately the sentiments and aspirations of Africa's liberation struggles and the struggle for national reconstruction, both of which were Africa's top priority."

Babu stood at the intersection of these two great movements - nationalism and socialism, which he saw as aspects of each other. Because for any country which had been a colony, reconstructing its economy, becoming self-reliant economic nationalism, in other words, would in itself pose a challenge to the forces of imperialist dominance; and at the same time be a central strategy of a socialist struggle[11]. This was true in the colonial and immediately post-colonial eras and is even more the case in the contemporary phase of globalisation of capital.

In the years following his release from prison, when he was living and teaching in the US, Babu wrote a number of articles about democracy. They appeared mainly in the New African magazine for which he was a correspondent. Their focus was human rights. "Unlimited power in the hands of the State" he commented, thinking perhaps of his own experience at the hands of the Tanzanian state, "which cannot be subjected to people's supervision and intrusion, inexorably leads to repression irrespective of the will of the holders who wield such powers" (The Obscenity of Preventive Detention p 189).

In Leader Knows Best, p 205 he discussed the repressive state apparatus common in so many African countries:

"there is the government of the "Presidential Palace" or the "State House", the all powerful state functionaries close to the top person in power, who can and do dictate orders with presidential authority. They are usually a clique of people renowned for their fierce loyalty because they have no other qualification or political history to be where they are".

However, he soon began a deeper analysis of democracy and the liberal state - one which he was to develop in the years ahead providing us with a way of understanding the ideologies which have arrived in the current phase of globalisation . "Democracy" he wrote "is about freedom but not unconditional freedom. It recognises the necessity to safeguard the security of the nation and the state; to safeguard public order, the rights of citizens and public morals but such restrictions are only allowed within limits"[12]. In 1992, he discussed this further, "the model of western democracy, in the form of universal franchise came long after the liberal state had been firmly established. Only on demand from the people...Such a democracy therefore had to accommodate itself to the cultural ground of an already established competitive market society and to the operation of the already established liberal state...the liberal state was democratised and democracy was liberalised".[13] He demystified the term in its present political context. "It is the lack of democracy which has enabled Africa's elites to accumulate millions of dollars in personal wealth by exploiting people and appropriate their national wealth in conjunction with the IMF, the World Bank and international money lenders...[Africa] must not confuse democracy and the free market. Democracy does not necessary mean a free market economy...All of Latin America, except Cuba, is operating on the basis of a free-market economy, but is far from being democratic. Nor is a planned economy necessarily a negation of democracy[14]."

For Babu, the people were the motive force which would transform society; victory belonged to them, of that he had no doubt. Their needs and their revolutionary creative energy were central to all his hopes and strategies, the relationship between the people and their leaders was therefore of crucial importance. He analysed it in a variety of contexts.In 'Bleak, Bleak Future for Africa' one of his most well-known articles from the 80s,he wrote:

"Anybody visiting Africa today will be astounded by the language of threat reminiscent of the colonial era, with leaders accusing the people of laziness. Only a decade ago these same lazy people built roads, dams, cleared bushes, dug canals almost 20 hours daily, all on the basis of voluntary labour and the spirit of nation-building.What has gone wrong between then and now? What has turned those active patriots into passive bystanders? ...Twenty years after colonialism...their standard of living is declining relatively; they see a deterioration of social life, with their leaders 'helping themselves first' while they are asked to sacrifice."

He also discussed the relationship between people and their leaders in the context of liberation movements. After a visit to Sri Lanka to commemorate the death of Rajani Thiranagama a civil liberties activist murdered by the Liberation Tigers of Tamil Eelam, he wrote:

"We saw with grief that the people actually feared the fighters, they were terrified by them. It seemed to us that they were all conscious of the fact that anyone of them could be a victim of indiscriminate killing tomorrow, like many of their fallen friends and relatives. The only thing that outsiders can learn from this situation...is by its demonstration as a negative example: that is, the danger of a liberation movement when it loses its sense of direction. It develops negative tendencies and, as it loses the respect of the people it resorts to anti-people activities".[15]

His internationalism was not some separate aspect of his politics but inherent to his thinking and his personal experience of violence and tyranny had made him sensitive to people's responses to oppressive power structures of a variety of kinds. Babu was at home everywhere, despite his sadness at his enforced absence from Africa and particularly from Zanzibar, he never saw himself as an exile. Throughout his political life Babu remained a communist, for whom Marxism was most crucially a method of analysis - a dialectical approach which enabled him to identify without dogma or sectarianism the forces of progress and change within any situation, while at the same time never losing his commitment to the socialist future of Africa and of the world.

The path to his "cherished goal" of a socialist and united Africa was based on a Pan Africanism shaped by "the united will and solidarity of the revolutionary people of Africa".[16] It encompassed many battles on many fronts in many different periods of time and across continents. Babu stood as a bridge between these struggles linking, through his own experiences, the Pan Africanism of anti-colonialism with that of today and the struggle for a united Africa with the African-American struggle.

He had been close to the African-American experience since the 60s after he met Malcolm X in the wake of the Zanzibar revolution, and during Malcolm's visits to Africa they had become close friends. Later Babu had spoken with him at mass rallies in Harlem. There had been discussions on the burning question of the time – what was the primary contradiction, race or class? Some ten years later after Malcolm was dead and Babu incarcerated in prison Imamu Baraka was to recollect those times in his poem 'Class War'.

> "Years ago, we both swore oaths, with one another,
> of revolution. You, Malcolm and I, one night
> in a room at the Waldorf. Where you had come as
> ambassador from New Afrika, when the fumes
> of revolution 1st opened our nose ...
>
> We still had not made the motion towards science, had not yet tracked the long distance to reality "[18].

There can be no doubt that Babu had been a powerful influence leading Malcolm towards a more explicitly anti-imperialist world view. At the same time he frequently emphasised the role and significance of the African-American struggle for Africa. Pan Africanism, he wrote, "the most popular political concept which in many ways reflects the true aspiration of the young generation of Africa ... is a wholly African-American ideal stemming from their long experience of struggle and from the self-confidence that struggle engenders.....However, to this day African leaders do not seem to have grasped the significance of the African-American contribution to Africa's future".[19] From 1984 on, Babu based himself in London. He became a close adviser and mentor to a range of progressive movements - in Eritrea, Uganda, Ethiopia and Rwanda. Unlike earlier struggles for liberation which were fought against settlerism and colonialism and which were supported by the OAU and even the United Nation's Decolonisation Committee, these movements were seen as separatists and as Babu writes "vilified, vigorously opposed and shunned by virtually the entire continent"[20]. Always looking for sparks of hope and ready to fan them, he took up their causes. In the case of Eritrea he travelled to the liberated zones and battlefront, living and talking with the fighters. Everyone knew him in this country in struggle. As one fighter put it later, "He had the courage to say what he thought, the foresight to be optimistic about Africa's potential and the integrity to live in accordance with the dictates of his conscience when doing all this was neither fashionable nor expedient".[21] As these movements surged forward to victory, Babu began to foresee a new phase of African unity. Writing of these new leaders –Ethiopia's Meles Zenawi, Uganda's Yoweri Museweni, Eritrea's Isais Afewerki and Rwanda's Paul Kagame he noted that, "They are civilians who took up arms to fight dictatorial military regimes and they have won. A unique feat in Africa dominated by the privileged military establishments whose roots are colonial in every respect...they have developed a solid identity of purpose, the purpose of regional stability and prosperity".[22] In the context of this new phase of national liberation Babu emphasised the importance of recognising difference. Writing of Uganda he commented: "A people's own leadership, to be successful, must be founded on a broad democratic alliance of various social groups, and must draw its strength and initiative among these groups; from retaining their identity; and from their contributions reflecting their own interests."

He described the Ethiopian constitution as a bold political experiment. Reporting from Addis Ababa as it was being drawn up in March 1994, he noted that it "sets up 14 regional self-governments each with its own parliament and president. Within each region are several linguistic groups, each of which is now entitled to use and develop its own language and culture...most important, within their own defined territories, all groups are free to exercise their own right to self-determination or independence if they feel these rights are being denied them" . This he regarded as an important alternative to the centralised state so common in African countries.

In this post-colonial period he emphasised the urgency of redrawing national boundaries to undo the problems created by the colonial borders which had divided linguistic and ethnic nationalities between two or more countries. These borders continued to facilitate interference in and control of countries by western powers particularly France and the US even though colonialism was long over.

In this context, he emphasised once again the need to restructure economies because otherwise "there was no basis for 'objective economic complementarity' ... a precondition for any meaningful economic cooperation." He castigated the OAU on its record: "Conflicts (have) become more and more common. The noble objective of attaining African unity seems to be even further out of reach..... Yet, the OAU has no conception of where Africa should be in the next decade or so. ....Its vision has been and continues to be obscured by the preconceived prejudices of the dominating states.... If it is to reactivate itself and be more relevant, it has to go to the people; it must cease to be a mere instrument of heads of state, most of whom have lost credibility; it must rekindle the spirit of Pan-Africanism, which will give it the zest and verve of the people instead of the cold emptiness of pompous diplomats, who serve no one but themselves. These are the necessary prerequisites for any African organisation which seeks to respond adequately to what is taking place in the continent".

His attitude to the OAU, however, was one of constructive criticism as he wrote in The Crowning of Emperor Mitterand, "African unity is too important to be left to the politicians and diplomats. The OAU must be placed under the firm control of the people by setting up independent "national OAU associations" in all member countries, rather like the UN associations to which the country's representative would be obliged to report regularly and which would be responsible for evaluating their diplomatic actions". This is now at last happening and the OAU though it is still not in control of the people has set up regional committees for regional participation and control.

For Babu, because Pan Africanism was a tool of struggle, it had to be reshaped with the changes in the nature of western dominance. In the early 90s, in the face of the intensifying economic stranglehold and ideological hegemony of international agencies he spoke and wrote of the need for a second liberation of Africa. He did not leave this at the level of theory. He was the driving force behind the 7th Pan African Congress held at Kampala in April 1994. It was he who coined its slogan "Don't agonise! Organise!" The Congress united all strands of the contemporary movement. His authoritative and visionary contribution to that Congress is in the section 'The Africa We Need' which was to have been the title of one of the chapters of the memoirs which he sketched out several times but sadly never wrote.

Why did those memoirs never really progress - was it lack of time? Was it his innate rejection of individualism? More than anything perhaps it was his conviction that his life and the collective struggles he was engaged in were still going on, and were not something over and relegated to memory. But we feel that this selection of his writings conveys something of that wonderful life. And we hope, as he would have, that it serves to strengthen the struggle he lived for.

Salma Babu
Amrit Wilson
London, February 2000

Notes

(1)   African Socialism or Socialist Africa, Zed, 1981.
(2)   Walter Rodney, How Europe Underdeveloped Africa, Bogle-

L'Overture Publications, 1972.
(3) Occasionally the same article appeared in more than one publication; we have in such cases acknowledged only one source.
(4) See, for example, Counter Punch p...
(5) In 1962 Babu was imprisoned on trumped up charges of sedition in an attempt to remove him from the political scene. He regarded this as a demonstration of the British fear of Chinese influence spreading to Africa
(6) Outline of memoirs, Appendix 1 Vol 2 of The Future that Works, also Review of African Political Economy, no 69, 1996
(7) Outline of memoirs, as in footnote 6
(8) For the full story see US Foreign Policy and Revolution, Pluto Press, 1989.
(9) Babu discusses the reasons why he accepted the post in his letter to Karim Essack p...
(10) This was a project which had been discussed by the Tanzanian and Zambian governments for some months in 1964/65. It was intended to reduce Zambia's dependence on white dominated regimes. The rail link would provide Zambia with an outlet to the sea as Dar es Salaam for its major export, Copper which would otherwise had to go via the Portuguese dominated territories of Angola and Mozambique, and Rhodesia and South Africa. It would also obviously expand Tanzania's infrastructure and facilitate the development of its countryside. On a Trade delegation preceding Nyerere's visit to China, Babu had thought of asking for Chinese help with the railway and it mentioned to it to Chou En-Lai. When Nyerere arrived in Beijing, he however never raised the question of the railway as expected by the Chinese leadership. Finally he was asked directly about it by Chou En-Lai. (For Babu's account of these discussions see US Foreign Policy and Revolution : the creation of Tanzania)
(11) Babu thought Zanzibar's attempts at self-reliance were regarded as a threat by the US
(12) A Conversation on Democracy, Africa Now, 1982
(13) This article was intended for Index on Censorship but was not published
(14) The Right to demand freedoms', p..
(15) Inqilab, South Asia Solidarity Group's magazine Oct 1990
(16) This was how Babu described Augustino Neto's Pan Africanism but it was equally his own approach
(17) Babu describes the role of the Nkrumah, Padmore, and others at the first All African People's Conference in Accra in creating unity in the struggle for independence in Zanzibar see Appendix 1. US Foreign Policy and Revolution: the Creation

of Tanzania, Pluto Press, 1989
(18) Babu Papers
(19) Black American influence on Africa, Africa Now, February 1985
(20) From 'A hopeful dawn of post-colonial initiatives' see p...
(21) Andebrhan Weldegiorgis's message to the memorial meeting for Babu, September 22, 1996, London
(22) Although the tragic war between Ethiopia and Eritrea proves that this solidarity is far from secure, it can be argued that if Babu had been alive he might have been able to intervene and mediate between the two governments.

ECONOMIC POLICY

Postscript to *How Europe Underdeveloped Africa*[1]

Are there short cuts to economic development for the underdeveloped economies? This question has occupied the attention of many interested parties during the last decade. These include University lecturers, international economists, the United Nations and its agencies, the O.A.U., planning agencies, Economic Ministers, etc. Many international conferences under various sponsorship have been held during the decade and volumes of resolutions, guidelines, learned documents and theses have been published. The end result has been negative. The developing countries continue to remain underdeveloped, only getting worse in relation to the developed countries.

By and large the question still remains unanswered. Are we going to repeat the same exercise all over again during this decade? From the look of it, it appears that we are. Already the UN has launched the Second Economic Decade with the same zeal and fanfare as they did with the First. The same appeal has gone out to the developed countries to be charitable and contribute '1 % of their national income' for helping the developing countries, as if the population of the world can continue to condone poverty so that the rich can be charitable! If past experience is anything to go by the seventies will experience the same disappointments which climaxed the end of the sixties.

What we may ask, has gone wrong? Is it inherent in the very nature of underdevelopment that makes development an impossible task? Among the many prescriptions that have been offered e.g., cultural, social, psychological, even economic - none has produced any encouraging results. In fact nearly all of them have had negative results, and made bad situations worse. Are we to continue with the same experiments at the expense of the people, who, let's face it, have borne the whole burden of these experiments through the last decade? This is the question to which all the developing countries, especially those in Africa, must address themselves. And the sooner the better, because there is very little time left before our economies become permanently distorted and probably too damaged for any meaningful reconstruction in the future.

Walter Rodney, in this very instructive book, provides refreshing openings for discussions which may well lead to finding the right solution. He is raising the most basic and fundamental questions regarding the nature of underdevelopment and economic backwardness. Unlike many works of this nature, which to all intents and purposes have approached the problem with a sort of metaphysical outlook (garbed it is true, in scientific terminology), Dr. Rodney follows the method of historical materialism, which in effect says: "to know the present we must look into the past and to know the future we must look into the past and the present". This is a scientific approach. We can at least be sure that the conclusions will not be marred by subjective distortions.

It is clear, especially after reading Rodney's exposition, that throughout the last decade we have been posing the wrong questions regarding economic backwardness. We did not "look into the past to know the present". We were told, and have accepted, that our poverty was caused by our poverty in the now famous theory of the 'vicious circle of poverty' and we went round in circles seeking ways and means of breaking that circle. Had we asked the fundamental questions which Dr. Rodney raises in this work we would not have exposed our economies to the ruthless plunder brought about by 'foreign investments' which the exponents of the vicious-circle theory urged us to do. For, it is clear foreign investment is the cause and not a solution, to our economic backwardness.

Are we not underdeveloped now because we have been colonised in the past ? There is no other explanation to the fact that practically the whole of the underdeveloped world has been colonised either directly or indirectly by the western powers. And what is colonialism if it is not a system of 'foreign investments' by the metropolitan powers? If it has contributed to our underdevelopment in the past is it not likely to contribute to our underdevelopment now, even if the political reins are in our hands? Put in this way the question of underdevelopment is immediately rendered more intelligible, even to the uninitiated. And this is how Dr. Rodney is directing us to pose our questions. The inevitable conclusion is that foreign investment not only helps to undermine our economies by extracting enormous profits, etc., but it does more serious damage to the economies by distorting them into lopsidedness and if the process is not arrested in time, the distortion could be permanent. As long as we continue, as we have done for centuries, to produce for the so-called 'world market' which was founded on the hard rock of slavery and colonialism, our economies will remain colonial. Any development will be entirely incidental, leaving the vast majority of the population wholly uninvolved in the economic activity. The more we invest in export branches in order to capture the 'world market' the more we divert away from investing for people's development and, consequently, the least effective our development effort. And since this type of investment does not contribute much towards the development of a material and technical base, internally, our economies are rendered always responsive only to what the Western world is prepared to buy and sell, and hardly responsive to our internal development needs. That is why, although most of our development plans make elaborate resource allocations for 'rural projects', invariably most of these resources find their way back to the urban projects and consequently accentuate the urban/rural disparities. Slums, unemployment, social maladjustment and, finally, political instability are our most outstanding characteristics.

Almost without exception, all the ex-colonial countries have ignored the cardinal development demand; namely, that, to be really effective, the development process must begin by transforming the economy from its colonial, externally-responsive structure, to one which is internally responsive.Where we went wrong is when we followed blindly the assumptions handed down to us by our exploiters. These assumptions can be stated briefly as follows: Growth in underdeveloped countries is hampered by inadequate growth in exports and inadequate financial resources and is made worse by 'population explosion' in these countries. And the solution is prescribed as follows: Step up exports, increase aid and loans from the developed countries and arrest growth in population. Throughout the last decade our efforts have been to follow religiously the above prescription, and even if our own experience continues to disprove it, we still adhere to it even more fanatically. The greatest need appears to be a process of mental decolonisation, since neither common sense nor sound economics, not even our own experience is with us in this. Experiences of other countries that have chosen a different path, a path of economic reconstruction, is most instructive here.

The Pearson Commission's Report - Partners in Development - has been hailed, even by the developing countries, as ushering in a new era, a sort of turning point, in international co-operation for development. Even if its recommendations were to be adopted and implemented in toto it is doubtful if it would make any impact on the ever-widening gap between the developed and the developing countries. This is because it has avoided tackling the most fundamental question, namely, 'can development take place when our production strategy is influenced by the demands of the world market which is determined almost exclusively by the pattern of production and consumption within capitalist Europe and America?' In other words, in distorting our economies to fit in with the demands of the world market, the demands which are not always compatible with the demands of our own development, are we not, in the process, depriving our economies of the capacity for a self-sustaining growth which is a precondition to development.

By posing the question in this style, it is possible to see through the smoke-screen of international do-gooders and begin to understand the real cause of our underdevelopment. It is, of course, too much to expect Pearson or people of his liberal inclination to pose the question in this way, since their training and outlook consider this way of putting the question to be almost morally sinful and economically subversive.

However, as leaders of the developing countries, we are obliged to adopt this style of posing the question since we have taken upon ourselves the responsibility for steering a development course whose success or failure will affect, one way or another, the well-being of hundreds of millions of the people who comprise more than two-thirds of the human race. For too long we have left their fate to be determind by the kind of production which is not based on the satisfaction of their wants but rather on serving external interests as expressed by the accepted laws of supply and demand of the so-called world market. We have twisted their education in such a way that the 'skills' we direct them to develop are geared towards serving the same ends of the world market rather than towards development of an internal material base with the result that technologically, and in relation to the developed world, we move backward rather than forwards. We have tamely accepted the international division of labour on behalf of our masses, and in doing so we have condemned them to specialise in 'primary' commodities whose production is conducive neither to the development of technological skills nor to the invention of advanced machinery, both of which are the pre-conditions to real economic development.

The significance of Dr. Rodney's book is that it is addressed, quite appropriately, to the masses and not to the leaders and one hopes that it will be instrumental in arousing some mass action by the people. In the absence of committed leadership, many African countries have fallen prey to military exploitation, to the extent that today the generals constitute the majority at the African summit. This is as it should be, because when the political leadership loses the sense of internal direction, when, in bewilderment, it gives up its efforts to find solutions to people's problems and begins to accumulate wealth for its own individual use, political leadership tends to get increasingly 'commandist' in its state operations. Logic and rationale become subversive. And when politicians become commandists, they too become redundant, because who is better fitted to giving command than the army?

With very few exceptions it is sad to have to admit that Africa is ill-served by the current conglomeration of what passes for leaders throughout the continent When Asia and Latin America produce giants, like Mao, Ho, Che, who inspire and excite the, imagination not only of their compatriots within their borders, but of the rest of the world, including the developed world, Africa has produced only one Nyerere and maintained him in power, while, we have murdered Lumumba and have locked up or exiled leaders like Ben Bella and Nkrumah in response to the wishes of the imperialists - our donors, our money-lenders, our patrons, our masters, our trading partners.

With all due respect, it is difficult to imagine, apart from one or two honourable exceptions, any of the present leaders being capable of standing up for the genuine rights of his people, knowing that these rights are of necessity directly opposed to the interests of imperialism. And yet such a stand is necessary if we are to really fulfil our obligation as leaders, otherwise we have no right to impose our leadership on the people. While most of the leaders on the continent have no sense of urgency in solving the problems of people's misery, since they don't bear the brunt of that misery, the masses, who do, cannot wait. That is why one hopes that Dr. Rodney's book will be read by as many people as possible because it has come at a time when it is most needed - for action.

After reading the harrowing account of the brutalities of slavery, of subjugation, of deprivation and humiliation, when whole civilisations were crushed in order to serve the imperialist interests of the West; when settled societies were disintegrated by force of imperialist arms so that the plantation owners of the 'new world' could get their uprooted, and therefore permanent labour force to build what is now the most advanced capitalist economy, it becomes absolutely clear that the only way out of our current impasse is through a revolutionary path - a complete break with the system which is responsible for all our past and present misery.

Our future course must be guided dialectically. If by looking into the past we have known the present, to know the future we must look into the past and the present. Our action must be related to our concrete experience, and we must not give way to metaphysical hopes and wishes, hop-

Economic Policy

ing and wishing that the monster who has been after us throughout our history will some day change into a lamb; he won't. As Engels puts it 'Freedom does not consist in the dream of independence from natural laws, but in the knowledge of these laws,... freedom of the will, therefore, means nothing but the capacity to make decisions with knowledge of the subject'. We know the subject only too well, and he is a monster. Do we have the capacity to make a decision now that Dr. Rodney has provided us with the knowledge of the subject? The people must answer.

Dar es Salaam, December 1971

Notes

(1)   Walter Rodney (1972) How Europe Underdeveloped Africa, Bogle L'Ouverture Publications,London.

Open Letter to Prime Minister Mugabe
New African, May 1980

Dear Comrade Mugabe,

Warm congratulations on your victory and comradely salutations from your admirers!

In the last five years or so since you took over the reins of ZANU you have shown magnificent qualities of leadership-resolute without being dogmatic, daring without being adventurist, and flexible without being lax.

But above all, you have revealed yourself during this period as an outstanding strategist and tactician both in political organisation and in war.

With all these rare qualities it would be presumptuous even to attempt to tell you and your gallant comrades-in-arms what is to be done in independent Zimbabwe. Moreover, you know better than any outsider the concrete situation in the country. This letter does not claim to tell you anything you don't know; it only seeks to re-emphasise some salient points which we may lose sight of in the euphoria of freedom.

The enemies of Africa are anxious to prove that every new African country is doomed to failure and, to ensure that this does indeed take place, they will want to entangle you deeply in their world system so as to destroy you. Proof? Look at what is happening in practically all sister countries: economic chaos, shortage of food and other basic necessities, corruption, and so on, is the order of the day. You, as a revolutionary, will be a special target particularly because of Zimbabwe's proximity to South Africa.

You are, however, fortunate in that Zimbabwe is the last but one arrival into the world arena as a proud, free country, and so you can learn from the mistakes of other countries that have preceded you. This is the purpose of this open letter. If you have thought about the problem along the lines discussed below then this letter is redundant. If you don't agree with it then it is irrelevant. In either case it will still be worth our while to repeat to ourselves all the points raised if only to keep them fresh in our minds.

Economic Policy

The other reason for this exercise is that we owe it to Africa and to history to share our past and present experience in order to arm ourselves against possible pitfalls which are all too common in the challenging period of national reconstruction. We have been struggling and continue to struggle against many odds, natural and man-made, and we need not be ashamed or scared of making mistakes. We learn through mistakes. Our task is to minimise them when we can, and this we can do by reminding ourselves again and again of the more obvious ones. This is the spirit of the letter.

Unlike many developing countries, you are taking over a country with considerable potential. Let me give some comparative statistics. Kenya, a fairly "prosperous" country, has double the population of Zimbabwe (14m. to your 7m.) and yet its Gross National Product is only $2,900m. compared to your $3,560m. (1976 World Bank figures), or a per capita income of $220 to your $550. (Incidentally, when the bourgeoisie took over France in 1792 the country's per capita income was just about $600).

Zimbabwe has a fairly solid industrial base most of which was made possible thanks to the "sanctions" which forced the country to look inward. It was what you might call a blessing in disguise. (Looking back, one wishes that sanctions had been imposed against all African countries soon after independence. What a happy people we would have been! It was "aid" that proved to be the kiss of death.) Your agricultural base, too, is fairly healthy.

From this level Zimbabwe has an excellent chance to move rapidly to a self-sustaining development. As a Socialist you will no doubt want this development to be accompanied with social justice. And here's the crux of the matter.

How do we restructure an economy whose social basis was to exploit the majority for the benefit of the minority? Seemingly the easiest way is to take over the "commanding heights" of the economy and transform it into a popular-based one. But this is easier said than done, with enormous potential dangers. We often tend to be overwhelmed by the magnitude of the task and consequently fail to raise the most essential, most basic question: Where to begin?

While it is impossible for outsiders to know the concrete situation without a thorough investigation, there are, nevertheless, generally acceptable principles that may be applicable to any country at a given level of the development of its productive forces. If the latter are at a low level then it is imperative that their development be regarded as top priority, even over that of the relations of production. In Maoist terms, development of the productive forces in this case becomes the principal aspect of the contradiction with production relations a secondary one. This strategy has variously been called the New Economic Policy, or N.E.P., or the New Democracy, in which capitalist relations are allowed to coexist with Socialist ones. And this was done for very practical reasons: to allow maximum opportunity and facility for the productive forces to develop as rapidly as possible without in the meantime causing economic dislocations and subjecting the people to unjustified hardships. It cannot be over emphasised that people are our most precious capital and, therefore, they must eat well, be housed and clothed well.

This, then, is our starting point. The economy must be so structured as to provide adequate food, good housing and cheap but good clothing. In the course of providing these the economy will also develop a good agricultural foundation, together with engineering and extensive textile industries. All of these will create vast employment opportunities for hundreds of thousands of people currently un- or underemployed, who in turn will help expand the home market-essential for further industrial and agricultural development.

For this to take place, one will of course need to generate investible resources or accumulation for investment. One of the most unfortunate experiences of developing countries is that they all sought these resources from external sources, either in the form of loans or aid, which has led to heavy and unbearable debt burdens (bankruptcy, you might say) which now threaten our very survival as sovereign states. To avoid this monumental pitfall, it is essential for a country to generate its investible resources internally, first and foremost.

How? There are two ways: by taxing (but not overtaxing) the private sector; and by utilising for this purpose the surpluses that will come from future state enterprises.

At this level of development it may be advisable to allow maximum (but disciplined) play of individual initiative in economic activity guided by the principle of "utilise, win over and control." You utilise the existing private skills and resources for rapid development of the productive forces; you win over through education and persuasion all good elements to serve social rather than individual ends; and you control private enterprise incomes through fixing the sale price of their products (allowing, of course, for proper incentives); tax their profits, control its repatriation and encourage ploughing back.

It could be made into a principle that at least 50% of the accumulation from this source should go into state productive investments annually and the rest can go into paying for recurrent expenditure and the building up of economic and social infrastructures. This principle will discipline the bureaucracy and prevent them from indulging in unnecessary low priority expenditure while, at the same time it will help to build step by step the state industrial sector that is nonexistent at the moment, for example iron and steel industries, machine tool industry, metallurgy, petrochemical industry, and so on; in short, heavy industry or Department No.1.

It will not be worthwhile to pay serious attention to such pundits as Rene Dumont[1] and their like who urge us to concentrate only on small-scale production based on the argument that small is beautiful. No country in history has developed on that basis. But given our condition of uneven development in Africa, perhaps the best way will be to combine large scale and intermediate production. Where, for instance, you already have large farms you either expand them where necessary or you maintain them at their present level and thereby enjoy the benefits of large-scale farming. Where production is still peasant based you may want to develop it to an intermediate level with producers cooperatives as their basic units.

Experience elsewhere has taught us that the taking over of ongoing viable farms has invariably led to almost total collapse of agricultural production and has forced the countries concerned to incur heavy foreign debt to import food. As foreign borrowing without repayment cannot be sustained for a long time the countries are forced literally to beg for food on an international scale. This is undesirable from both the economic and political standpoints, to say nothing of national dignity.

It is a painful historical fact that in Zimbabwe such large-scale farms are owned by White settlers, some of whom are liberal and others incorrigibly reactionary. To expropriate them will amount to economic disaster, at least in the short run. To allow them to continue as before will amount to perpetuating a national injustice. This is a serious dilemma. Probably you and your party have already made up your minds on how tackle it. To an outsider it will seem possible to avoid both of these undesirable consequences by:

* where possible, surrounding all these settler farms by producer agricultural cooperatives;

* making obligatory for the settler farms, as a condition for their existence to share their facilities (farm implements, expertise, marketing, dispensary service etc.) with the newly-established cooperatives.

This will help; first, to develop viable cooperative farms at a minimum cost and make maximum use of the existing stock of agricultural implements in the country. Secondly, it will help diminish the imbalance between settlers' and people's production and thereby correct the existing situation in which the settler farms are isolated like prosperous islands in the midst of mass poverty. Thirdly, it will help distinguish between good elements among the settlers who are genuinely willing to work with the new government in improving the living conditions of the people, and the diehards. It will then be possible to win over the first group and isolate and eventually ease out the latter. Fourthly, and this is most important it will help consolidate people's as opposed to individual production without any large-scale economic dislocation (and its attendant consequences) during the transition.

The rising rural incomes entailed in this strategy will expand the home market for industrial consumer products as well as broaden the tax base. It will then be possible to accumulate from the latter to pay for further development of the former. Which means not only the development of nationally integrated, independent industrialisation but also the rapid rise of the proletariat. All this, of course, is based on the assumption of a planned and proportional development of the national economy.

Going by your public statements since you took over, it appears that this is broadly what you have in mind. If so, you are definitely on the right track; and all well-meaning people will back you in your obviously very difficult task. We will all wish you the very best.

Yours fraternally,

Notes

(1)   Rene Dumont (1966) False Start in Africa, Andre Deutsch

The Tanzania that might have been
Africa Now, December 1981

Tanzania is renowned for its honourable aspirations which even its worst enemies dare not question. It has aroused huge vistas of hope among young and poor countries by its bold and innovative experiments. By the same token, however, it has attracted world attention to its economic and social performance. This is not an enviable position to be in. Every action, every move and every setback comes under close scrutiny and is often magnified out of proportion. This in turn forces its leaders into trying to show results as quickly as possible in order to prove the validity of their experiments.

Unfortunately, the pressure to show results tends to lead to overlooking concrete conditions in the country and trying what is impossible at a given historical junction and this inevitably leads to economic disruptions.

The objectives of the "Arusha Declaration" adopted in February 1967 are beyond any doubt the most worthy ones any country can hope to achieve. They became world famous not because they were unique but because the manner in which they were to be pursued was exemplary, i.e. through "self-reliance". For a poor country like Tanzania with its economy wholly reliant on external market forces any attempt at self-reliance was bound to attract world curiosity.

It turned out, however, that there was a serious misunderstanding about the meaning of self-reliance among the Tanzanian leadership which later turned the whole experiment into a near disaster.

At the time of the Arusha Declaration there was a distinct divergence in approach to development within government leadership between the Right Wing and the Left. The former represented "Modernisation" thinking which was then still popular among liberal bourgeois theories of development. The outstanding component of these theories was the creation of a favourable environment for foreign investment and secondly export promotion of our agricultural produce. To the Rightists therefore, the idea of self-reliance sounded rather silly and impracticable. The Declaration was regarded as a big joke with serious potential dangers.

The Left, on the other hand, received the Declaration with a lot of enthusiasm and accepted its declared policy of "socialism and self-reliance" as a good start on the long journey to the development of an independent national economy.

Until then the "Centre" had not emerged as a significant political trend, but the enthusiasm of the Left was so overwhelming and widespread that President Nyerere, who was slowly and cautiously moving away from the extreme right, got stuck somewhere in the middle and resisted moving any further to the left.

One of the shocking experiences of the Rightists was the mass support for the Declaration by the workers which was manifested in the monster demonstration a day after it was declared It was organised by the country's official trade union NUTA. It surpassed anything the country had ever seen in size or vigour. The enthusiasm of the workers knew no bounds. At one point it was even suggested by Western observers that the workers were about to take over state power, and many Rightists thought so too.

It was then that President Nyerere decided to deliberately create and strengthen the Centre as a decisive factor in Tanzania's political equation; it was to block the move to the Left of Centre. This is in keeping with the traditional classical philosophy before the spread of experimental science which saw the correct path as necessarily lying between two extremes. He therefore incorporated the Rightist's views and some from the Left in an eclectic mishmash which led to the evolution of the doctrine which became the official policy of the Arusha Declaration, as he put it, " a policy of revolution by evolution", whatever that meant in concrete terms.

If to the Rightists, self-reliance meant wishful thinking, to the Centre it meant reliance on our own traditional ways with some innovative improvements here and there. It is the position of the advocates of "intermediate technology" school, of Professor Dumont, and of the "rural development" ideology. In fact, Dumont 's "False Start in Africa"[1] became Tanzania's development blueprint . The Left however, gave a much wider application to the meaning of "self-reliance". They perceived it as a policy of gradual delinking of our economies from the pernicious subordination by the metropolitan markets over which we had no control. They advocated self-reliance in food and in the production of surplus food grains for export in the early period of restructuring the economy in a barter arrangement with the centrally planned economies in the advanced socialist countries in exchange for the establishment of: (a) Basic industries such as iron and steel, machine tool industry, etc.; (b) Light industry such as textiles, food processing, etc. (c) Development of state-farms so as to modernise agriculture and move away step by step from peasant farming into large-scale scientific farming.

In the course of this stepped up economic activity, the prosperity which would be generated would then filter down to the rest of the economy. The resulting era of rising incomes would give the economy an impetus which would lead to the takeoff stage. Once this occurred the economy would be freed from the shackles of underdevelopment and would enter into the more advanced stage of a high-consuming society which is a characteristic of a "developed" economy as exemplified by Europe, Japan and North America.

The Tanzania First Five Year Plan launched in mid-1964 reflected this strategy but was abandoned half way in late 1966 as an unworkable proposition. The anticipated flow of foreign aid (more than two-thirds of the total envisaged investment) had failed to materialise and most of the country's surplus was wasted in useless and unproductive investments.

The Arusha Declaration was a massive rejection of the above strategy. President Nyerere in rejecting it declared that foreign investment would in fact give foreign governments or individuals a stranglehold on the economy and would lead to a large number of the people becoming paid servants of another nation or another person. This had to be rejected as it would infringe upon the freedom of the country and violate the principle of human equality of all citizens to which Tanzania was committed from the days of its struggle for independence as far back as 1954.

However, this was the farthest Left he would go. He rejected any idea of restructuring the economy, of rapid industrialisation (heavy and light industry) or rapid mechanisation of agriculture for which the Left was pressing. On August 5, 1967 in an address to the University of Dar-es-Salaam students where leftist ideas were dominant, he defined the meaning of self-reliance as development dependent principally upon ourselves and our own resources, i.e. "land and people". It would be unrealistic to dream of "developing Tanzania through the establishment of large, modern industries", he said. It would be a mistake to "think in terms of covering Tanzania with mechanised farms, using tractors and combined harvesters." If there were industries or mechanised farms they would be the exception, not the rule, and they would be entirely to meet particular development needs of Tanzania. We would "develop from our own roots" and "preserve that which is valuable in our traditional past" and we "have to stop thinking in terms of massive agricultural mechanisation and the proletarianisation of the rural population."

He stressed the development of agriculture independent of industry, using the hoe until it is "eliminated by the ox-plough before the latter can be eliminated by the tractor. We cannot hope to eliminate the jembe (hoe) by the tractor".

On trade he said that this self-reliance "is unlikely to reduce our participation in international trade, but it should over time change its character to some extent" - i.e. move to primary processed commodities - and continue to import "things which we cannot produce and which are necessary for the development and welfare of our whole people". The ideology of "Rural Development" which was developed more elaborately later was based on the above premise.

To the Left this definition of "self-reliance" was a sure prescription for economic stagnation and perpetuation of external dependency. History has proved them right. It was the sort of self-reliance favoured by our trading partners, by the World Bank, the IMF and by GATT. In fact McNamara, the then President of the World Bank was so impressed by Tanzania's concept of self-reliance that he elevated it to a model worthy of emulation by the rest of the developing countries.

The Left's position, broadly outlined in a series of articles in The Nationalist was based on a rationale which first questioned the structure of the state which we had inherited and the social relations of productions that corresponded to it.

The colonial state was designed to suppress the entire people and it was based on the use of violence. Violence was latent in the colonial structure. That kind of state was not intended to develop the people but to undermine their self-respect so as to make it easier to rule them. Its economic activity was limited to the production and export of agricultural commodities for the consumption and production needs of the metropolitan countries. Needs of the people were ignored by such an economy except for the provision of a minimum of social services essential to keep the system of exploitation functioning. In other words, to transform the state into a real people's state the one we had inherited had to be "smashed" as a first priority.

The second priority was to do away with the colonial economy and in its place develop an independent national economy whose first prerequisite was to provide for the basic needs of the people, namely, food, clothing and shelter, and to continually raise their standards.

The means to attain this goal is by propelling the development of technology and production by observing the essential internal links between production, exchange and consumption which determine the ultimate direction of the development of the economy. This requires as a precondition the unity of objective possibility and subjective initiative.

The essential links are brought together under a strategy of planned and proportional development of the national economy, involving the allocation of manpower and material resources among various productive sectors. These in turn are guided by the sectoral and inter-sectoral proportional relations, the main ones of which are those between agriculture and industry; within agriculture and within industry; communication and transport; education; health; and the relations between town and country. The key and determinant proportional relation is that between accumulation and consumption.

What all this means in practice is a serious restructuring of the state and economy based on a correct appraisal of the concrete situation in the country and then planning the economy on the basis of these conditions. We should take into account the obvious fact that if industry is backward then agriculture, which involves over 90% of the population will remain backward, and vice versa, and that such a situation will yield very limited, if any, surplus that can be allocated to the improvement of the well-being of the people, i.e. to health, education, etc.

If on the other hand, the allocation in the social service sector is greater than the economy can afford then there will be insufficient accumulation to go into advancing agriculture and industry. Unless both sides, i.e. accumulation and consumption, are proportionally balanced the country will remain in a permanent state of indebtedness.

The essential balance between revenue and expenditure, and between supply and demand can be obtained only if the principle of adapting construction to the concrete condition in the country is observed strictly. In Tanzania, for example, the scope of capital construction (large buildings and fancy houses for bureaucrats and businessmen, airports, building of a capital city, "tourist roads", etc.) was overextended and did not go directly into production of new value. The result was that the country was pushed deeper into external indebtedness and a loss of billions of shillings because costs far exceeded the growth of value in agriculture and industry. It is a cardinal rule in development that production must precede capital construction and that the country must first utilise all its existing potential before embarking on new projects.

What would have happened if this Left strategy were adopted in the immediate aftermath of the Arusha Declaration?

By modernising agriculture, especially with large scale

state-farms along the river belts, with the construction of flood controls and irrigation, Tanzania would have strengthened its position as the food-surplus producing country that it used to be. Natural hazards, floods or droughts, would have had very limited damaging effects. Having neglected that cardinal rule, natural hazards have become the scourge of our economy.

If we had invested in the exploitation of our coal and iron ore resources, which are in abundance by any standards, Tanzania would now have been well on the way towards developing several industrial complexes, employing scores of thousands of our young people, daily creating new national wealth and gaining new skills in the process, and the effects of the "energy crisis" would have been reduced to a minimum. We would have been able to supply most of our development needs locally, especially the most basic ones like tractors, trucks, water pumping machines, construction, transport and communication implements, machine tools, and so on.

Our agriculture would have been less dependent on small-scale, inefficient peasant production and our countryside would have been flourishing with emerging industrial towns producing most of the amenities of modern life - healthy food, good and permanent housing, running water, hygienic environment and most important of all, the emergence of educated and skilled young Tanzanians, liberated from the shackles of rural environment.

This does not mean we would have no problems; far from it. The struggle for controlling our environment, that is to say, the journey from the "realm of necessity to the realm of freedom" is a protracted and difficult one; it is uphill and zigzag and beset with many and complex problems. But they would be problems of a different character. They would not be problems of struggling merely to feed ourselves; that would have been long overcome. Nor would our problems have been ones of trying to extract the most from other countries' wealth through aid, grants and credits. They would be problems of improving our knowledge of the natural environment (i.e. science) and of improving our skills and tools to control it (i.e. technology).

In conclusion, it is relevant to ask, if it sounds so straightforward, why is it that there was so much reluctance to follow this path? The answer is obvious: it was the difference in world-outlooks. The Centre had the world-outlook of small-scale commodity producers, of looking to the past for inspiration, of accommodating with the natural environment. The Left on the other hand, have the world-outlook of large-scale production, of controlling and transforming our natural environment to satisfy and expand social needs, of looking to the future; in other words of introducing a process which would have led to the beginning of our society consciously creating its own history.

Most 'developing' countries chose the first path - which leads nowhere. It entrenches us deeper into neocolonialism, at best. Those that opted for the second path, the path to the future, are well on their way to developing independent national economies. Tanzania might have been one of them; instead it chose the path to Blunder land.

Notes

(1) Rene Dumont (1966) False Start in Africa, Andre Deutsch

Bleak, Bleak Future for Africa
Africa Now, November 1984

An African diplomat remarked the other day that the reason why the OAU has refused to mark the 100th anniversary of the Berlin Conference which legitimised the division of Africa by European powers in November 1884 is that such a reminder would embarrass some African countries which are already on the slippery slope to re-colonisation this time by remote control. Although the diplomat said this with tongue-in-cheek the essence of his remark is clear and to a large extent quite correct. The only difference between then and now, however, is that while the old Chiefs, Sultans, Mwinyis, etc. - the predecessors of our present rulers - were free people forced into colonial bondage, our new rulers enter the new bondage virtually bankrupt, already half enslaved by an unbearably huge foreign debt that neither the present generation nor several generations to come can ever hope to repay.

Every African child born today carries debt burden of $200 (about 3,500 East African Shillings at official exchange rates) which grows annually at 22% with the obligatory annual debt service ratio averaging about 13%.

This child moreover is born into economies with 11% declining per capita output, which in plain language means our governments have to seek more external loans in order to remain static. No wonder the OAU does not want to be reminded of the struggle for independence and the sacrifice entailed in that struggle since the formalisation of African colonialism 190 years ago this month. To all intents and purposes, for the masses in Africa today, independence has lost its meaning and direction.

The people are no longer responsive to the hoary explanation of their misery which blames it on the international economic order. They see their countries getting more and more integrated into the very "economic order" their leaders condemn; they are daily being urged - even forced - to produce the "cash crops" intended for the same "economic world order" their leaders blame for their misery. In the meantime. they see their leaders doing very well under the system in which they, the masses, continue to suffer. (In East Africa, indigenous millionaires are cropping up everywhere like mushrooms while the masses, hundreds of millions of them, are degenerating into absolute poverty.) Scarcity, which is general, is generally only for the people, while those in power live in a world of conspicuous consumption - a world of videos and stereos, of washing machines and dryers, of Mercedes and private mansions and beach villas; they see a disgusting world of luxury in the midst of poverty.

It is becoming increasingly clear to the people that the massive debts that they carry on their almost broken shoulders are largely contracted by the ubiquitous "Messrs. Ten Per Cent" (the new indigenous millionaires, that is) who ruthlessly burden their countries and people with useless projects, costing billions of dollars. Ten per cent of this goes into their pockets and the pockets of the organisers of this criminal conspiracy: politicians, bureaucrats, diplomats, local "consultants" and their so many hangers-on.

It is no longer a secret that these conspirators who shed so many crocodile tears when they advance the case for their countries' poverty (over caviar and champagne, of course) have made themselves rich and their countries insolvent by the simple expedient of privately colluding with international financiers and publicly condemning their institutions.

When the inevitable pressures are put by the international lenders to further squeeze the masses by lowering their already meagre standard of living and so breaking their resistance, the lenders mandate the abolition of what few social welfare programmes exist and the decontrol of food prices and other necessities. The leaders tow the line, although not without kicking and screaming (for public consumption).

At the same time they impose severe restrictions on wage increases, harsh penalties for striking workers and students, continuous devaluation of national currencies and, as a final national humiliation, direct control of financial and monetary policies right down to the level of revenue collection. In many instances the international lenders actually appoint specific Ministers in specific Ministries to do their job for them.

Unfortunately, no country in Africa is free today from this humiliating experience in one form or another. It is immaterial whether a country describes itself as "capitalist" or "socialist"; in the final analysis they both go through the same humiliation. The former usually suffer from a lack of export outlets, having already saturated the world market with their agricultural commodities which constitute "inelastic demand." They suffer from rapid and extreme social and class differentiation between the rich and the poor; from land-grabbing where the land is scarce; from corruption; and they are permanently in balance of payments difficulties.

The latter suffer from internal economic dislocation; bad management; over-bureaucratised and top-heavy state institutions; from excessive and uncontrollable economic and political power of the politicians and bureaucrats and from the inevitable corruption. Both systems end up, at best, in stagnation, but very often in absolute deterioration, expressed in the current crisis by the 11% decline in per capita output.

Force is increasingly becoming the means of making the reluctant population work both in agriculture and industry. Anybody visiting Africa today will be astounded by the language of threat reminiscent of the colonial era with leaders accusing the people of "laziness". Only a decade ago these same "lazy" people built roads, dams, cleared bushes, dug canals almost 20 hours daily, all on the basis of voluntary labour and the spirit of nation-building.

What has gone wrong between then and now? What has turned those active patriots into passive bystanders? The reason is not far to seek. We have only to look into what is happening to the vast majority of the people, the peasants, the small farmers, and so on, who constitute more than 90% of our population.

Under colonialism the people were forced to produce for the world market in order to satisfy the import needs of the colonial power that dominated them and also to earn cash for the maintenance of the state that oppressed them.

Twenty years after colonialism, peasants see the situation as having not changed decisively except for a few cosmetics. Their standard of living is declining relatively; the "education" of their children is irrelevant to their immediate and long-term needs; they see a deterioration of social life, with their leaders "helping themselves first" while they are asked to sacrifice. Their spontaneous reaction to this obviously unjust situation is to contract out of production for the market and resort to subsistence agriculture, with serious consequences to the "national economy".

The most serious and most damaging effect of this on the ruling groups is the inevitable decline in foreign exchange earnings. On these depend the satisfaction of their consumption needs; the behind-the-scenes wheeling and dealings and the eventual "10%" in hard currency to be stashed in foreign banks; and then there is the national obligation to service their debts to international lenders and so on. The other damage is the contraction of internal demand which has a direct effect on home industries with serious consequences for employment revenue, and so on. It is this nightmare which is compelling the leaders to resort to force, to resort to the colonial language of threats and to castigate the people as "lazy".

But the method of force or threat of force has never been the most effective way of mass mobilisation. On the contrary, it results in mass disenchantment, apathy and passive resistance. It is producing the very results the leaders seek to prevent; and this is exactly what we are witnessing today. The devastating and unprecedented drought is claiming its toll; masses of people, especially children and old people, are perishing in thousands, and governments seem to be unable to handle such emergencies without massive external aid - not only material but also in personnel. In an environment of the mass enthusiasm we experienced a decade ago, a lot of damage that we are going through now could have been avoided by the actions of the people themselves.

The World Bank's current document on Sub-Sahara Africa entitled "Towards Sustained Development in Sub-Sahara Africa" exposes, through facts and figures, the grim but real situation which is now being experienced in the continent. Between now and the end of the century it is bleak, bleak and bleak all the way. We are reaping the bitter fruit of the prior decisions our leaders have taken which made neither political nor economic sense. The only people who benefited from our misery are the foreign partners and their local representatives, the "Messrs. Ten Per Cent."

No wonder the OAU is not inclined to remind Africa about the Berlin Conference and the struggle that followed it. Those who have fallen in order to make Africa free did not realise that they were fighting for a cause that would be highjacked by a handful of people who would turn Africa into a continent of hunger and starvation. Re-colonisation is taking place under our very noses and very soon we shall be treated to a feast of double talk in which a retreat will be called victory.

From China with Lessons for Africa[1]
Africa Now, November 1984

Many African countries may soon be passing through the "crucial threshold" of their development which may help or hamper our growth process, depending on our ability to absorb our own or others' experiences and to utilise them to our benefit. Every experience is useful, but some experiences are more beneficial than others.

For instance, experiences gained in the US or USSR are useful but in many instances inapplicable to our circumstances. But experiences gained in, say, China or India are both useful and practicable to us because they have been gained from circumstances and environments more or less similar to our own.

Such experiences are also instructive both positively and negatively. For instance, both China and India have largely peasant economies, just like ours. But what can we learn from their experience where in the first case (China) the peasants are an asset and in the second (India) they are a liability?

Some 25 years ago China was engaged in the "Great Leap Forward"; an attempt to jump over several stages of development in order to achieve a minimum economic base essential for ushering the country into the early stages of Communism. It was argued that since China had a largely peasant economy with backward agriculture and very little industry, it would be very difficult to embark on serious Socialist construction without changing this backward base. It was further argued that since Capitalism was a dying social system and Socialism was a new emerging one, to attain rapid development it was necessary to introduce, as soon as possible, Socialist relations of production in order to achieve the objective as fast as possible.

So some time in 1956 the Communist Party of China announced the "Great Leap Forward" campaign to the surprise of many overseas comrades as well as some leading members of the party within China. The latter were particularly disturbed because until then they had been operating on the theory of the 'New Democracy' which argued that in the process of creating Socialism, the state would be obliged to utilise Capitalism and capitalist relations side by side with socialist relations and that this process would take a very long time until finally Capitalism would atrophy. In spite of these apprehensions, the campaign was pursued vigorously by the party and state cadres as well as by the rest of the population.

In 1960 the campaign was at its highest, and so was production enthusiasm of workers and peasants. China did achieve some great leaps forward but also a lot of destruction of the old forms. For instance by introducing the "People's Communes" in the rural areas a great advance in agriculture was achieved but also a lot of destruction of the old forms which had sustained China for thousands of years. As a rule peasants everywhere are fiercely individualistic and they cherish individual enterprise; they all harbour some hopes that some day they are going to be rich and prosperous and so ensure that their children would never again be raised in the hardships that they themselves went through.

To change this deeply-felt outlook requires years of persuasion by word and deed, otherwise the state will be introducing innovative systems when the people are not yet ready for them; and that is a blueprint for social disaster. Peasants react negatively when they feel pressured into a system about which they are not yet convinced; and in a peasant economy the last thing the state wants to be confronted with is peasants' apathy. They will resort to subsistence agriculture or cultivate only what they are obliged to cultivate in the collective form. Although they may express verbal enthusiasm (for survival reasons) in practice they will do everything to avoid doing their best.

China went through this experience with considerable damage. In the 60s and much of the 70s these activities were climaxed by the 'Cultural Revolution' and further massive social dislocations. Anybody who urged caution or who advocated a practical approach was branded a 'Capitalist roader' and would be discredited and humiliated. Even the head of state at the time, Liu Shao Chi, was similarly treated and later died in prison branded a 'Capitalist roader'. Chou en Lai, the Prime Minister, escaped that fate because he was too popular among the masses and therefore could not be touched without serious consequences. One might say that the Cultural Revolution was a carry-over of the "Great Leap" without the doubters and the cautious.

When Chou en Lai died and then Mao himself, a new situation was introduced. Only one month after the latter's death his widow and her colleagues, dubbed in China "The Gang of Four," were arrested and were later accused of being responsible for all the mess of the Cultural Revolution. Deng Xiaoping, who himself had suffered various forms of humiliation during the cultural revolution, now emerged as the strongest and most respected leader in the country. He and his colleagues who had suffered similar fates decided their time had come to introduce their version of the process of transition to Socialism. Without destroying the Socialist structure that had been built over the years, the new leaders encouraged some form of private initiative, especially in the rural areas, rather like what had occurred before the Great Leap, i.e. during the era of New Democracy.

This change of course was greeted with some serious misgivings among overseas comrades and even some elements within the country who thought that a new form of "revisionism" was under way. In the West the new policy has been hailed as a victory for Capitalism and an admission of failure of Socialism. This interpretation is of course necessary in the ideological battle between East and West to win over the minds of the people of developing countries as well as those of the West's own poor.

The new Chinese leadership, however, argue that there is no serious departure from the course laid out by their revolution which introduced the People's Republic in 1949, all that they are doing now is to correct the mistakes that were committed in the past which departed from the original path. The real course to Socialism begins with understanding the concrete reality of one's country and devising policies suitable to that reality.

A largely peasant and backward society like that of China needs as a top priority to develop 'productive forces,' to develop the material basis for Socialist construction and, in order to achieve that end, every means available to society must be utilised to the maximum. Socialism, they emphasise, is about abundance, not about poverty. You cannot divide poverty; you must first develop the 'national cake' before you can divide it; and to develop it you must have advanced means of production plus advanced technology. In this effort everyone has a role to play in raising production: private enterprise, co-operatives, state enterprises, trade unionists, and so on.

To use economic terms, they say that an economy based on the law of 'planned and proportionate development' can legitimately use the law of value in the early stages of economic construction without distorting the law of planning or debasing its ideological foundation. The principal instrument of the economy still remains the central planning mechanism and the objective still Socialist.

To someone from Africa, who has been engaged in the struggle for rapid development and who went through various experimentation stages in economic construction, this was a most thrilling experience. It is more so when one has been to China on several occasions and seen and discussed the various eras that that country went through since 1949.

The New Democracy period (1949 - 56) was exciting precisely because it was so relevant to Africa's needs. This is the period (the theory goes) in which all democratic parties in the country came together under one United Front to ensure a strong central co-ordination during the creation of the new nation, new state, new national ethics, new foundations for national construction, and so on but at the same time avoiding the stifling experience of a one party state. It is also a period when the various trends and tendencies within the country which are not used by external interests are given an opportunity to make their contribution to national construction, as Socialists, as Capitalists, as peasant producers and so on.

China went through this period with impressive results and has aroused the enthusiasm of many social theorists in Africa and elsewhere in spite of the massive negative

Western propaganda at the time. Those who visited China then saw the future being created under their very eyes; all sections of Chinese society were in one way or another involved in the creation.

When the Great Leap interrupted New Democracy few foreigners noticed any discontinuity and it came at a time when China was developing an independent position from Krushchev's USSR and therefore enjoyed the sympathy of all the parties that were opposed to the new leadership in Moscow.

Reality apparently was submerged under deafening patriotism and no one had the true picture of what was going on in China. It was in fact massive dislocation side by side with massive construction. The resultant 'balance' meant stagnation. This period (1956 - 66) was characterised by China's heavy involvement internationally - Vietnam, Indonesia, Albania, liberation movements in Africa, socialist and communist movements in Europe, the Americas, Asia, Australasia, and so on. China was a world figure to be reckoned with, although materially a weak and backward country.

The era of the Cultural Revolution (1966 - 77) was most exciting too, no matter whether you were for or against it, It was a period of unprecedented mass defiance, ostensibly to destroy the old and build the new, a period of scientific innovation in the midst of chaos (China's nuclear development, space technology via intercontinental ballistic missiles, etc., were achieved during this period). The "Thoughts of Mao" became universal; you either supported it or opposed it but were never indifferent. In Africa, the Tanzam Railway (TAZARA) was under way, the biggest single Chinese investment overseas, and completed two years ahead of schedule. But the revolution also meant a setback for China's rapid development because here, too, the negative counterbalanced the positive which resulted in stagnation.

The current era, intended to correct most of the past mistakes and has also been received with a lot of enthusiasm internally and internationally. Individual incentives are producing excellent economic results in agriculture and handicrafts; the responsibility system guided by the principle of "to each according to his work" has led to increased productivity in industry, both light and heavy, and consumer goods are in abundance. The policy of "opening to the world" has attracted a lot of interest in the country and a lot of investment in the allotted enterprises designed specifically to attract capital and technology.

Visiting China now, one cannot help being involved in the excitement and in the optimism for the future. China is determined to be a "modern nation" by the turn of the century and, if the ongoing examples are anything to go by, the 21st century will indeed see a new China and a new world. There is a useful lesson here to be learned by Africa, especially now when we are going through the most difficult experience economically and financially since independence.

Notes

(1) Babu wrote this article after visiting China after a gap of 16 years

The Masses are Hungry
Africa Events, January 1985

Once again the UN has, on 3 December, unanimously carried yet another emergency declaration on the economic situation in Africa. Its main emphasis is on food production but a special UN conference will be convened at the end of December to concretize the details of the declaration. It is a reflection of the genuine concern of the international community for the plight of the millions of people who face imminent death or permanent brain and physical damage and the unfortunate children who have become the primary and the most vulnerable victims of the famine.

This is comforting although it is necessary to be aware that no amount of UN resolutions can really redress this ugly situation if no drastic change in our thinking and in the order of our priorities accompany these well-meaning resolutions and declarations There is a tendency among diplomats and politicians to smugly congratulate themselves with a sense of victory as soon as a resolution they have sponsored or supported is adopted. Once one resolution is over and done with, they move on to the next, quite oblivious to what happens to the first one - as long as it is on record, all's well.

Beginning from the early 1960's, this practice has developed almost into a habit among our politicians and diplomats. Even in those days when the situation was not yet as bad as it now is, it was already clear that we were heading for a calamity if no action was immediately taken; the rumblings of the impending disaster were loud and clear. It was then that the UN declared the 1960's as the First Development Decade with the intention of mobilising world resources to help developing countries improve their economic and social conditions. By the end of the decade, however, the situation in the developing world worsened. The UN and the World Bank were so alarmed that they hastily appointed Mr. Lester B Pearson, a former Canadian Prime Minister, to head a UN Commission to inquire into the causes of, and recommend remedies for the crisis of underdevelopment.

On the basis of the recommendations of the Pearson Report, the UN adopted the Second Development Decade (1971-1980). But just before the end of the decade, the situation became so obviously bad that the UN once again resolved to appoint yet another Commission. This time it was headed by the veteran and internationally involved West German Social Democrat, Willy Brandt, former Mayor of West Berlin and later West German Chancellor and a Nobel Peace laureate. Brandt selected a handful of notables from the developing world, as well as the developed, to be members of his Commission and by 1980 they had tabled their recommendation, later to be known as the Brandt Commission Report. This became the blueprint for the Third UN Development Decade and was known as the New International Development strategy for 1981-1990. Halfway through the decade we are already in a much worse situation than we were at the beginning.

Side by side with these new development strategies for the 1980s, the UN had another programme for the Least Developed Countries (LDCs) the substantial New Programme of Action which was formulated at the special UN Conference in September 1986 and later endorsed by the UN General Assembly which also adopted a Special Measures Fund to help the LDCs. As we know the deterioration has now turned into a plunge. Starvation has worsened, although everybody including our governments, knew then of the impending disaster.

Earlier that year, in April 1980, the 2nd Extraordinary Session of the OAU had adopted the Lagos Plan of Action (LPA) which outlined development priorities as human resource development, food, self-sufficiency, and protection of the natural environment. LPA pledged the commitment of the OAU member states to implementing yet another UN programme known as the Transport and Communication Decade of Africa. All these resolutions and programmes precede the declaration of 3 December 1984.

Scanning through all these new strategies, declarations and programmes one cannot help suspecting that firstly, they have all been written by the same people with the same mental habit and secondly, that they were all intended rather as an exercise in public relations than a serious attempt to find solutions to our plight.

The people who run international institutions, regional organisations and even our bureaucracies normally argue their cases from the same logical premises; they all think alike, use the same categories, view the world from more or less the same perspective and enjoy roughly the same standard of living. They have about the same educational and cultural background -in some cases they went to the same colleges and universities in Europe and North America, probably guided by the same teachers and professors. In short, whether they work for the US State Department, Whitehall, the UN, the World Bank, the OAU, or any government in Africa, from Algeria to Zimbabwe, they bring with them the same perspective implanted by the same source.

As a public relations exercise these documents are superb and up-to-date. A couple of generations ago, the pundits of the psychology of salesmanship found out that if you put the word "new" to any of your products it was bound to sell like hot cakes. For some reason, anything new has a magical impact on our psyche, and it is more so in societies in dire hardship and in a state of hopelessness. New is somehow accompanied with hope. Hence the new strategies, new economic order, new development decade, etc. They all have the effect of intoxicating the starving people with hope. However, while it is necessary for our existence to have some hope in life, it becomes extremely counter-productive if it is empty, not accompanied with tangible results.

And this is the situation we are in now. For the last two years, everybody concerned with the matter was certain of the impending famine but apart from declarations and resolutions, hardly any of our governments took appropriate measures to prepare for the disaster. It is a fact that some leaders take it for granted that the "international community" would not passively let us starve and would come to our aid at the critical moment. Some are simply overwhelmed by the magnitude of the organisational work which crises-management entails and just give up in despair and wait for "something to turn up". Some just have no time to think of the future, having totally absorbed themselves in the day-to day manouvering for positions in their petty struggle for power. Some have quite different priorities, such as building Club Mediterranean's, tourist towns and gambling casinos. Others who are more serious and genuine in their efforts to find the solutions are confronted with insurmountable structural obstacles because their economies are still conditioned to produce for the world market and not for internal consumption.

And when the inevitable happens, as it now has, hundreds of thousand of people perish daily or are on the move from one border country to the next in a hopeless search for food. Millions of TV viewers around the world are daily subjected to generous portions of harrowing scenes of children dying in their mothers' cadaverous arms while sucking the shrunk and dangling skin which once adorned a distended human breast. A human degradation made worse because it could have been averted or at least minimised if our priorities were properly ordered to serve people's welfare.

Most of the leaders have already lost any real hope for the future and have left the initiative to the "international community". They already claim the right to be fed off the surplus grain from the EEC countries and they do so by making the Europeans feel guilty for producing so much grain, milk and butter while we are starving. This mentality of dependence, the mentality of asking for alms and charity, which is becoming universal in our countries, must be combated vigorously before it evolves into a habit. As an antidote we must cultivate the spirit of genuine, as opposed to rhetorical self-reliance, especially among the up-and-coming generation, our future leaders, who will have to bear the brunt of past and present mistakes.

We must, for instance, try to learn by asking ourselves: What makes Europe, with such limited land area and the highest population density in the world, still capable of producing so much surplus food? Why is it that Africa, with such vast human, material and physical resources with the lowest population density in the world, is still unable to feed itself now and that by the turn of the century we shall be needing three times as much food aid from overseas? Is it an act of God? The answer is quite simple: it is not. The fact is that Europe, unlike us the victims, has long realised one fundamental truth, which is that internal causes are the basis of change, and external causes are only conditions of change. That is to say, an economy must have internal material basis for it to develop and then, and only then, can external causes create conditions for such development. It is rather like an egg: it must have an internal basis before the incubator can turn it into a chicken. No amount of external causes can transform a stone into a chicken.

But we do the opposite. We say once the external conditions are right - for example, the New International Economic Order - then our development will follow irrespective of the internal basis. It is this topsy-turvy way of looking at things that we must combat if we are to utilise our resources to our maximum advantage No amount of UN resolutions can achieve that for us. The solution is within our own reach.

Similarly, with all the best intentions in the world, alms and charity cannot sustain us for long. While we must remain grateful to all those wonderful and generous human beings who came forward with selfless aid and assistance of all kinds at the height of our worst tragedy in recorded history, the best way to show our gratitude and appreciation is to prove to the world that we are determined to achieve food self-sufficiency by next year or at most by the year after. That is achievable It requires not only tripling our effort but more importantly, a drastic change in the order of our priorities, as well as in the style and type of leadership. Leaders with villas in Paris or who rely on brute force to stay in power are not the type who can transform disaster into prosperity. In the final analysis it is not the leaders who will deliver the goods but the people, and they must feel masters in their own countries before they can transform themselves from passivity into energetic actors on nature. That requires, as a precondition, a different type of leadership.

Counter Punch
Africa Events, June 1985

The OAU Summit this July will be concerned almost exclusively with the problems of food (or the lack of it) and external debt, both of which have become the major scourges of Africa. Both of which, moreover, are man-made and can be rectified by sound economic policies. This article will be concerned especially with agriculture, with industry, with general economic development, with emphasis on food.

In discussing this topic, it is important to bear in mind a few pertinent observations at the outset.

Egypt, as a rule, has no rain to speak of; it is in "permanent drought" if you like. But Egypt, with its population of more than 40 million, the second largest in Africa, can feed its people and have a lot more extra to spare. They hardly have any tractors either. So what is their secret? Well, they utilise to the maximum the water resources of the Nile for irrigation and they use draught animals instead of tractors.

China, up to the end of the 1940s, suffered famine every year and millions of its people would perish annually. The tragedy was so constant that in the end nobody was ever shocked by the horrors that China was going through. One quarter of the human race lives in China. Today, China is a major grain-exporting country with a possible export sale of 5m tonnes this year. How did they achieve this spectacular success? Simply by way of reordering their priorities. They did not wait for the New International Economic Order to bail them out.

Ethiopia is suffering severe famine with millions of people either perishing or likely to suffer permanent physical and mental damage for the rest of their lives owing to malnutrition. Yet in the midst of all this suffering, Ethiopia still exports coffee and exotic vegetables to the tables of the rich world. What brought about this grotesque contradiction? Simple: stubborn refusal by the policy-makers to reorder their priorities in production. Whereas land reform in China had positive results and meant prosperity for the broad masses of the people, land reform in Ethiopia had negative results and meant disaster to millions of its people. Why? Because in the former, production priorities were correct and in the latter not. Ethiopia is as old as China (or Egypt) with as long and rich an agricultural tradition which disproves any possible assertion that China has greater skills in agriculture than Ethiopia.

These three examples tell us that the argument that we are starving because there is no rain is untenable when we have some of the major rivers of the world crisscrossing the entire continent; and we have lakes second to none in size and depth. That we have so many mouths to feed is equally a false argument because Africa has the lowest population density in the world. That we are less capitalist or more socialist makes no sense either, because both 'capitalist' and 'socialist' countries in Africa suffer more or less equally. That we suffer because of the unfair international economic order holds no water because China, North Korea and others like them have moved ahead towards prosperity in spite of the unfair world economic order.

In the final analysis, needless to say, the reason why there is famine and starvation in Africa is that our economies are backward and that they have remained backward or worse since independence because the order of our priorities has not changed in essence since colonial times. Most of the surplus that our economies produce is drained out of our countries to the industrial countries of the West. The current estimate by the London-based World Development Movement is that $35bn per annum is drained in this way from the so-called Third World countries - or $4m per hour.

It is obvious, therefore, that firstly the inflow of aid and credits to our countries is far outstripped by the outflow of wealth and secondly, that capital accumulation virtually does not take place; consequently, there is nothing to invest for extended reproduction, the essential prerequisite for any development.

All international efforts, including the Brandt Commission, the Lagos Plan of Action and the New International Economic Order, are destined to fail because they refuse to face the crux of the matter, namely, that as long as there is this drainage there can be no development; and that this drainage cannot be remedied through negotiations since capitalist relations which govern capitalist world economy of which we are a part cannot change by negotiation.

This is how the Summit in July must approach the situation, to come up with a serious attempt to grapple with the problem. It is wrong to tackle the problem of agriculture or food in isolation from other aspects of the economy, especially the question of capital accumulation. If you continue to expand production for the world market instead of gradually reducing it; if you leave capital accumulation to emanate from international money lenders and donor countries instead of depending on locally generated capital; then you will be committing a crime against the people of Africa of the same magnitude as that of Ethiopia.

Of course, the OAU can hardly do much to remedy the situation since the solution ultimately and fundamentally lies with individual countries and their internal policies. However, it is important that our leaders are at least meeting to take stock of the tragic situation facing the continent. There will, of course, be the usual appeal to international agencies for help and appeals to foreign governments; there will be discussion on how to confront immediate needs of the affected countries and so on. But these are only temporary measures. The long-term solution to our plight is the more important aspect of the problem. And the solution, let it be repeated, can only be achieved by individual countries.

The real constraint to our development is lopsided development. It must be our immediate task to rectify it. Our productive sector, i.e., agriculture and industry, is not only backward but also not complementary: our agriculture is for export and our industry is for import substitution; consequently the development of the former is separate and unrelated to the development of the latter and vice versa. This automatically leads to uneven development and its damaging effects.

To correct it, we must organise our production so that agriculture supports industry and industry agriculture on the basis of planned and proportionate development; by strictly observing the principle of balanced and proportional relations of all the major sectors of the economy while constantly recognising the key links in each of the following main proportional relations:

1. The relations between agriculture and industry, the two basic, mutually dependent sectors. It is the key link in national development.

2. The relations within agriculture i.e., between small and large-scale; between modern and traditional; between private and cooperative. In all these relations you cannot abandon one at the expense of the other. You can only phase out gradually that which represents the past, the inefficient and the uneconomical as the economy moves step-by-step towards a balanced and even development. The key link in agriculture is the production of FOOD.

3. The relations within industry between light and heavy industry; traditional technology and modern technology; between urban and rural industrialisation; between capital and labour intensive industries. The key link in industry is the production of steel.

4. The relations between industrial and agricultural production on the one hand and communication and transport on the other. The key link is industrial production.

5. The proportional relations between education and cultural construction on the one hand and economic construction on the other. The key link is the development of modern science and culture.

6. The proportional relations between increased population and increased social facilities. Family planning is not for reducing population growth but for planning people's livelihood; for the reproduction of the work force; and for the protection of the health of the mother and child. The key link is the mother.

7. The proportional relations between accumulation and consumption. The key link is the development of production capacity.

8. The proportional relations among various regions through rational distribution of production capacity. The key

link is the development of production capacity.

Of the eight proportional relations, the relations within agriculture, within industry and that between agriculture and industry are the three most important relations in the entire national economy and must be handled with great discipline and competence. This is because of all the economic links, in production, exchange, distribution and consumption, the determining link is production.

The solution to our financial and monetary crises; to our inflation; to our chronic deficit financing; to our internal and external indebtedness, also depends on production and not on financial juggling to which our economics constantly resort.

To achieve maximum results we must exercise vigilance by avoiding waste; and we should economise in manpower, materials and funds. Manpower is live labour; material is embodied labour; and funds mean live and embodied labour manifested in currency circulation. Frugality, in other words, means economising labour time; every waste in labour time has its penalty.

In advanced capitalist economies where labour time is wasted in chronic unemployment, the penalty is manifested in economic and monetary crises. These economies do not collapse because we are there to nourish and sustain them through our neocolonial relations and exploitation of our wealth through sale of our national resources at giveaway prices at the expense of our own economic development.

In our case, however, we have no one to exploit or plunder - although many leaders in our countries collaborate with external forces to exploit and plunder our people. We must rely for our capital accumulation on the diligent labour of our people, on frugality and on constantly creating new wealth.

If we continue to waste our labour-time in diverting resources to export branches, or large bureaucracies or excessive military spending and secret police; in pompous living and unbridled travel by our politicians and diplomats; in unproductive investment in useless projects and on borrowed money; in corruption; in umpteen conferences and all the fanfare attendant to them, and so on, the penalty is manifested in our universal hunger, in disease and in chronic underdevelopment.

Our leaders at Addis may wish to ponder on all this; once they do, they will begin to realise how easy it is to change from their usual approach to development to the one recommended above. It is the only way that can save Africa and which can lead to the full utilisation of our national resources for the benefit of our people. Do not let drought be the major cause of our disaster; our ancestors survived worse droughts every 10 or 20 years by utilising their own ingenuity. Let Egypt and China be an inspiration to catapult us to truly self-reliant economies. It can be done!

Basic Needs Approach[1]-arguing for the sake of argument, *Africa Events*, September 1988

Academics are probably the only people who are paid to argue for or against any crazy idea simply for the sake of argument. This is as it should be since one of their tasks is to challenge old ways of thinking, to incite new ideas and promote intellectual excitement among students. The trouble begins when they take themselves too seriously and attempt to put those, often half-baked, ideas into practice. Since, as a rule, their pet notions have never been tried out in the real world, any attempt to implement them often ends in disasters.

Nowhere has this disastrous academic adventure been more widely practiced than in Africa. Here, the experimenting academics have a field-day since the ground is virtually barren. Most political leaders have no time to think seriously about development strategies and much less of development itself; they are often too busy either enriching themselves by managing and exploiting the status quo - at the expense of the people, or organising and re-organising their political and repressive institutions to consolidate their autocratic rule and ensure a firmer social control. All serious thinking is therefore left to the academics.

The worst type are the well-off, well-fed, well-endowed, and very often well-meaning academics from the industrially developed countries, working in Africa as teachers or as advisors to governments. If they are ideologically on the Left they tend to be ultra-Left; or ultra-Right if they are on the Right: both having the damaging effect of distorting the concrete African reality. The liberals in the middle are often muddled sentimentalists, with neither experience nor vision on how the present can be projected into the future. This book is a typical example of this total lack of vision.

The book's main thesis, as the title implies, is about building an economy with emphasis on the promotion of what is now commonly referred to as basic human needs.

They call this the Basic Needs Approach (BNA). The author distinguishes between "strong" and "weak" BNA, describing the first as advocating "a new style of development which was radically participatory and in which land reform, asset redistribution and other necessary preconditions set the stage for the poor to take control of their own development, usually through grassroots organisations." This approach is said to be favoured by the radical critics of growth theory.

Whereas the strong BNA implies "popular political action", the "weak" BNA which, according to the author, is "promoted mostly by the bilateral and multilateral aid agencies", sees "participation as a limited, formalised process, stripped of the political volatility of direct popular involvement." Also, (horror of horrors!) the author sees this weak approach as bearing "an uncanny resemblance to the old modernisation model of development." This then tells you the whole story of the book's projection: Modernisation is out. "Production First" is out. No large-scale hydroelectric plants; no massive irrigation schemes; no large-scale flood-control projects. Indeed, no iron and steel, or machine tool industrialisation, or indeed any such basic industries essential for any form of development of an independent national economy. All these the author calls "grandiose" projects, and presumably unnecessary.

According to the author, the peasant must be left alone to fight, first against the interventions of the state officials whom the author calls the "elites" and "bureaucratic bourgeoisie" (both meaningless terms to describe those elevated and privileged sons and daughters of the peasantry whom the peasants themselves are proud of) and then to struggle against nature, presumably all on his/her own, or jointly with one or two surrounding villages, in order to procure basic, subsistence needs.

But the author's favourite peasants happen to be part of the same system - in fact a product of this same system - i.e. colonial economic relations. How then can they change this relation if they are "half rooted in what has to be changed"? To repeat the famous question: "How can the peasant understand that isolation and the commodity economy are no good to him if he himself is isolated and works at his own risk and responsibility for the market"?

There is not a single indication in the book to show if the author even remotely understands the significance of this question to development strategy.

The author's many examples of bad "modernisation" are drawn from his Kenya experiences, and he is at pain' to refute the favoured IMF and World's Bank's repeated assertions that Kenya and Ivory Coast are the shining examples for Africa to emulate. But does it really need a whole book to prove the obvious? Apart from this futile preoccupation, the author does not make any attempt to at least indicate to us where on earth this BNA thing has worked. His only example is the defunct Ruvuma Development Association (RDA) in Tanzania which, in fairness, can hardly be said to be an outstanding development model. He also mentions the Mbarara Ujamaa Village in Tanzania (and the Lushoto Integrated Development Project) as showing how "attempts at investments and farm planning were crushed by regional 'experts'." But like the RDA, no one who knows anything about these projects can seriously talk of them as outstanding examples in development, for God's sake!

Let us be clear of one thing, though: There is another form of Basic Need Approach, which has worked historically and continues to work today. It has worked in most advanced settler economies in the USA, Canada, Australia and, yes, even in South Africa and Rhodesia. It has worked to a certain extent in Kenya and Algeria too. Needless to say, all of them are historically oppressive and unjust slave and colonial societies, but that was not the key to their development success. All Portuguese and Spanish settler colonisation in Latin America were based on slavery, but to this day they are still underdeveloped neo-colonies. Turkey too was an extensive colonial empire but its legacy, both at home and abroad, is marked by underdevelopment.

No, the real motive force of their success was their development approach forced by necessity to produce for the settler's Basic Needs. They were the same needs as for the rest of us, i.e. food, shelter, and clothing. But the provision of these needs was linked (again by the necessity of building an independent national economy) to the development of the rest of the economy, and not as isolated, village-exclusive, welfare ventures, as is advocated by the BNA people. This kind of development-orientated Basic Needs Approach has also been pursued in countries like China with impressive results.

Housing the masses, for example, has resulted in the development of construction industry as a major national enterprise employing millions of workers who continually develop new skills essential for other forms of development activity. The policy of clothing the people has developed a vast and viable textile industry, employing millions of peasants and urban workers. A policy of food self-sufficiency to feed the people the development of large-scale irrigated state farms, entailed supplementing but not replacing the old traditional peasant farming. This too opened up vast employment opportunities to the peasantry ensuring them regular income and learning new skills.

Ultimately, all industrial activity, both heavy and light, was effectively and creatively linked to the provision of the Basic Human Needs. And because such industries provide employment on a massive scale, they have contributed enormously to the creation of the essential prerequisite for any development to take place: the home market.

Provision of health service, education and other welfare services directly accompanied the development of the flourishing agricultural and industrial enterprises. In this model, production takes the principal and leading role, while consumption, social or otherwise, assumes a secondary, but no less important, role.

The rationale of this model is clear. If agriculture (which in our countries occupies 90% of the population) is backward, then inevitably industry will be backward, and the economy will yield limited surplus for health, education, etc. If, on the other hand, the social welfare allocation is greater than the economy can afford, there will inevitably be insufficient accumulation to go into advancing agriculture and industry

Clearly, the proper balance between accumulation (production) and consumption is a prerequisite for any development. This we may call a Dynamic Approach to Basic Needs Strategy, but it cannot be achieved by relying on spontaneous, haphazard local initiative without any centrally coordinated strategy.

But this is a long way from the advocacy of the book under review - a confusing, wishy-washy fantasy which, if pursued, will inevitably create more problems and worsen our underdevelopment. The book is probably good for students' intellectual exercise, but not good enough as a strategy for development. It has no precedence in economic history, and it makes no strategic sense

Notes

(1) A review of *Power and Need in Africa* by Ben Wisner, Earthscan Publications Ltd, London, 1988.

Aid perpetuates dependency
Southern Africa Political and Economic Monthly, November 1994

Perceptive students of international relations have discerned new realities emerging in relations between rich and poor countries in this age of aid-culture. The most outstanding of these is the nature and form of both bilateral as well as multilateral aid flowing from the rich to poor countries. This aid flow seems to have developed its own momentum which no one is able to control. Hence the appearance on the aid scene of what has come to be known as "aid dealers, aid pushers and aid addicts".

The inference of this categorisation is that aid has become addictive and a self-perpetuating phenomenon in international relations. Its addiction is as pernicious and long-lasting as drugs. The only difference between the two is that the former is acceptable, and practised openly and legally, while the latter is not yet acceptable, and its activity is still clandestine and illegal. But the amounts of money involved in their respective transactions is equally overwhelming. In both cases, some of the money is visible, but most of it is laundered in secret deposit banks worldwide: and in the case of aid, it simply disappears! Both have the same effect of dulling our critical faculties.

In the early days of independence, some visionary leaders of the newly emerging African countries could foresee the possible damaging effect of aid-dependence to national reconstruction. So much so that they even coined a popular slogan "Trade, not Aid". The slogan at least expressed a desire for national self-esteem which came with trade in place of the humiliations of remaining permanently as aid-seekers. This slogan became the theme of the newly formed "Group of 77" at the first UNCTAD conference in Geneva in February 1964. However, trade turned out to be equally damaging to the economies of primary-commodity-exporting countries - in fact, the need for aid has become a necessary concomitant to our trade relations with developed economies: we trade with them, we lose, and we beg them for aid, and more aid! Aid is damaging to both givers and receivers. In most cases, especially in the case of voluntary agencies, aid is given in good faith, with a genuine desire to do good and to feel good. The aid donor, though, does not realise that his or her high standard of living is often maintained at the expense of the aid receiving countries whose cheap exports to developed countries are largely based on slave wages and where the peasant producer of coffee or cocoa earns less than eight cent for every dollar's worth of processed coffee or chocolate sold in Western supermarkets. In fact, the aid given to relieve the disastrous impact of this kind of exploitation of the poor by the rich only helps to consolidate the former's poverty.

We must make a distinction between disaster-relief aid as given to Rwanda, Somalia, Ethiopia, where food and medicine are in urgent demand, on the one hand, and the "development" aid on the other. However, even in the case of aid for disasters arising from famine, civil war or floods, some would argue that such emergencies are the direct or indirect consequences of the lopsided development of our economies which favour production of cash crops for export instead of food for local consumption.

Trading cheap primary commodities for expensive, high-wage industrial goods from the West always favours the latter, i.e. the aid givers. Their businesses flourish while the former wallow in endemic poverty.

To take one glaring example. Bob Geldof, the British musician, was so moved by the Ethiopian famine of 1984 that he launched a massive charity campaign worldwide that raised US $400 million. But, generous as no doubt it was, this amount is only equivalent to two days' transfer of wealth from Africa to Europe and America, thanks to the composition of our exports and imports, and the misguided trade policies, which rob the continent of nearly US $200 million per day. The converse of the old adage "fair exchange is no robbery" is unfair exchange is robbery! Consciously or not, aid in effect helps to make this massive robbery acceptable.

The situation in the official aid from Western countries is worse than that of the voluntary aid agencies. If the damage by the latter is unconscious, the former's is deliberate. Developed countries' governments have established ministries for "overseas development", dishing out "aid" to tackle effects, not causes, of unfair exchange. The purpose of this kind of "aid" is to maintain intact the international regime of robbing the poor in the North/South relations. Graham Hancock in his Lords of Poverty[1] shows not only the extent of corruption in the official aid, but also that this kind of aid is not always motivated by compassion as it is claimed: rather, its purpose is to block our way out of the status quo, out of underdevelopment.

If the official aid agencies are the "aid dealers", the voluntary aid agencies are the "aid pushers". They are known as the non-governmental organizations or NGOs. While most of them are motivated by honorable intentions, the effect of their aid to poor countries, as shown before, is not wholly positive.

They started modestly and humbly in the early days of Africa's independence, but now the aid agencies have become the beneficiaries from Africa's poverty. Although they themselves are not poor, poverty is their business, with rich returns. Recently, during the Rwanda emergency, a British company was exposed to be making £23 000 per day, as a fundraising agency for the British Red Cross in Rwanda. Many other charity agencies are of no higher moral rectitude.

The NGOs have virtually become neocolonial powers. They dictate the kind of aid offered and its location and insist on themselves managing their projects, even if competent management is available locally for the purpose. These NGOs are spread all over Africa, hundreds of them! In one capital city I visited recently, there were about 120 NGOs! Similar numbers are duplicating each other's functions in practically every African country. The majority of them are expensively located in capital cities, living it up like millionaires in the midst of poverty. These expatriates are to be seen in their fashionable four-wheel Suzukis, driving around in search of the best black market exchange rates for their dollars. They are everywhere pushing their "aid drug" which perpetuates the addiction. (For full documentation, see *The New Protectionism* by Tim Lang and Colin Hines, *Earthscan*, London, 1993).

So much for the "aid pushers". Their victims, the "aid addicts", are aplenty! With the honourable exception of Libya, all African countries are serious aid victims. They cannot do anything without it. Like all drug addicts, they are almost paralysed in agony at the threat of aid withdrawal. They will agree to anything to avoid it. The habit was initially formed by administering the aid-drug in small doses over the years. At first it came, via Oxfam, CIDA, SIDA, NORAD, DANIDA, etc., in the form of complementing government's "development programmes", at project level. It slowly worked its way into the entire state system, reaching the highest levels to become the most important component in our national economies. It is operating at the macro level where it directly influences the direction of the national economy through its contribution to the national recurrent budgets. Most African governments today cannot even pay their civil servants without a massive dose of foreign aid. In some extreme cases; foreign aid accounts for up to 80 percent of the national budget!

Aid agencies have thus become the policy makers of our countries. They dictate policies not only on financial management, but also on population, on human rights, on democracy, on party policies, on ideology, on religion and above all, they even dictate the directions of our economies so as to attune them to the political and economic strategic concerns of the G7 industrial powers. Because of their addiction to the aid-drug, our countries obediently follow the aid barons' instructions, without giving a thought to their implications on our short-and long-term interests. In the final analysis, the quest for aid is seriously compromising our economic prospects and undermines our national self-esteem in the process.

Is Africa condemned to the intoxicating rule of aidocracy? Is it possible to kick the habit, get rid of the pushers and be liberated from the dealers? It is not impossible, but the task is tough. Like kicking the other drug habit, it requires will, determination and self-discipline. Unfortunately, a lot of national leaders have developed a vested interest in living under the lulling comfort of aidocracy. As sub-pushers and as addicts, they are too dependent on it to have the necessary will to resist.

Aid-addiction is rapidly spreading to the civil society as well. Already there is a proliferation of "local NGOs", who are funded entirely by foreign aid agencies. They are virtually foreign agents, for better or worse. As new recruits in the business, they tend to be most enthusiastic sub-pushers, which has qualified them to the donors as the most favoured recipients of aid.

If both aid and trade have let us down, then the only way out is to rekindle the long forgotten, but honourable, notion of Self Reliance. We must reorder our economic priorities and place the satisfaction of our internal needs at the top of the list - food, clothing and shelter. This is the real foundation of all developed economies. We must aim, not at "sustainable growth", but at *self-sustaining development*. As Malaysia's recent experience has shown, we must learn to utilise our social labour-time, which is our social capital, more effectively and efficiently, instead of wasting it in the production of useless "cash crops". We must gradually, but temporarily, retreat from the world economy which, through our trading in primary commodities. deprives us of the opportunity to accumulate and invest for growth. Instead, we must concentrate on strengthening the internal base through what the Chinese call: Readjusting, Restructuring, Consolidating and Improving. A strong internal foundation is the precondition for change from our "natural economies" (dependent as they are on cash crops and aid), to "development on an extended scale". Once the internal basis is firmly consolidated, then, and only then, can we profitably re-enter the world economy from a position of relative strength. This is the only way to overcome the pernicious aid addiction and to liberate ourselves from aidocracy which not too long ago we used to call imperialism. It can be done! We must organise to do it!

Notes

(1) Graham Hancock (1993) *Lords of Poverty*, Manderin

Panafricanism

Speech to the 4th PAFMECA[1] Conference in Addis Ababa as General Secretary of the Zanzibar Nationalist Party[2]

As an old veteran of PAFMECA I am glad to see the growth of this organisation both in membership and influence. We have moved from an obscure hall at Mwanza in Tanganyika where we held our first PAFMECA Conference, via Zanzibar where we held our second to Mbale in Uganda where we held our third, right up to this exalted and magnificent Imperial Capital.

At the first historic Conference we were gathered as a band of 'rebels' and agitators; we were insignificant in the eyes of the imperialist world We quietly plotted and schemed, as rebels would, with determination and purpose. We set ourselves a goal, namely complete liberation of our countries, and we were determined to realise this goal by all means, fair and foul.

We are now well on the way to achieving that goal completely. It is highly significant that having held our first conference in Tanganyika, Tanganyika should be the first among our member countries to achieve independence. This is no accident it is indicative of the revolutionary spirit of the Tanganyika people which encouraged the first PAFMECA Conference to be held in their country, in spite of the oppression of the British imperialists

A lot of us who were then "rebels" are now ministers and statesmen. We have Mr. Kiwanuka here as the Chief Minister of Uganda. We have Mr. Maswanya as a Minister without Portfolio - and in Tanganyika it is a stepping stone to Prime Ministership! We have Mr. Monanka the old guard of PAFMECA, as Parliamentary Secretary to the Prime Minister of Tanganyika. A lot of others are back home engaged in affairs of State. The only genuine "rebel" from among the original "rebels" whose organisations met at the first historic Conference at Mwanza is perhaps Mr. Kaunda

Thus, Mr.Chairman, while at the Mwanza Conference the circumstances were such that it was but natural that we should approach our problem in a certain frame of mind we will be unrealistic, and it may well prove dangerous, if we pursue that same frame of mind in dealing with our present problems.

The circumstances surrounding us in our struggle at present have raised it to a different level and we must find that level and raise ourselves to it in order to deal with the new situation effectively. In other words we must plan our strategy. But we cannot plan our strategy if we do not know the enemy against whom we are fighting. To fight without a strategy is like fighting blind folded - you may blindly line up with your enemy in his fight against your brother!

Imperialism is on the retreat as far as direct rule is concerned, but imperialism as a system is still creating havoc in our struggle to regain Africa We have forced imperialism into a retreat through our unity. Unity is our strongest weapon. The imperialists know this fact too and they are determined to rob us of our weapon.

Luckily the whole of Africa today is vigilant in safeguarding this unity An independent state in Africa feels the burden of subjugation as acutely as a dependent state. As Dr. Nkrumah, that uncompromising fighter for Pan-Africanism said "We are not fighting for African liberation only, we are fighting also for the political unification of Africa, for without unity there can be no future for the African People".

Our enemy, therefore, is anyone who wants to disrupt that unity. In their attempt to divide Africa the imperialists tried to classify us into two groups. Africans North of the Sahara and South of the Sahara. The creation of the All African People's Conference dealt a decisive blow to this imperialist scheme. Africa is Africa and the Sahara is in Africa!

Our Conference here will also deal a blow to the imperialist machinations. As part of the All African People's Conference we are helping to push forward the ideology of unity We are neither South nor East, neither North nor West we are one.

But the imperialists are trying again to divide us in a slightly different form. They are referring to us in terms of blocs But we tell the imperialists that we in Africa have only one bloc an African bloc. A bloc dedicated to complete liberation of Africa. And if we should talk in terms of blocs Africa is a bloc against the imperialist bloc. I referred to Mr. Kaunda as the remaining "rebel" because the struggle of PAFMECA is now centered in Rhodesia in its ugliest form. Mr. Kaunda and Mr.Nkomo deserve our fullest support - material and otherwise. So long as Rhodesia is in the hands of the fascist regime neither Tanganyika's nor Zanzibar's independence is safe. We all know the attempts by Welensky to consolidate Tshombe and disrupt the Congo unity We all know about the pressure of Welensky on the British Government to delay the independence of Kenya as long as it is possible for Britain to delay it.

Rhodesia must be free under any circumstances for as long as that regime of fascists remains, the unity of the whole of Africa will be difficult to achieve. Brother Kaunda has told us about his programme of action. Now it remains on us to support it fully and support it we will. My delegation is pledged on behalf of the Zanzibar Nationalist Party to give the people of Rhodesia our fullest support in their struggle for liberation. We suggest that a "Rhodesia Freedom Fund" be set up at once so that all who wish to support the Rhodesian struggle can contribute. All the people in our regions must be made conscious of the Rhodesian struggle by being asked to contribute to this fund. We must leave this conference determined to see to it that when we meet next time Rhodesia will be firmly in the hands of the African people. That is the challenge facing us.

For the countries that are on the threshold of independence a new and dangerous situation is arising - namely, the intrigues of the neocolonialists. The imperialists having been frustrated politically are actively trying to regain their position economically. Through cajole and flattery, with offers of "financial assistance" the imperialists are trying to corrupt our leaders into dancing to their tune. Happily, our leaders and people are alert to this danger. But we must intensify our vigilance. Essentially the neocolonialists are our oppressors and we, the oppressed, cannot reconcile our interests with the interests of the oppressors.

The greatest blow to the neocolonialists is the unity of Africa. It must be our urgent duty to strengthen this unity. Already we have the All African People's Conference, and in strengthening this body we shall be strengthening our position in the battle against neocolonialism. The imperialists want us to feel that we cannot exist without their support. This is the psychological mood they want to perpetuate in the people's minds. But, in spite of the neocolonialist efforts, the people of Africa understand quite clearly that the only way to salvation is to rely on their own efforts. We have unlimited strength and once we make full use of this strength the imperialists will once again be frustrated in their economic aggression. We must defeat our enemy - imperialism - in all directions. And we must crush it so it never again raises its ugly head.

In unity lies our salvation.

Notes

(1) Pan-African Movement for East and Central Africa was set up in 1958 see 'Pan Africanism and the New World Order' p...
(2) At this time Babu was still officially known as Abdul Rahman Mohamed. In 1957, he changed his name by deed poll to Babu, the childhood nickname given by an Indian neighbour, which was how he was always popularly known

Patrice Lumumba
African Concord, 29 January 1987

The rise of Patrice Lumumba to political prominence in the Congo (Zaire) coincided with, or was probably a result of, the anti-colonial ferment that had engulfed Africa at the time. Less than two years before his debut to international eminence, hardly anybody knew of Congo's political scene, and much less of Lumumba.

In the Congo itself he was known to only a handful of his comrades who had formed a half-hearted political movement with very limited political objectives. Belgian colonialism was probably the worst form of paternalistic colonialism, which regarded its "colonial subjects" as just slightly more than children. Their whole rule in the Congo was shrouded in secrecy, with hardly any news going in to or out of the country. The Lumumbaist movement was therefore wholly unknown outside his immediate circle of comrades and who in turn knew hardly anything about the political movements in the rest of Africa.

Thus, when the delegations of the Pan African Movement for East and Central Africa (PAFMECA) stopped over for 3 days at Leopoldville (now Kinshasa) in December 1958 on their way to Accra, Ghana and the first All African People's Conference, the Belgian authorities gave them what amounted to a royal welcome. The delegates came to know later that the purpose of that hospitality was really to keep them as far away as possible from the nascent political movement in the country. They were introduced to all the "Africans that mattered", the so-called evalue who had attained the "civilised levels" approved by the colonial master. These had nothing but praise for the Belgians who were "helping the Africans towards maturity".

The Belgians kept repeating to the East and Central African delegates that "there is no politics in Congo; no trouble-makers. We are all one family". This blissful situation, however, sounded strange and even unreal to the emerging African politicians who were on their way to declare war on colonialism.

On their second day of their stay, they made discreet enquiries among hotel workers if there existed any political movement in the country. This resulted, very late that night, in their being introduced to Lumumba and his comrades at a nightclub in the African section of the city. The Congolese politicians were naturally suspicious at first and they wanted to know what brought these East African politicians to the Congo. It soon transpired that the Congolese comrades had heard nothing about the impending all-African conference in Accra that month, although it had been widely publicised all over Africa for the previous six months or more.

After outlining the political objectives of their movement, the Lumumbaists expressed the desire to also attend the Accra conference but were financially constrained, as their movement was still very young. Thereupon the Kenya delegation offered to pay for the air fare for all five of them and from then on Congo politics took a most dramatic turn in modern African history. Events came crowding in quick and momentous succession from that day in December 1958 to the tragic and untimely death of Patrice Lumumba at the hands of the CIA and their local agents.

For, as soon as Kwame Nkrumah was informed of the impending participation of the Congolese delegation to the Conference, he gave instruction that they should see him as soon as they arrived, and when he eventually met them, he requested them to stay longer in Accra after the Conference was over. Ghana's commitment to Congo's independence henceforth was to become Nkrumah's obsession.

Lumumba returned to Congo a few weeks after the Accra conference, and his arrival turned into a political event of national and far-reaching magnitude. He immediately emerged as the national leader – an unknown phenomenon in a Congo that was deliberately kept divided by the colonialists. He became the "trouble-maker" who was to disrupt the bliss that the Belgians had nurtured for many past decades. He ignited the spark of freedom that led to Congo's independence much sooner then the whole of East and Central Africa whose delegates had helped to put him and the Congo on the political arena of the world.

It was not Lumumba's fault that Congo's independence was marked by the chaotic menace of foreign mercenaries,

CIA, Tchombeism, and the death of the UN Secretary General, Dag Hammerschold. Congo has always been and will always remain a key factor in Africa's geo-politics, for better or worse. Too many interests were at stake, too many pundits, African and non-African, were involved and too much ignorance about the country as a result of Belgian rule of secrecy – all have conspired to make the post-colonial Congo history what it is.

It will be useful to recall that at the time of Lumumba's advent to power the world was witnessing a most dangerous period of East/West global confrontation. The US was just emerging from the anti-communism hysteria of McCarthyism. The "Cold War" was raging and US power was being challenged internationally. The Soviet Union had just made unprecedented diplomatic and psychological gains by her dramatic advance in space technology with her Sputniks and "walks in space" achievements. In Asia, colonialism and imperialism were being challenged by China and Vietnam both of whom were then identified with the Soviet Union. And in Algeria, the revolutionary war was teaching Africa that French colonialism was only "a paper tiger".

Technological successes of the Soviet Union meant demoralisation in the US as this was taken to mean that the US was "loosing out to the Russians". At the same time, the US was being challenged by her own allies in Europe as de Gaulle of France was warning the whole of Europe against the emerging "menace of US colonisation of Europe".

Thus any shift in the balance of forces in Africa was interpreted in terms of East/West "numbers game" – a "plus" to the Soviets meant a "minus" to the US and vice versa. The "loss of Congo to the communists" would have meant a serious setback to the US's global "credibility" as well as to military strategy as conceived then. The US therefore took it upon herself to fight on all fronts – against the "Soviet encroachment", against European and especially "de Gaulle's meddling", and against the emerging African nationalism which took the form of anti-imperialism. Although Lumumba symbolised and stood for the latter he was deliberately identified with advancing Soviet encroachment in order to find a pretext for his immediate liquidation.

The Europeans propped up Moise Tchombe to advance their interests in the Congo; the US had to make-do with Kasavubu while grooming a more ruthless surrogate to take over the country on her behalf. It was in this atmosphere that Lumumba was sacrificed by fellow Africans to advance the contending interests of foreign powers.

What Lumumba will be remembered as is his leadership in the calibre of the great pan-African leaders. Although his prominence as a national leader was very short-lived, his image as an uncompromising fighter against imperialism and as genuine leader of African masses will undoubtedly continue to inspire the emerging generation of African fighters whose principal task will be the attainment of Africa'' most cherished goal of Pan-Africanism. Lumumba at independence was a leader of the people of Congo; Lumumba after independence and after his death has been transformed deservedly into a towering leader not only of Africa and the African people the world over, but also into a leader of oppressed people everywhere. This will be the legacy of this great son of Africa.

Regional Co-operation in Africa
African Concord, 1 October 1987

Ever since independence, African countries have been attempting in one way or another to form some form of regional co-operation but without any outstanding success. The objectives have always been the same: to foster regional co-operation as a means of promoting the well-being of the people through regional economic development.

Various forms have been thought of, or even in some cases, implemented. These include free trade area, customs union, common market, economic community, economic union, political union, and federation.

Apart from the Organisation of African Unity (OAU) which is a political organisation of the whole continent minus white-ruled South Africa, other organisations are mostly economic and are limited to some areas or regions of the continent.

In West Africa there are several such organisation, some dating back to the colonial period, like the African and Mauritian Common Organisation (OCAM). Most of the member states emerged from French colonialism with the exception of Somalia. There is the West African Economic Community, or in its French name: Communaute Economique de l'Afrique L'Ouest (CEAO), which comprises six French-speaking African countries – Burkina Fasso, Mali, Senegal, Mauritania, Ivory Coast and Niger.

Previous to CEAO these countries were grouped in some other French-speaking organisations most of which are now defunct. They include the Federation of French West Africa (dissolved in 1958); the Conseil de l'Enttente (CE), comprising Benin, Ivory Coast, Niger, Togo and Burkina Fasso; the Mali Federation of 1959 comprising Benin, Senegal, Mali and Burkina Fasso.

There is also the Douaniere Economique de l'Afrique Centrale (UDEAC) which is a customs union of French speaking West African states of Ivory Coast, Benin, Mauritania, Senegal, Niger, Burkina Fasso and Togo. But when it was realised that the elimination of trade barriers within UDEAC was leading to "polarisation", ie the more developed states derived benefits from the Union at the expense of the least developed, the Union was dropped to be replaced by CEAO in 1973. The CEAO became a sub-grouping within the larger Economic Community of West African States (ECOWAS) which includes English-speaking and Portuguese speaking West African states. ECOWAS treaty provides for the establishment of a customs union which would abolish customs duty among member states and a common external customs tariff from countries outside the community. The envisaged customs union, however, would be achieved gradually after the achievement of a free trade area.

Other African regional organisations include the West African Monetary Union (UMOA), Organisation for Senegal River development (OMVS), Lake Chad Basin Commission (LCBC) and Niger River Commission (NRC).

But the oldest and most experienced regional grouping was the East African Economic Community (EAEC) which collapsed in 1977. It is worth paying closer attention to this organisation because of the useful lessons that can be learnt from its experiences.

This organisation stemmed from its colonial predecessor, the East African High Commission which comprised of the three British colonies of Kenya, Uganda and Tanganyika. Kenya and Uganda had formed a customs union as far back as 1917 when Tanganyika was then still a German colony.

After the First World War Tanganyika became a UN Trusteeship colony under the British and in 1927 it joined the two others in the customs union. Throughout the colonial period the British had prepared grounds for an East African Federation, but the idea was opposed by the people of all the three "territories" because the federation was designed to be dominated by the Kenya white settlers in much the same way as the Central African Federation was later dominated by Rhodesian settlers.

Still, owing to a strong and viable settler economy of Kenya, that country's capital Nairobi became the Headquarters of the High Commission, with the British Governor of Kenya its permanent Chairman. Consequently, Kenya enjoyed most of the benefits, especially the free trade. As independence was approaching Uganda and Tanganyika launched a campaign to rectify the imbalance brought about by the polarisation. As a result, in 1960 the Raisman Commission was appointed to look into the matter. In its report, the Commission recommended the setting up of a budget revenue distribution system whereby each country would get 94% of its own customs revenue and 60% of its own tax revenue. Half of the collected amount would go towards the operation of the common services and the other half would be divided equally among the three countries.

In 1964 the Kampala agreement was signed as a further attempt to rectify the imbalance, since, in spite of the Raisman's arrangement, industrial development in Uganda and Tanganyika still lagged behind that of Kenya. The Kampala agreement emphasised the redistribution of industrial activity. But by 1966 it was seen that Kenya still enjoyed greater benefits. Export of manufactured goods, for instance, within the community was: Kenya 68%, Uganda 23%, and Tanzania 9%.

In 1967, as a result of the Phillips Commission, the East African Economic Community was formed with a three-pronged strategy, which was also designed to rectify the imbalance. First, the Headquarters of the common services were to be distributed fairly. Second, it established the "Transfer Tax" which provided for the deficit country like Uganda or Tanzania to levy a tax on the imports of the surplus country. Third, the establishment of a Development Bank to be subscribed equally by the three countries, but Tanzania to have 38.75% of the loan, Uganda also 38.75% and Kenya 22.5%.

By 1977 the Community came to an undignified end, with each of the three countries literally grabbing as much of the Community's assets as it could lay its hands on. Among the shared common services were East African Airways, E.A. Railways, (hosted in Kenya); the E.A. Development Bank and the E.A Post and Communications, (hosted by Uganda); and Tanzania hosted the HQ of the

Community at Arusha, and the East African Harbour Corporation.

From a community of friendship the E.A. states degenerated into a community of hostile camps, and all the three suffered serious economic setbacks. Moreover, the petty competitions and jealousies which had existed prior to the break-up of the Community developed into serious self-destructive rivalries which threatened their respective security. Each of the countries suspected the other of plotting to undermine their sovereignty. In 1978 the situation deteriorated to armed hostilities when Amin's Uganda invaded Tanzania and occupied some of her territory. The war ended in Tanzania's victory and the overthrow of Idi Amin as President of Uganda.

Of the three countries Tanzania turned its attention southwards soon after the break-up. She took the initiative to form an informal political organisation to be known as the "Frontline States". This was facilitated by the collapse of the Portuguese Empire in 1975 which led to the independence of Mozambique and Angola, who became part of the Frontline states. When Zimbabwe won her independence in 1980, the Frontline States expanded into a new politico-economic organisation, the Southern African Co-ordinating Conference (SADCC). The original six frontline states, namely Mozambique, Zimbabwe, Zambia, Angola, Botswana and Tanzania were now joined by Lesotho, Swaziland and Malawi to form the SADCC.

Whereas the objective of the East African Economic Community was to bring about economic co-operation of the three countries in a future East African federation, the objectives of the SADCC are less ambitious; they are to lessen their dependence on South Africa's economy.

Side by side with the development of SADCC there also developed a free trade area (FTA) among the SADCC countries, this time including Kenya and Uganda. Tanzania, however, was reluctant to join, presumably guided by her unfortunate experience in the EAEC.

Can SADCC and FTA succeed when other regional co-operations have virtually failed elsewhere in Africa? Will not

Zimbabwe and Kenya end up by reaping most of the benefits and the rest bearing most of the costs? Would the polarisation effect, in addition to accelerating the prosperity of the more prosperous, also accentuate the uneven development in the region and aggravate the lopsided development of the least developed member countries?

There is no doubt that Zimbabwe and Kenya will benefit from the FTA which promoted the free entry of their manufactured goods to the markets of the member states. Sooner or later the interests of the more developed and those of the least developed will necessary come into conflict as the latter begin their import-substitution industrialisation and feel the need to protect infant industries.

Although the SADCC is less ambitious in its objectives, it is very expensive in its establishment. The objectives are limited to the minimising, and finally the cutting off, of all forms of economic dependency on South Africa, especially in transport and communication. Billions of borrowed dollars will go into building new harbours, roads, railways and so on, and it will take years to complete the delinking process. But taking into account the rapidly changing political situation in South Africa, it is likely that half-way between now and complete delinking, South Africa will be either a free country or at least enjoying some form of majority rule, both of which situations will make delinking unnecessary and co-operating with Black ruled South Africa essential politically and economically.

Unless the SADCC leaders assume that South Africa and Namibia will never be free for the next generation or two (the time it will take to complete SADCC's objectives), this projects look like a gigantic and very expensive white elephant, for which generations of their people will burdened with the debt incurred. Secondly, South Africa's domination in the region is due to economic strength and not to its transport facilities. The way to extricate the neighbouring countries from their subordinate position to South Africa is not via duplicating an independent transport system, but by accelerating rapid economic development, utilising all the existing facilities to that end with minimum capital expenditure. The vast capital which now goes into funding the SADCC infrastructure could be more gainfully invested in industrial and agricultural development projects that would make their economies, in as short a period as possible, as strong and viable as that of South Africa.

To sum up then, experience has shown us that there can never be lasting regional co-operation as long as these economies remain "colonial". Secondly, each country must first undertake to change that colonial economy structure and lay the foundation for the development of a nationally integrated and independent economy, before it can begin to think in terms of regional economic co-operation or integration. Thirdly, a viable and credible regional integration can be achieved only by means of objective economic complementarily, whereby the stronger helps the weaker, this is not available through the mechanism of foreign trade, but by means of planned economic co-operation.

The OAU's Lagos Plan of Action for economic co-operation among African states and the 1985 OAU's Special Addis Summit on the same subject, which is now even more serious because of the mounting debt crisis, were both a colossal disappointment. They have both failed to tackle the most fundamental obstacle to development, namely the colonial economy and the need to change the very structure which sustains and nourishes it. Unless each of our countries changes this structure of colonial economy into an independent, internally integrated national economy, there is no hope for development, and much less for regional co-operation.

The Visionary Neto
Africa Events, August 1988

Agostinho Neto will be remembered by all those who knew him as a man of great vision; a leader committed to revolutionising Africa in a more profound manner than that advocated by petty-bourgeois Pan-Africanists. He saw Africa's challenge really beginning after the attainment of independence to which the struggle for national independence was only a prelude. His political training enabled him to analyse Africa's situation more realistically than many other leaders of his time who viewed the struggle only within the context of anti-colonialism. Indeed he was far removed from the calibre of leaders who, soon after colonialism, so enthusiastically joined hands with their erstwhile enemy to continue the exploitation of their own people. This brutal exploitation taking the form of the net transfer of value from "poor" Africa to the rich Western world has now reached the astronomical figure of $36 billion annually or $100 million per day.

The united Africa that Neto envisioned was not to be created from a "union of African states" but from the united will and solidarity of the revolutionary people of Africa. Africa's post-colonial states, as instituted by the departing colonialists, were not the proper instruments for bringing about unity. On the contrary, they were meant to intensify divisions and competition among themselves for the benefit of the imperialist forces and for international finance capital. Not only have the leaders developed a vested interest in the status-quo, but also the very nature of their colonially orientated economies is not conducive to unity; it is conducive to disunity and competition.

I personally will remain eternally thankful for my good luck in having known Neto during the peak of the Angolan liberation struggle when he was confronted with a myriad of problems of supply, and transport, of arms; of political and military training of cadres some of whom, like Chipenda, were of doubtful ideological persuasion and loyalty; of dealing and negotiating with hostile African states who preferred

Savimbi's UNITA to his own MPLA.

He lived under constant threats of assassination by the Portuguese "hit men"; of expulsion from or prison detention in some African countries whose leaders had been poisoned by foreign intelligence services and so treated him as a dangerous communist. He faced all this with supreme serenity and reassuring self-confidence; and he would be just as calm on receiving the sometimes disturbing news of ups-and-downs from the battlefield. This strength of character was most inspiring, and I would always draw on it to strengthen my own resolve during the most difficult periods in my political life.

Among the many instances of bureaucratic obstructions which faced him daily at his transit headquarters at Dar es Salaam, there was one in which I was personally involved. He had complained to me that he had been anxious to see President Nyerere for several months, on a very urgent matter but the bureaucrats were obstructing him and he was extremely worried. The reason for his worry was that during the transit of MPLA supplies to the border of Zambia from the Tanzanian port of Dar es Salaam, there would always be a few submachine guns missing. He wanted to draw President Nyerere's attention to this, not because MPLA would suffer from this shortfall, but because that there was a possibility of some sinister design against the State.

We were all going to Addis that week for the OAU Summit, and on our way back I literally smuggled him into our plane and made him sit next to President Nyerere, who was now freed from the bureaucrats. When Nyerere heard the complaint, action was immediately taken on his arrival in Dar. This was in 1970 at the height of the liberation struggles in Southern Africa, and when the CIA was worrying over the activities of the "Lubumbashi Group" consisting of Nyerere, Kaunda and Obote whom they regarded as radical Left and about the future course of Africa. Who knows, this timely warning from Neto to Nyerere probably saved Tanzania from falling victim to external and internal bloody subversion.

Like many other leaders of the liberation movements at the time, Neto was not too happy about the April 1969

"Lusaka Manifesto" issued by the east and central Africa's Heads of State. He thought the document was full of legalism and "humanism" but short of anti-imperialism. It reduced the struggle in Southern Africa into a struggle between South Africa's apartheid and Portuguese colonialism on the one hand, and the rest of humanity on the other. It did not put it in the context of the worldwide capitalist system of exploitation of which South Africa and Portugal were only a most concentrated expression.

Consequently, the Declaration had the effect of ideologically disarming the masses in the region and rendering them defenceless against future economic onslaught by international finance capital. This conclusion was prophetic. Viewing the situation in the region now, with the creation of SADCC and the intimate involvement of the EEC, Chester Crocker and, yes, even Mrs. Thatcher's Britain, in the campaign to "save the region from South Africa's destabilisation", the masses are bound to be utterly confused in distinguishing between friend and foe.

His analysis of the Portuguese situation at the time, especially concerning the struggle between the merging national bourgeoisie and the landlord class represented by the Caitano regime has been accurate when it was concretised by the military uprising in Portugal in 1974[1]. The impulsive need of that emerging industrial bourgeoisie to take Portugal into the EEC, with the support of Anglo-American capital, was bound to intensify the class struggle in which the Portuguese workers and peasants would naturally support whichever force was in conflict with the ruling feudalistic landlord class whose domination kept the country as an anachronism in the midst of an industrially thriving Europe. In 1972, Neto saw this revolt as imminent, especially as the liberation movement in Angola, Mozambique and Guinea Bissau was intensifying.

Neto was a principled leader, conscious of his responsibility to his movement. Consequently he would submit to nobody's bullying, even in countries where he took refuge. He would not allow any Head of State to use him for any purpose other than that of advancing Angola's independence. He would not compromise his principles in order to win favours, and he regarded all actions by African states in support of genuine liberation movements not as favours, but duty in the service of the people of Africa everywhere. This did not make him very popular among many heads of state, some of whom tended to use liberation movements to advance their own ends.

There was also confusion among some African Heads of State on whether to support Savimbi or Neto. Many leaders regarded Savimbi as an "authentic" African nationalist while Neto was regarded as "pursuing alien ideology", i.e. Marxism. In Zambia, the MPLA was tolerated but not liked; and support for it was at best lukewarm. Tanzania too preferred Savimbi whose military cadres were trained at her Arusha military academy. President Nyerere admitted to Zambian journalists in 1978 that Tanzania gave Savimbi enough arms to equip ten thousand soldiers at a time when UNITA was fighting MPLA. It was not until Savimbi sided with South Africa that Tanzania stopped its military assistance to him.

Neto, however, accepted this state of confusion among some African leaders with the dignity and generosity of a seasoned political leader who knew what he was doing. He did not blame them; he simply said that history would prove them wrong. In his view, this support for Savimbi was not given because of malicious intentions against MPLA, but out of ignorance of what was "authentically" African. He thought the root cause of this confusion lay in a mistaken world outlook and not due to any sinister motivation.

Would the current rapprochement between Angola and South Africa have happened if Neto were alive? Yes, most likely. First, because the MPLA is a very democratic party and its decisions do not depend entirely on the views of the leader of the party, as is the case in many one-party states in Africa. Secondly Angola is now negotiating from a position of strength and not of weakness, having inflicted severe blows on the enemy on the battlefield. Any seasoned statesman would go to the negotiating table if this had the chance to lessen human losses and economic devastation. And Neto was too much of a consummate statesman to let this opportunity slip by. That is why he will be remembered by both Angolans and the rest of us for a long, long time to come.

Notes

(1) See Portugal's Empire p...

Challenges Ahead for the New Secretary-General of the OAU
Africa Events, September 1989

The tasks confronting a secretary-general of an international organisation are vastly different from those confronting a Foreign Minister of a sovereign state. A Foreign Minister has some definite policy reflecting the national interest of his country, whereas the head of an international organisation necessarily has none; and if he tries to devise his own policy he will definitely end up in serious trouble. His role is simply that of being able to interpret the various policies of member states, define the main threads, weave them into a sort of coherent blueprint, and package it in way that most members states would feel comfortable to be identified with.

No Secretary General of the OAU, from Diallo Telli to Ide Oumouru, (otherwise Idi Umari, in Kiswahili), has been able to achieve this feat, largely because, except for Ethiopia and Egypt, the countries that comprise the OAU have no definable foreign policy. And these two exceptions have evolved their respective foreign policies as a result of their participation in the scramble for colonising Africa. Consequently, their foreign policies are tinged with predatory designs. Both had imperial monarchies with expansionist ambitions; both claimed that their ancient histories were a justification for colonising what they regarded as the more backward parts of the continent; both were used by the competing big powers to advance their colonial interests in the region; both took part in most of the major Big Powers conspiracies of the last century which determined the fate of Africa.

Moreover, since all international organisations, including the OAU, are based on the legal precepts of the last century which were largely designed to minimise conflicts among the predatory 'Big Powers' – i.e., the five European powers who not only dominated but also changed the course of history of the entire world – it is difficult for a leader of an organisation bound by such legality to distinguish between a policy based on predatory objectives and that which is based on principles of liberation. The confusion is worse in an organisation of ex-colonies like the OAU, whose Founding Fathers, far from creating conditions for the evolution of a doctrine of resistance in the Charter that brought them together, have on the contrary swallowed hook, line and sinker all the trash from the so-called Geneva Convention which was designed to oppress them in the first place. The posture of "running with the hares and hunting with hounds" which projects itself in most of the OAU initiatives is a direct result of this confusion of principles of resistance and the predatory principles of dominance.

Salim Ahmed Salim, the new Secretary General of the OAU, will therefore take over the administration of an organisation lacking any clear cut position on all major international issues, except perhaps that of Southern Africa; and even on this ready-made one there is no well defined policy with which member states can identify without much hesitation. It is unfortunate, moreover, that his first year on the job will be under a President whose country is virtually tied to a superpower; a country which is also deeply involved in the complexities of the Middle-East crisis from a very complicated and compromised position of being at once on both sides of the conflict – officially with the Arabs, unofficially with the Israelis. The confusion will be even worse confounded by the fact that, while the new President of the OAU leads an organisation which has no diplomatic relations with Israel, his own country, Egypt, of which he is the President, is the only one among the Arabs which has diplomatic ties with this arch enemy of the Arabs. The Secretary General will find himself in a most unenviable position every time such questions are inevitably raised.

Those elements who are keen on dividing Africa on such irrelevancies as 'Black' and 'Arab' will have a field day with this new awkward situation, especially when Salim himself is a product of both. Kaunda has already been the first on record to jump in with this racial approach by cynically 'advising' Mubarak to ask his Arab colleagues to stop supporting the Eritrean liberation struggle against Ethiopian colonialism, as if that has been the essence of the Eritrean struggle these last twenty-eight years. Similarly, those with vested interest in splitting the continent on religious lines, Muslim vs Christian, will also have ample opportunity for mischief in that direction, especially when Mubarak's Egypt is itself deeply involved in the Sudan conflict with its traditional Muslim/Christian division which has been thoroughly exploited since the inception of the Sudan as we know it today. The timing for the Mubarak/Salim take-over is most unfortunate too. Most of the conflicts that currently face the OAU have racial colouring. In addition to the Sudan conflict, the latest and worst is the Senegal/Mauritanian racial war in which citizenship in the two countries has ceased to have any validity – it is a free-for-all war between Black-African and Arab-African, of either country. Then there is the Libya/Chad conflict which verges on the Black/Arab divide, but which has been taken over by foreign powers who came on the side of Chad because of Libya's uncompromising anti-imperialist stand. The OAU has no clear-cut stand on either of the two conflicts because most member states are themselves involved having taken sides in both disputes.

But the most serious and paramount issue which faces the OAU is of course the Eritrean question which has a more far-reaching destructive potential than President Kaunda's simplistic approach will have us believe. Throughout his presidency of the OAU Kaunda took a position of out-and-out support for Mengistu, crowning him as the most outstanding revolutionary leader in Africa. He has accepted the Ethiopian propaganda that Eritrea was simply a question of Arab interference in the internal affairs of Ethiopia, full stop. This position has deprived the OAU of an excellent opportunity to mediate and save Mengistu a humiliating defeat on the battlefields of Af-Abet and Tigre, and a coup attempt which nearly toppled him. The circumstances that led to his humiliation are even worse for him now and the situation may once again flare up during the Mubarak presidency of the OAU. And indications are that any such new offensive by the Eritreans will probably mean the final battle of the war, an African Dien Bien Phu. The mediation initiative has now been taken over by Ex-President Carter, very likely on behalf of the US State Department, and the OAU has absolutely no role to play in the matter. And it is doubtful if Mubarak can initiate an African attempt at mediation on this or any other major issue which involves the superpowers, one of whom is his benefactor.

Salim Ahmed Salim will require all his diplomatic skills to steer the OAU through the stormy period ahead, but he must never attempt to devise an 'OAU foreign policy'. People with his wide experience in foreign relations, both as a diplomat and as a political head of department, are always prone to succumb to the temptation of trying to 'set things right'. However, in an international organisation it is not a predetermined policy which sets things rights, but rather a skilful and timely intervention in unanticipated events determines the degree of success. In other words, what is needed in an international organisation is not the formulation of a distinct set of policies, but a capacity to anticipate. Luckily for the OAU, it is this rare endowment which Salim Ahmed Salim will bring to the organisation to good effect, and it will be to his own advantage as well to make full use of it while the opportunity lasts.

Of course there must be a well defined framework of principles within which negotiations, mediation, reconciliations, etc. are conducted, but these must in principle be tipped in favour of the oppressed. The colonial principle of "noninterference in internal affairs of member states" which is entrenched in the OAU Charter at the behest of Emperor Haile Selassie, has been thoroughly abused and some of the worst crimes against the people have been committed by some ruthless leaders, while the OAU was silenced by the clause. It took President Museveni's courageous intervention to ask the OAU Summit: "Where were you when Uganda was bleeding?" to bring the point home. Perhaps, with a little encouragement from the OAU secretariat, the situation can be rectified. For instance, independent African lawyers may look afresh into the Charter with a view to giving it an Afrocentric basis. Let them 'brain storm' on the subject, freed from state obligations for the purpose of liberating the OAU Charter from 19th century conventions. The Secretary General can take the initiative on the matter without overstepping his mandate.

But apart from political and diplomatic questions, the most challenging problem that faces the OAU, is of course, Africa's mega economic crisis. This crisis has been looming since the mid-1970's and it is daily getting worse. The debt problem continues to mount and no solution is anywhere in sight. The OAU made several futile attempts to adopt a collective African position, culminating in 1980 in the Lagos Plan of Action. The last OAU Summit in July was directed to consider a "blueprint" prepared by the UN Economic Commission for Africa as a last chance for Africa to have its own alternative solution to the crisis which is now seen to be aggravated by the World Bank's structural adjustment programme (SAP). But, regrettably, this initiative too, like the others before it, is destined to end in failure. And the reason is obvious. None of the proposed "solutions" has ever attempted to show how we can stop the massive net outflows of wealth from the continent to our Western 'trading partners'.

The core question remains unanswered: "Is it possible to build a national economy on the basis of a colonial economy?" If the answer is negative, which obviously it is, then what do we do about it? The colonialists have built colonial economies throughout Africa designed to serve Europe's interests. All the anti-colonial struggle seems to have achieved was to get rid of foreign administrators and planted ourselves in their place to administer the same colonial economy, and in a less 'cost effective' way. Even if we were to be more efficient than the colonialists, the gains would still continue to go to our 'trading partners', because that was the aim of the structure of that economy. So what the World Bank is telling us is to be more 'cost effective', and we respond by arguing how best to achieve it, without raising the key questions. If the OAU is to give Africa meaningful guidance on economic emancipation, then it must depart from the jaded path which leads only to a dead-end. It must initiate new thinking, starting from the vital question: How to change a colonial economy into a national economy. The rest will follow.

But in all aspects of the OAU tasks, whether political, diplomatic, economic, social or cultural, to attain positive results the Secretary General will find it useful to be guided by the universal, all-purpose principle, which is also the irresistible trend of history, namely, that countries want independence, nations want liberation and people want revolution – the last being the KEY LINK to the rest. We all wish Salim Ahmed Salim a very successful tenure at the head of the OAU's administration.

Speech at the International Conference on Malcolm X: Radical Tradition and a Legacy of Struggle, 1 - 4 November 1990, New York

Comrades and Friends, in the last three days of this conference I have been constantly thinking what Malcolm would have been doing, or how Malcolm would have been inspired by seeing this conference almost wholly dominated by youth. This is a very significant event. Not only to the American struggle, but to the struggle worldwide. Because it is happening at a historic moment, when the United States, for the first time since the end of the Second World War has complete hegemony over the rest of the world. This is a very, very dangerous moment in history. And we are seeing what is happening in the Gulf[1] - it is only an expression of what can happen if the people, especially the Black community in this country, are not prepared to fight.

I knew Malcolm at a very interesting moment. I met him for the first time in Cairo, when there was a crucial meeting of the second summit of the O.A.U., as well as the summit of the non-aligned movement, which was to follow immediately after. Malcolm came to my room in a very ambivalent mood, because at that very moment Harlem was burning. The youth in the uprising in Harlem were calling for Malcolm. This was in July 1964. And Malcolm was in two minds. He wanted to go back - to come back and lead the struggle and be with the people in the struggle. But we wanted him to remain there in the conference so as to give us the 'feeling of the struggle' and to convey to all the Third World leaders what America, the real America, was going through. I'm glad to report that we succeeded in detaining him there.

But this meeting of Operation Solidarity also gave us an insight into Malcolm's own evolution. As you know, Malcolm started his political struggle, at a community level. But he evolved into a national and international figure... Malcolm had the vision to see the threat that a united Third World would pose to imperialism. That threat has been expressed continuously since the end of the Second World War.

For instance, although American imperialism was supposedly fighting communism throughout this period you'd find that American presidents - *every* American President - had to have a Third-World leader as a villain. They never fought the Russians. Truman had Kim Il Sung, the North Korean leader, as the villain and he mobilized American forces and international forces to fight this villain. Eisenhower had Mao Tse Tung as the villain, not the Russians but Mao Tse Tung. Kennedy had Castro as the villain, not the Russians but Castro. Then came Johnson - he had Ho Chi Minh as the villain, not the Russians but Ho Chi Minh as the villain. Then came Nixon. His villain was Sihanouk of Cambodia. He had to destroy that country in order to prove Sihanouk was his villain. Then came Carter. He chose Khomeini as villain. He was followed by Reagan and he chose Ghaddafy as his villain. And now we have Bush with Saddam Hussein as his villain

But is this accidental? Is this accidental or is it a part of U.S. policy necessitated by the significance of Third World countries in relation to the United States? Not because Third World countries have nuclear weapons, but because United States contains a large population from Third World countries in its own borders, more than any other country in the Western World.

And this population is never reflected positively in its foreign policy, it is always reflected negatively in that foreign policy. The United States has a positive policy toward Poland, it has a positive policy toward Israel, because they reflect an internal situation. No foreign policy can be viable if it does not reflect internal needs - the needs of the people that it contains. And U.S. foreign policy reflects all these needs except the needs of the Black people of this country.

When the rest of the world was clamoring for sanctions in South Africa, United States was the one to refuse in spite of the fact that it has its massive population of 25 million Black people in this country, daily and hourly being insulted by the very existence of apartheid in South Africa. The significance of the presence of Third World people in this country is something we need to reflect on seriously, and I think this is what Malcolm X wanted to promote.

When Malcolm X came to Tanzania, I took him to meet President Nyerere, on another historic date. Because that very day, China had exploded her first nuclear bomb. Nyerere said, "Malcolm, for the first time today in recorded history, a former colonial country has been able to develop weapons at par with any colonial power. This is the end of colonialism through and through."

And Malcolm replied, "Mr. President, this is what I've been thinking all the way as I was coming from my hotel to this house."

It just shows you the thinking of Malcolm, that international struggle is not limited just to one or two countries but it must be universal- literally and effectively universal. This is what Malcolm had in mind: To promote internationalism in the Third World. He saw what American policy meant and what it could mean in the event that the Third World population inside America could be politicised and mobilised.

The situation is becoming even more critical at this moment, I am saying it is becoming critical because, with the Cold War over, Mr. Gorbachev keeps repeating the phrase, "Common European Home". Now this phrase is very frightening to us in Africa especially, because we remember the period when Europe was unified ideologically, when, before the Second World War the five great powers were dominating Europe, i.e., Czarist Russia, the Austro-Hungarian Empire, Germany, France and Britain. We remember what this meant to the rest of the world, especially Africa. When international trade, or world trade shifted, in the fifteenth century, from the Mediterranean to the Atlantic -that marked the beginning of the tragedy of Africa. Europe was at that time unified ideologically to dominate. And the history of that period - slavery, to be followed by colonialism, to be followed by neocolonialism - this is *our* history of the Common European Home.

But this situation was saved, or at least was minimised

or relieved after the Second World War when there was tension between East and West. And some of us (Third World countries) utilized the tension, utilized the contradictions between East and West, and had some relief. But when that tension is over, that relief is gone.

That's why I'm saying we are passing through a very serious phase in history. Certainly Third World countries and especially Africa, is going through crisis now. And this brings me to the significance of this conference.

We have lost Big Brother, the Soviet Union, to put the fear of God into U.S. foreign policy. We have lost that tension which kept some kind of peace and stability on a world scale. Where are we to turn to now when America is extending its hegemony in a very, very vigorous way? America is unifying or is it trying to evoke a unity of purpose in foreign policy with an emerging 'unified' Europe. Europe has had a very damaging relationship with Africa, and a damaging contractual relationship through the so-called Lome Convention. The Lome Convention ties the entire continent of Africa and the Caribbean and Pacific islands to becoming neocolonies of Europe. Do we toe the line that the IMF and World Bank prescribe, and in the process do the masses suffer? Who is to salvage the situation? Who is to act as the bastion to stop the degradation? The significance of this conference is that it highlights that that responsibility lies with the progressive forces led by the Black population of this country.

Your nationalism and our nationalism in Africa are the same; Our nationalism and your nationalism have nothing to do with jingoism. It is a nationalism of resistance It is a positive nationalism. And this must be expressed within the context of American hegemony.

What is affecting an African in Lagos, in Tanzania or anywhere is the same as is affecting a Black person in this country. And therefore, while we are conducting our revolutions - and young forces are emerging to conduct our revolutions in Africa - we hope the young generation of Black militants in this country will lead the struggle to ensure that United States domination does not extend to humiliating Africa once again.

This is a great responsibility, which does not need spontaneous reaction, but organized action. And if Malcolm was around, I am sure this is what he would have emphasized. Because as Imamu Baraka mentioned the other day, just one month before Malcolm was assassinated the three of us were sitting in a hotel in New York from 8 p.m. 'til 8 a.m. the next morning talking about nothing else except this issue and the relationship between race and class. At that time there was some confusion about which is leading - race or class. And I'm not going to tell you what were our conclusions! But I'm telling you one thing that Malcolm had always emphasized: that if there is a class, an oppressed class who should lead the class struggle, then Black people should, *will* be in it. They have nothing to lose, literally, nothing to lose but their chains. And that message, I think we should revive that message now - that Black population in this country have a specific and unique responsibility to liberate themselves. And in the process of liberating themselves, they will be liberating the rest of us.

Thank you very much

Notes

(1) The US led invasion of Iraq took place in the second half of January 1990

Organisation of African Unity – help or hindrance?

East Africa and the Horn, August 1993

Eritrea, Africa's newest independent state, stunned the opening session of the Organisation of African Unity summit on June 28 in Cairo by declaring that the organisation had been an utter failure for thirty years.

"The sad fact remains that the OAU has become a nominal organisation that has failed to deliver on its pronounced objectives and commitments," the Eritrean president told a hushed conference hall. "Although the OAU has often championed the lofty ideals of unity, cooperation, economic development, human rights and other worthy objectives, it has failed to seriously work towards their concrete realisation.... Thirty years after the foundation of this organisation, our continent remains affected by growing poverty and backwardness.. The African continent is today a marginalised actor in global politics and the world economic order." He continued to say, "Africa is not a place where its citizens can walk with raised heads but a continent scorned by all its partners, a continent that seems to endlessly produce the wrong manuals for economic development, democratisation and political management."

Issayas' frustration and anger is understandable. Eritrea fought for its independence throughout the thirty years of the OAU's existence, achieving it in spite of the organisation's opposition.

The weakness of the OAU is ultimately due to the fact that the leaders of most of its member states are routinely replaced by one kind of military junta or another. Consequently the OAU has never taken a consistent stand on any of the major issues affecting the continent.

When the OAU was formed in 1963 it aroused great hopes among the people of Africa. The majority of the people felt that Africa was finally going to eradicate the divisions created by colonialism which had been formalised at the Berlin Conference of 1884. The divergent ideologies of the organisation's members has prevented this from becoming a reality. Africa is as divided today as it was thirty years ago resulting in the devastation of the nations' self-esteem and the livelihoods of their people.

The idea of 'African Unity' was conceived as a means of fighting two scourges inflicted on Africa by colonialism. One was the fragmentation of the continent, which resulted in weak and unviable states; the second was poverty, which was a consequence of fragmentation, extensive colonial exploitation and an illogical and primitive colonial economic structure which obstructed development. These two scourges were inter-linked, designed to facilitate colonial domination and exploitation. It was impossible to abolish one without abolishing the other - both had to be tackled simultaneously, beginning with the institution of a basis for a continental unity, like the establishment of an African 'Unified Command' as proposed by Nkrumah.

Kwame Nkrumah, the then President of Ghana, was the architect of this radical formulation. It was his untiring effort which led to the creation of the OAU. Owing to the division between radical and conservative tendencies among independent African states at the time, the radicals had to compromise on a number of their basic principles of unity so as to persuade the conservatives to join the organisation. Unfortunately the inclusion of the conservative states turned the OAU into the moribund institution it is today.

Conservatives take hold

The conservatives' first success in obstructing the move towards continental unity was achieved at the OAU Cairo summit in 1964. It was at this crucial conference that Nyerere, the then president of Tanzania, cunningly pushed through a resolution which urged the OAU to accept the colonial borders as the permanent, recognised frontiers of OAU member states. This move was in collaboration with Emperor Haile Selasie of Ethiopia who one year earlier had annexed Eritrea, forcefully including it within his brutal 'empire'. He was now seeking to legitimise this barbaric act through the OAU. The underlying motive of the resolution was to frustrate Nkrumah and his Pan-Africanist ideals though Nyerere claimed that the intention was to minimise border conflicts in Africa. The resolution was carried by a simple majority and became a key binding principle of the OAU Charter. Ironically, instead of abolishing Africa's primary malady of disunity, the OAU encouraged it.

Second, the conservatives strove to make the OAU serve their interests and not those of Africa as a whole by altering the balance of forces on the continent in favour of the conservatives rather than the radicals who were still dominant in African politics. Beginning with Ben Bella of Algeria in 1965 and Nkrumah in 1966, the conservatives, in collaboration with their ex-colonial masters, engineered the overthrow of radical leaders via military coups. Henceforth the OAU ceased to be an instrument of Pan-African revolutionary change and became an apologist for the status quo. Even the liberation of the remaining colonies was conceived in the context of maintaining this status quo. It did not take long for Nyerere himself, the architect of the OAU status quo, to publicly admit in 1972 that the OAU had become no more than a "trade union of Africa's heads of state".

As a result of a series of coups against progressive heads of state, especially after the death of President Nasser of Egypt in 1970, the OAU became completely dominated by reactionary military heads of state, most of whom were politically illiterate and knew nothing about economics except how to fill their pockets. It was a disaster for Africa because it deprived the continent of seasoned and committed leadership during the critical period in 1972-1973 when the world economy was shifting decisively. Europe and Japan were emerging as strong and self-sustaining economic powers while the collapse of the dollar led to an oil price explosion. The OAU had no policy except to weakly and humbly plead for more aid and credits to compensate for the loss of foreign exchange which non-oil-producing African countries had incurred as a result of the astronomical rise in oil prices.

Failure of the OAU

Because it had failed to tackle the core problem of African unity at its inception, the OAU degenerated into a huge and expensive bureaucracy without any sense of direction. It helped to hasten the process of decolonisation, but since Ghana's independence in 1957 the process was already in motion and would have continued with or without the OAU. Many observers now believe that in some instances the OAU made serious strategic blunders. In 1972 it helped to delay the independence of Namibia and South Africa which led to the devastation of Angola and Mozambique by South Africa. The strategy, which could be called the 'salami approach', was to concentrate on the liberation of the so-called the 'weakest link' first, i.e. the Portuguese colonies, followed by Rhodesia (Zimbabwe) and Namibia, and ultimately South Africa. This proved to be disastrous. Leaving it as the last target allowed South Africa to destroy the socio-economic foundations of Angola, Mozambique, and even Zimbabwe to a certain extent.

The OAU did make several attempts to create institutions for economic cooperation among its member states. All of them failed for the simple reason that no African country undertook the structural changes required to move away from a colonial economy There was no basis for 'objective economic complementarity' among member states; a precondition for any meaningful economic cooperation. Consequently, the OAU's call for an 'African common market' sounds rather like a pipe dream.

The Future

Now in its thirtieth year the OAU has degenerated into a useless institution, in spite of the dynamic leadership of its Secretary-General, Salim. It is politically and financially bankrupt and with its role in 'decolonisation' now in the past it has been left with no significant purpose. it has become no more than a mere instrument for 'conflict' prevention and resolution. The 1964 resolution which sought to minimise conflicts has had precisely the opposite effect as conflicts become more and more common. The noble objective of attaining African unity seems to be even further out of reach. The real danger is that Africa may disintegrate even more as some of the existing states subdivide. Yet, the OAU has no conception of where Africa should be in the next decade or so. They are presently confined to 'crises management'. Its vision has been and continues to be obscured by the preconceived prejudices of the dominating states. Eritrea's thirty year struggle for independence, achieved with considerable human and material loss, went 'unnoticed' by this African organisation. Somalia has been bleeding to death but the OAU has not lifted a finger to 'resolve' the conflict. The Nigerians are obliterating Liberian villages, killing innocent children, women and the aged, in the name of West African unity under ECOWAS with the sanctioned of the OAU.

Unless the OAU ceases to be the 'headquarters of intrigues' and a conveyor-belt for ambitious African diplomats, it is unlikely to survive for long. The member states of the OAU are now individually weak, exhausted and lacking any vision themselves. This state of affairs is inevitably reflected in the OAU. If it is to reactivate itself and be more relevant, it has to go to the people; it must cease to be a mere instrument of heads of state, most of whom have lost credibility; it must re-kindle the spirit of Pan-Africanism, which will give it the zest and verve of the people instead of the cold emptiness of pompous diplomats, who serve no one but themselves. These are the necessary prerequisites for any African organisation which seeks to respond adequately to what is taking place in the continent. Unfortunately, as it is, the OAU's future seems to be bleak.

Notes

(1) This was a quarterly bulletin published by Babu — 3 issues appeared *Panafricanism and the New World Order*

Pan Africanism and the New World Order
Africa World Review, November 1992 - April 1993

At no time has the need for wider amplification of the theory and practice of Pan Africanism been greater than now. Africa and Africans everywhere, whether on the continent itself, in the Americas, in Europe or the Caribbean are faced with new challenges as "natives" as "ex slaves" and as "immigrants". In all these categories, they have been singled out as objects of exploitation, oppression and humiliation Is this because the world is unfair to Africa and its people? Not at all. There is no fairness or unfairness in the world where relations between peoples of different nationalities or races (in the broadest sense of the word) are concerned. Africa and Africans have been subjected to all these degrading treatment simply because historically they have been disunited, fragmented, partitioned, disenfranchised, separated, all of which rendered them vulnerable and often defenceless in the face of predators, local or foreign, or in an unholy alliance of the two.

Revolutionary Africans especially those who have suffered the worst of these degrading treatments after being kidnapped and then subjected to slavery, realised that the only way to fight back was through unity and organised resistance.

PanAfricanism came into being in order to effectively pursue the twin objectives of unity and organised resistance. This was due to the realisation that, although there have been heroic resistances here and there, they were mostly spontaneous or reacting to individual acts of oppression and therefore ineffective in the long run.

The current on-going struggle for the Pan-African ideal is essentially a continuation of the old struggles but under a different world setting. The new struggle is necessarily more complex, more demanding and multifaceted. There is the struggle of the African-Americans in the Americas both for their civil rights and for power-sharing in the ordering of their destiny.

There is the struggle of the independent states in Africa and the Caribbean in relation to the big, predatory powers. There is the struggle of the underprivileged people within these independent states who have remained the target of all forms of exploitation and oppression in their own country.

The identity of our struggle

What is the common identity of all these seemingly disparate struggles? Is it colour? No; there are many colours among Africans and the descendants of Africa as there are among many other groups in the world. Race? No; there are many races in Africa; i.e. Bantus, Nilotic, etc. Culture? There is no single "African culture" any more than there is a single Asiatic, Europe or Latin American culture, although there is a need for one.

The common identity of the Pan-African struggle is none of these things. Rather it is the common history of oppression and its modern manifestations and the common struggles against them. This is the foundation on which the theory and practice of Pan-Africanism is based. Its history is most interesting. For conceptual convenience, it can be divided into two phases, the Old and the New. The old one started roughly from the fragmentary movements of the past, via Garvey to DuBois and the 1945 Manchester Conference. In other words, the era prior to post-colonial Africa The new one comprises the era of the struggles for and the attainment of independence in Africa and the Caribbean. This was effectively ushered in by the All African Peoples Conference (AAPC) in Accra in 1958 soon after Ghana's independence. In theoretical terms the Old Phase can be described as the one which set out the need, for a Pan-Africanist movement and it laid the foundation for its existence: its aims and objectives; it outlined the principles and philosophy guiding the movement; it pointed out areas of operations and set the "terms of engagement". The New Phase, on the other hand, was to give the philosophy its deeper orientation in the context of the new world situation (i.e. the demise of the traditional "great powers" and the new alliances for "spheres of influence"; the era of world wide struggles for independence and social revolutions). As well as give it a new orientation, the New Phase also gave the movement its practical application i.e., the "mass movement" against colonialism and against "all forms of oppression". Months before the convening of the AAPC in Ghana its preparation and publicity created favourable conditions for the mushrooming of the regional Pan-African mass movement in the continent. There emerged the powerful Pan-African Movement for East and Central Africa (PAFMECA) which, for the first time in East African politics, brought all political movements in the region under one umbrella. After the Sharpville massacre in 1960 and the banning and exile of South African political parties, South African liberation movements joined PAFMECA and turned it into PAFMECSA and went to the Accra meeting as one movement. PAFMECA became the first Pan African movement on a mass scale which helped to usher in the era of the New Phase of Pan-Africanism in practice.

While some of the immediate objectives of the New Phase such as decolonisation have been achieved, the struggle against "all forms of oppression" is yet to be won, not just in Africa but throughout the world where Africans and the descendants of Africa are to be found. This therefore is the remaining task for the New Phase in the era of what might be called the "era in search of a new world order". How is this struggle to be effectively put into action?

Currents in the movement

At present there are two currents in the Pan-African movement which need to be identified and then unified. One is "political" and the other is "cultural". They are not mutually exclusive; essentially, they are complementary. The cultural tendency seems to take the view that unless Africans realise the greatness of their cultural contribution to civilisation, unless they are fortified by this awareness they will not be able to effectively challenge the onslaught of the West on their dignity and self respect. Hence the emphasis on cultural revival - on delving into the African heritage, and the study of the Nile bank communities as the origins of humankind; on what has come to be known as "Afrocentricism", the idea that we must view the world from an African world outlook; and so on. A body of profound knowledge on all these topics is emerging which will contribute enormously to African scholarship. However, the pursuit of these cultural revivals and studies tend to be exclusivist; that is to say "outsiders" e.g. Western scholars, must not be accepted as authorities in this field since they have always distorted our history to suit their imperialist and predatory ends. Some go even further and they exclude even North Africans from their "project" on the grounds that they are not authentic Africans.

The political tendency, however, is much broader and it includes North Africans as an essential part of the Pan Africa and as an essential part of Pan-African struggle. The reason for this distinction between the two tendencies is obvious. Whereas the cultural tendencies leans more towards academia where "knowledge is power" (the fewer the experts, the more powerful and dominant in the subject they are!) The political tendency, on the contrary, seeks wider participation. The cultural tendency is more common in the Diaspora where Africans are in the minority and powerless. Here the struggle is to maintain what is theirs, exclusive of others. In the continent where Africans are in the majority and in power, the political tendency is more common. As Malcolm X once described these two tendencies: the cultural is "ghetto politics" and the political is "national politics".

African nationalism and Pan-Africanism are one and the same thing. National power is the prerequisite to internationalism which is the essence of Pan-Africanism. If modern Pan-African struggle is about fighting against "all forms of oppression in the era in search of a new world order" then obviously the political tendency with its internationalist stance is more likely to be effective because the struggle against "all forms of oppression" is world wide and it must be tackled on an international scale. However the two tendencies necessarily complement each other.

What are the immediate and long term targets of the

modern Pan-African struggle? Imperialism or in the post-modernist terminology, hegemonism, still remains the main threat as well as the main obstacle to our well being. Its current aim is to reduce Africa to a "fourth-world" and to exclude it from the global process or production and exchange. Already their main theme now, being inculcated into the minds of Africa's elites, is that Africa no longer has any strategic role in supplying the North (i.e. the imperialist, the "hegemonic powers") and our new role is simply to cooperate with them in the areas of "the environment, population and AIDS", albeit, at the expense of Africa.

Africa is tied to Europe in a colonial relationship through the "Lome Conventions"; we do what Europe tells us to do, failing that the IMF and World Bank will impose the sanctions through "conditionality" and "structural adjustment". We have to be "democratic" by which they mean paving the way for their puppets to get into power; we have to "modernise" by which they mean to be submissive to their dictates; we have to "liberalise" by which they mean abandon the struggle for social justice. This is to toe the line of Western neo-liberalism. The new stars to do this are greedy self-serving individualists ready to sell themselves and their country for a pfrnnig. As Edgar Pisani, former EEC Commissioner and Minister in the French Cabinet arrogantly put it after touring Africa recently: "...I didn't come across monkeys, that's what I call people who are black and talk posh-but genuine Africans who have espoused modern civilisation but remained authentically African. Monkeys I've seen, but there are few of them now"[1]. In other words the "monkeys" are the former leaders who fought for the liberation of Africa and who put the interests of their people first. He certainly doesn't mean those African leaders who traditionally served French interests throughout the post-colonial era. The dignity of Africans everywhere on the continent or the Diaspora, ultimately depends on the state of the African continent. If it is humiliated through starvation and famine all Africans are humiliated. If it is liberated from these indignities all Africans everywhere will be dignified. The task of the modern Pan-African struggle is to uplift Africa, to salvage it from "fourth-worldisation". To do this we need a proper world outlook and a proper strategy. And it is for this reason that we must look forward to the proposed Seventh Pan-African Congress, which may well be the vehicle to launch a decisive struggle in the same way as the AAPC became the landmark to Africa's decolonisation. It is equally encouraging that Dr. Tajudeen Abdul-Raheem, has been appointed as Secretary General of the International Preparatory Committee to take care of the organisational work in preparation for the Congress. Congratulations to him and Africa is waiting hopefully for the great occasion, not individualism, but solidarity is our strength. Don't Agonize, But Organize, is our war cry!!

Notes

(1)   Quoted in *The Courier* No. 134 of July/August 1992 issue.

Visions of Africa
Red Pepper, July 1995

When Britain and Europe were celebrating their victory over German imperialism 50 years ago, Africans and people of African descent were making preparations for their fifth anti-imperialist Pan-African Congress in Manchester. The victors in the Second World War against German occupation and oppression in Europe - the British, the French, the Belgians and the Americans - were themselves occupying and oppressing black people everywhere, on the African continent, in the Caribbean and in the United States. Nevertheless, the end of the war in 1945 was seen as the beginning of the end of all forms of oppression, ushering in the epoch of great expectations.

The Labour Party in Britain had just won a landslide victory against Winston Churchill's Tories, Socialist parties in the rest of Europe were scoring massive political victories. The United Nations was drafting its celebrated Charter and Universal Declaration of Human Rights. The international labour movement had just held its first World Trade Union Conference in February 1945, in preparation for the formation of an all-embracing World Federation of Trade Unions (WFTU) in Paris in October of that year. The dark era of fascism and right-wing extremism was over. There was hope for the oppressed worldwide.

It was in this atmosphere of goodwill and optimism that Africans believed the time for their liberation had arrived. The Black community in Britain, the Caribbean and the US decided to convene the Fifth Pan African Conference in Manchester, taking advantage of the World Trade Union Conference, which would bring many African trade union leaders to Britain.

The predominant theme of the conference was radical anti-imperialism in the context of nationalism. There were two distinct nationalist tendencies contending - political nationalism and racial nationalism. The former was led by people with strong socialist convictions such as WE

Burghardt DuBois (US), George Padmore (Trinidad), Kwame Nkrumah (Ghana), Peter Abrahams (South Africa) and Jomo Kenyatta (Kenya). The other tendency was led by the Garveyist group, followers of Jamaican radical Marcus Garvey. As most of the delegates from Africa were labour leaders, the socialist tendency inevitably dominated the conference. Their slogan was "Forward to the Socialist United States of Africa!"

It was not until 1947 when Nkrumah went back to Ghana, and 1948 when Kenyatta went back to Kenya, that Pan Africanism was elevated from the realm of an ideal to that of concrete, mass-based political practice. Nkrumah launched the Convention People's Party (CPP) on 12 June 1949, after a brief and fruitless stint as the national organiser of the United Gold Coast Convention, an elitist political organisation. In Kenya, Kenyatta launched the Kenya People's Union (KPU). These two movements immediately inspired a vision of liberation and socialism in Africa.

Nkrumah's CPP won independence for Ghana in 1957, and in December 1958 he hosted the All African People's Conference in the country's capital, Accra. It was the first post-Manchester conference, backed by a newly independent African government, which sought to put into practice on the African continent that vision of liberation and socialism expressed in 1945.

The AAPC brought together for the first time all liberation movements in Africa. I was one of the three delegates from Zanzibar as Secretary General of the Zanzibar Nationalist Party. On our way to Accra from east Africa, with other delegates from the region, we "discovered" Patrice Lumumba, who became prime minister of Congo in 1960 and was later murdered by Zairian president Mobutu Sesseku in collaboration with the CIA. The Congolese had never heard of the Accra conference, so oppressive was Belgian colonialism. We organised to have him and his delegation of five come to Accra. It was a historic decision which was to change the entire political atmosphere in sub-Saharan Africa.

Only 14 months after Lumumba's visit to Accra, the vast

and backward territory of Congo was liberated, and the rest is history. But the significance of the Accra conference was even deeper than the liberation of Congo. With the influence of Frantz Fanon (the Algerian revolutionary who wrote *The Wretched of the Earth*) and the Algerian delegation, who were then fighting for independence from France, the theme of the conference was transformed from nonviolent liberation struggle to "struggle by any means, including violence". This was a decisive departure from the Manchester conference of 1945 which favoured Gandhian nonviolence and passive resistance to colonialism.

This changed the form of the liberation struggle and there was a proliferation of the Africa-wide, Ghana-inspired, "mass parties" involving entire populations, as distinct from the Soviet-style elitist "vanguard party" concept. It forced the colonialists to accept, in the words of Harold Macmillan (then British Prime Minister, speaking to South Africa's white-dominated parliament in 1961) that the "wind of change was blowing across Africa"

If the 1945 Manchester meeting ushered in the epoch of hope and great expectations, the 1958 Accra meeting concretised those hopes and expectations by making Africa no longer governable by the colonialists. One by one, African and Caribbean countries began to win their independence.

However, throughout the post-colonial era, the two contending tendencies in Black politics which revealed themselves in 1945 - racial versus political nationalism - continued to dominate African politics with devastating consequences. The political nationalists tended to pursue progressive socio-economic policies, with a strong bias towards social welfare, while the racial nationalists tended to be reactionary and backward-looking. While the former continued the anti-imperialist struggle even after colonialism, the latter declared the struggle was over with the end of colonialism. This latter stance provided a fertile ground for the advent of neo-colonialism.

The Nkrumahs, the Ahmed Ben Bellas (of Algeria), and all the progressive leaders of Africa were one by one overthrown in military coups, engineered by neocolonial interests. Where military coups failed to topple the progressive leaders, as in Angola and Mozambique, the neocolonialists unleashed wars of destabilisation, headed by their willing agents, the racial nationalists - the Jonas Savimbis (of Angola), the Mobutus (of Zaire), and the Afonso Dhlakamas (of Mozambique) and their ilk in the rest of Africa. They succeeded in reducing the richest continent in the world to the most poverty stricken one in history.

Looking back to the 1945 Manchester Pan-African Congress, whose deliberations and analyses have been excellently produced in a new book (*The 1945 Manchester Pan-African Congress Revisited*, edited by Hakim Adi and Marika Sherwood) it is with sadness that we have to admit that the vision and hopes which the congress inspired have yet to be attained. Independence has been achieved, but after reading this book, it is clear this is not the kind of independence which the "founding fathers" of Pan Africanism had in mind.

But take heart, all is not lost. In April last year, at Kampala, Uganda, the Seventh Pan-African Congress was duly convened, while next door in Rwanda, the massacres were just beginning, with the French and the Belgians doing their best to exacerbate them. The ongoing struggle between the forces of progress on the one hand, and backward, neocolonial forces on the other, could not have been more dramatically clear. (This Seventh Congress followed the inconsequential Sixth, held in Dar-es-Salaam, Tanzania in 1974).

More than 1,500 delegates descended on Kampala from all over the world. It was the biggest congress of its kind, with far-reaching but practical deliberations. Its most outstanding feature was the absence of the corrupt old-guard, replaced by the younger generation who are the likely leaders of tomorrow's Africa. (The 31-year-old secretary of this PAC, Dr. Tajudeen of Nigeria, is the youthful reflection of this new generation).

At the state level, such new respected and progressive leadership is represented by Isaias Afwerki of Eritrea, Meles Zenawi of Ethiopia, Yoweri Museveni of Uganda and Paul Kagame of Rwanda. The emergence of this new type of leadership is categorised by Africa's political scientists as the "post-neocolonial" leadership. Unlike the neocolonial leaders, these new leaders are not cynical, which makes them less corruptible. All of them came to power after protracted revolutionary armed struggle against oppressive regimes, so they tend to be closer to the people and they identify themselves with the people's problems.

While the neocolonial leaders are isolated from and are not respected by their people, these post-neocolonial leaders are popular, enjoying the overwhelming esteem and trust of the people. Their respective economic policies are establishing innovative and viable models of development which may well set a future trend for the rest of Africa. In addition, they have developed admirable ways of dealing with the allmighty multilateral corporations and aid agencies to ensure dignity and national self-respect.

So at last the progressive forces of Africa are re-emerging, moving away from the defensive position they were put in by neocolonialism and the monetarist orthodoxies of the World Bank and International Monetary Fund. They are now on the offensive, reasserting progressive leadership, and making Pan Africanism once again the beacon of hope for hundreds of millions of oppressed black people the world over.

A Hopeful Dawn of Post-Colonial Initiatives
Southern Africa Political and Economic Monthly (SAPEM), April 1996

While most of Africa is pre-occupied with its separate and individual internal struggle for survival – desperately trying to deal with problems of security, development and the devastations of structural adjustment programme (SAP), debt servicing, repayment of military rules and of the hopelessly endemic political instability arising from them – East Africa and the Horn, on the contrary, is emerging as an area of clear vision and hope.

This is the region which only recently saw some of the worst upheavals in Africa in Somalia, Rwanda, Burundi and Sudan. Before that, it had witnessed protracted wars in Eritrea, Ethiopia, Uganda and Rwanda. Upheavals are not new to the area but - with only a few exceptions – these upheavals were qualitatively different from those elsewhere in the continent. They were revolutionary upheavals: deliberate, disciplined and organised.

A collective wisdom has arisen out of these protracted and revolutionary struggles and has bestowed the region with some of the best leadership in Africa. The previous African liberation struggles against colonialism and settlerism, were fought against the external enemy, and they enjoyed total support of the people and the continent. The movements were supported and funded by, among others, the OAU Liberation Committee. They were even given the green light by the United Nations' Decolonisation committee.

Not so, however, with the Eastern African region's postcolonial revolutions. Far from being supported by Africa, they were vilified and vigorously opposed and shunned virtually by the whole continent. They were even condemned as "separatists" and not infrequently named the "enemies of Africa". Their "crime" was that they were fighting against internal oppressive regimes – against the corruption of neocolonialism. And they won these wars against all odds – against the powerful and well-established indigenous armies and in an unfavourable international diplomatic climate. The OAU, being the servant of the regimes under attack, dutifully condemned these movements with all its diplomatic ferocity. The revolutionaries enjoyed no external support and no sympathy. They were virtually alone, depending entirely on the justness of their cause and on their own ability, ingenuity and sound leadership.

Their total collective experience is enormous. In Eritrea, the struggle lasted for more than thirty years; in Ethiopia, for 17 years; in Uganda, for five years; and Rwanda three years – a total of more than half a century of collective struggle. Again, unlike other African liberation struggles, these were fought, organised, supplied and administered within their own countries – in the liberated areas – gaining a wealth of experience in the process.

They have, as a result, mastered the rudiments of self-government, of administration, of building essential institutions and the skills of self-reliance. They have through experience developed the ability to identify reliable leadership material under severe and stressful conditions. They have developed the mature skills of give-and-take negotiating for survival whether on the battlefield or at a round-table. That is to say, they have mastered the intricate art of flexibility, or being firm when firmness is required, and of compromise and reconciliation when no strongly held principles are at stake.

Tough and rough experience has enabled them to develop the ability to constantly distinguish and make a choice between primary and secondary contradictions, and to act on them according to the needs of the required objective. In other words, they have developed that very rare capacity to be able to reconcile the seemingly irreconcilable.

This rare wealth of experience is now seen in action. Eritrea's Isaias Afwerki, Ethiopia's Meles Zenawi, Uganda's Yoweri Museveni and Rwanda's Paul Kagame are the most outstanding examples of leaders who went through the rigid experiences of war. They are the new type of leadership in Africa. They are civilians who took up arms to fight the dictatorial military regimes, and they have won. A unique feat in an Africa dominated by the privileged military establishments whose roots are colonial in every respect. They have come to know and trust each other only after the victory of their respective struggles, but not during those struggles. They fought and won their wars separately without any common strategy, but now in victory they have developed a solid identity of purpose, the purpose of regional stability and prosperity. These leaders respect each other because each sees in the others similar qualities and traits which they themselves value most – honesty, courage, determination, single-mindedness, organisational talent and administrative skills.

The organisation that has brought all these talents together is the IGADD, The Inter-governmental Authority on Drought and Development. IGADD is dynamic. Having started with a particular emphasis on drought, the organisation is now being reorganised and revitalised into IGAD by de-emphasising drought – a necessarily transient phenomenon – and integrating it on development – which is lasting. At their Heads of State and Government meeting in Nairobi on March 21, the organisation's leaders decided to rename the revitalised organisation as the Inter-governmental Agency for Development (IGAD).

IGAD is confronted not only with a war situation in Burundi, Somalia and Sudan, but also by foreign interference, particularly from France and the United States. The former tries to restore to power the overthrown and discredited murderous ex-leaders of Rwanda in the hope of using them for the advancement of French interests in the area. The US for its part, seeks to mould the region to conform to its Middle-East and global strategy. These two powers, together with Britain, are in a powerful position as permanent members of the UN Security Council to form and influence what has euphemistically come to be known as the "international community opinion". To work with them and at the same time safeguard one's own national interests, as IGAD members will constantly be obliged to do in the current international climate, calls for diplomatic dexterity of the highest calibre.

Moreover, these imperialist powers have influential friends in the region both within and outside governments, and to keep them at bay without exposing them or making them "know that you know" also requires a lot of skill. The Nile symbolises this situation. It is one of the world's most strategic rivers, which links almost all the IGAD countries, and which has also been used effectively by the imperialists throughout the era of their domination of Eastern Africa.

Somalia poses a serious threat to the stability of the region. The IGAD countries cannot interfere in Somalia's internal affairs, although the affairs of Somalia spill over into neighbouring countries. How to ward off this threat from spreading without hurting the sensitivities of Somalia? Ethiopia, a member of IGAD, has an answer. It is resolving the Somalia problem in its region of the Ogaden by conceding to the Somalis a right they have never enjoyed since coming under Amhara hegemony in the last century – the right to self-determination.

Siad Barre, the former President of Somalia, invaded the Ogaden in 1974 to "liberate" Somalis and suffered ignominious defeat and disgrace. If the Ogaden Somalis wanted liberation then and never got it, now they are given it on a silver platter, but they are rejecting it. Why? Because the Somalis are beginning to renounce separatism in favour of self-determination within regional integration. It is a small step, but a good beginning with far-reaching implications for Somali nationhood and regional unity.

Sudan, a founding member of IGAD, is another potentially destabilising factor in the region as the war in Southern Sudan spreads to Uganda. Sudan shares its borders with nine other African countries of different ideological persuasions and varying strategic interests. On its southern flanks it borders Kenya, Uganda and Zaire, which brings Sudan right into the politics and strategies of Eastern and Central Africa. On its western front it borders the Central African Republic and Chad which brings it into the midst of those countries' rather confused politics of instability and constant changes of government. In the north and north-west it borders Egypt and Libya, which involves it not only in the politics of those countries but also makes it a significant actor in the politics of the Middle-East and, by extension, impinges on the security concerns of the US, Russia and the European powers. It borders Eritrea and Ethiopia in the east which made Sudan a willing or unwilling participant in the major civil wars that have been raging in that area for the last thirty years. It also carries most of the scars, memories, prejudices and suspicions left over by those bitter wars.

Sudan is quarrelling with its IGAD partners, Uganda, Eritrea and Ethiopia, the first two have already broken off diplomatic relations with it, and Ethiopia is almost on the verge of doing so. But the most significant threat to the region, with vast international implications, is Sudan's quarrel with Egypt. This Egyptian equation dramatically brings the US into the picture.

The origins of US deep involvement with the "Egyptian Question" takes us out of the IGAD region and here we must meander briefly into the jungle of the Middle East politics and superpower strategies. During 1952-1970 under President Nasser, Egypt was a bastion of anti-imperialism and a leading force in the non-aligned movement.

Then came Anwar Sadat, after whose assassination in 1981 by Muslim revivalists, Egyptian leadership was taken over by Hosni Mubarak. Post-Nasser Egypt has warmed up to the US in the hope that the latter might more profitably replace the USSR as the main supplier of Egypt's military and economic aid.

At first, the US did not want to appear to be too enthusiastic towards Egypt, whose leader Sadat only in 1973 had launched a decisive war against Israel which precipitated the Oil Crisis and dramatically changed the global economy. The unpredictable international events soon forced the US to embrace Egypt with almost indecent enthusiasm.

It came in 1979 when the Shah of Iran was overthrown after a mass uprising which installed Ayatollah Khomeini in his place, an event which changed the whole picture of the Middle East conflict, and brought the US right into African politics, and specifically the IGAD countries. Until the Shah's overthrow, US relations with Iran had been unique. Because of Iran's huge size and its geographic position *vis a vis* the USSR and the Middle East, with the Shah being so anti-Arab and anti-communism with equal intensity, it suited the US perfectly to make Iran an ideal centre to locate her entire Middle East strategy and intelligence.

With the removal of the Shah from Iran the US had to seek new allies in the region big and strong enough to counter-balance Iran, whose new rulers had turned out to be fiercely anti-US and anti-Israel. Egypt became the chosen ally for the purpose. The US accordingly made a strategic shift in favour of Egypt where the Arab and Middle East politics were concerned.

Egypt, however, is faced with a serious internal threat from Muslim revivalists, the so-called Muslim "fundamentalists", whose movement is seen to be also threatening the rest of the Arab world, from Algeria to the Gulf States. If Egypt falls to the Muslims revivalists, the rest of the Arab states of the kings and Sheikhs in the area are likely to fall too, which will spell doom to the economic and military strategy of the US and its NATO allies. The US is therefore determined to ensure the survival of Egypt's present leadership, by all means, up to and including, military intervention if necessary.

Geography was destined to link Egypt to Sudan very intimately, so much so that its security in many ways is dependent on what is happening in the Sudan and other counties joined by the Nile. It so happens that Sudan is also the ideological headquarters of the Muslim revivalist movement worldwide. Egypt's quarrel with Sudan stems from its suspicion that Sudan is helping to train and to provide a "rear-base area" to the Egyptian Muslim revivalists. This makes Sudan the prime suspect and a potential threat to the US strategic and security interests, not only in the Middle-East, but worldwide. It is this reckoning that, ipso facto, brings the US right into the politics of the whole region. IGAD diplomats with all their dexterity will inevitably be subjected to severe political, economic and even military pressure to persuade them to yield to the US strategic priority to undermine Sudan. And there are still many areas of conflict in the region which the US can exploit for the purpose of applying pressure.

The most serious one is the SPLA, the armed wing of

Southern Sudanese fighters against the North. This war is as old as Sudan itself, which typically started one year before the country's independence from Britain in 1956. The war was started then by the Anyanya movement who fought over the years until 1972 against the "Arabising" of the South by the North. There was peace for a decade before the war flared up again, but this time the movement has transmogrified into the Sudan People's Liberation Army fighting the North over the Shariah Law, and/or Muslim Fundamentalism. This war seems to be the only "actually existing" *Permanent Revolution* in history, leaving in its wake severe devastation and massive human suffering in the area.

Sudan accuses Uganda of helping the SPLA fighters, and Uganda believes that Sudan is arming the Lord's Resistance Freedom Army, a Ugandan dissident Christian "fundamentalist" group who have been terrorising Northern Uganda ever since the Obote regime in 1986. This tension has led to the break off of diplomatic relations between Uganda and Sudan, although both are members of the IGAD.

Again, soon after Eritrean independence, Sudan sent a high powered delegation to Asmara to congratulate the Eritreans on their independence and to urge them that they should now move on to the next step and declare Eritrea a Muslim state. Eritrea not only refused to oblige, but it also decided to recognise Israel. This led to serious tension on the Sudan/Eritrea border as dissident Eritreans tried to take advantage of the situation to infiltrate their fighters into Eritrea. As a result, Eritrea too broke off diplomatic relations with Sudan.

The traditional tension between Ethiopia and Sudan had been aggravated when Egyptian dissidents attempted to assassinate President Hosni Mubarak in Addis Ababa while attending the OAU Summit in July 1995. Ethiopia blamed the incident on Sudan and the two countries are now at loggerheads.

In any region these serious inter-state conflicts would have ended in war. But in the IGAD area war cannot happen because the leaders have tested wars and fully appreciate the implications. Moreover, their experience compels them to resort to diplomacy, or to indulge in what Winston

Churchill called "Jaw, Jaw, rather than War War". This approach will be especially suited in dealing with what are regarded as the intractable problems in the area, eg Burundi or Somalia – the UN interference and that of hundreds of NGOs who invaded the area on the pretext of helping to solve the problems and have actually aggravated them. France on its part, is trying everything in the book to destabilise the area, especially in Rwanda and Burundi, but to no avail, thanks to the patience and diplomatic skills of the leaders. Even the OAU, with its newly found conflict "management" approach, seems to be redundant and unable to do much in the area which has not already been done by IGAD.

In the meantime there is a new attempt to revive the old East African Community. Until its demise in the 1970s, the Community was the oldest, the most experienced form of regional cooperation on the continent. It had common services like post, communications, transport, and a common currency. The Presidents of Tanzania, Uganda and Kenya are re-establishing a new headquarters at Arusha in Tanzania, to prepare the groundwork for closer integration. Although Tanzania is not part of IGAD, it is linked to it through its East African credentials. All these developments seem to reflect African people's demand for a greater African integration, and hopefully a Pan-African solution to Africa's problems of backwardness and extreme poverty within a continent of enormous wealth and human resources. Such an evolution will be the greatest reward to the leaders who are today struggling to normalise and stabilise their area.

Imperialism:
Strategies of Control,
Strategies of Resistance

INTERNATIONALISM

Twenty years after the non-aligned movement
Africa Now, September 1981

The non-aligned countries are due to commemorate the 20th anniversary of a series of conferences, the first one of which was initiated in Belgrade in September 1961. At that time the towering champions of non-alignment were the famous big five - Nasser, Nehru, Nkrumah, Sukarno and Tito. The world then was in the midst of the Cold War between imperialism, headed by the US and the Socialist camp headed by the Soviet Union. The US then still enjoyed nuclear superiority and sought to fashion the world in its own image. To that end it often took the world to the brink of world war.

Many countries in Africa and Asia had just then won their juridical independence mostly under the leadership of the anti-colonial petty bourgeoisie. Their policies at independence in many instances were a confused amalgam of economic nationalism, international parasitism and progressive rhetoric.

Internally they did not depart significantly from the colonial administration with more or less the same objectives of producing for the consumption and production needs of the metropolitan economies. Internationally they took an ambivalent position between East and West. On the one hand they would not openly side with the imperialist camp so soon after leading their masses against colonial rule. But on the other their class interests prevented them from siding with the Socialist camp which was then the leading anti-imperialist force in the world.

Marshall Tito of Yugoslavia had broken away from the Socialist camp in 1948 but he could not side with the imperialist camp. It would have been too much for the masses of Yugoslavia to swallow double treachery in one gulp. Tito then enjoyed enormous international prestige after victoriously leading the Yugoslav people almost single-handedly in resistance to fascist Germany during World War II.

Isolated from the Socialist camp and unable to join the imperialist one, Tito emerged as a prestigious leader without an international role. Moreover, Yugoslavia had embarked on an ambitious programme of indiscriminate industrialisation which was not compatible with internal need. Consequently he was laden with industrial goods for which there was no internal demand. Deprived of the markets in the Socialist camp and unable to compete in the technologically advanced Western market which was then coming under the domination of the US multinational corporations, Tito turned to the newly independent countries as a potential outlet for his industrial products.

Nehru in India in the meantime was busy devising his "socialistic type" policies of a mixed economy as a means of pre-empting a Socialist revolution. China had just won its earth-shaking revolution and solidly sided with the Socialist camp. This event electrified the masses of Asia who saw in Socialism the only way out of their poverty and misery. Thus caught between the mass demand for a decisive change and his desire to serve class interests (India's landlords and national bourgeoisie) Nehru opted for his so-called socialist approach as a way of resolving the conflicting economic and social class interests.

Nkrumah, Nasser and Sukarno were in a similar dilemma in their own respective countries. The needs of the masses and those of their rulers were in constant conflict and the rulers were caught in a delicate situation of a permanent balancing act. They were reluctant to cut their link with imperialism but did not want to appear hostile to the Socialist camp either.

So it was a marriage of convenience between the ex-socialists and the ex-anti colonialists who needed each other in their quest for legitimacy. The concept of non-alignment was therefore seen as a way out of resolving the antagonistic and hostile confrontation between labour and capital at international level. Then there was the fear of nuclear annihilation. The threat of third world war was real with the US provocatively calling for the "rolling back" of the Socialist camp. In South East Asia the US had launched an aggressive war against the Korean people who were immediately joined by revolutionary Chinese volunteers to resist and finally defeat the aggression. In Indochina the French colonialists had been annihilated by the Vietnamese people at Dien Bien Phu with the US threatening to use the atom bomb in support of the French. This was the beginning of the Domino Theory which sought to justify US intervention in popular uprisings in Asia.

The US was furiously mobilising the newly independent countries to join its ubiquitous military alliances designed to encircle the Socialist camp. But the fear of involvement in a World War forced many of these countries to back out and they opted as usual for a compromise solution of remaining "neutral" in military confrontation but aligned to the West in economic and diplomatic institutions of the Cold War - i.e. the British Commonwealth, the French Community, the World Bank, IMF, GATT, etc.

In the last 20 years several attempts were made to turn non-alignment into a movement but without success. This was due to the conflicting interests represented in the group as well as to the amorphous character of the petty bourgeois leadership. But the most serious obstacle was that the group lacked social basis. It did not involve the masses of the people and to this day it remains at best an instrument for diplomatic skirmishes at the UN and other international fora. The big five are no longer with us but their spirit lingers, for however irrelevant the grouping is, it at least brings the poor nations together to grumble and lament in unison.

Notes

(1) The Domino theory asserted that if one country 'fell' to Communism, this would push neighbouring countries to similarly fall and so on.

Cancun: A postmortem
Africa Now, December 1981

By turning the Cancun Conference in Mexico into a Seminar on the Virtues of Private Enterprise, President Reagan has undoubtedly shown once again his well-known adroitness in making the impossible possible. He assumed his role as the Lecturer to the Seminar quite admirably too, all things considered.

He had a captive audience, in more senses than one. In the first place, he captivated them with his famous flamboyance and charm. Secondly, the setting was more than perfect. Isolated from the rest of mankind by the most elaborate security cordon Mexico had ever seen since Zapata – put together by the combined ingenuity of top secret police agents of the participating countries – there was simply no way that these world leaders could wriggle out of his harangue.

He accidentally humiliated them by arriving at the opening session 14 minutes late, which nevertheless managed to prepare the necessary psychological mood of anticipation. The fact that the meeting had no agenda also worked in his favour because he was then able to ramble on, on any subject to which his rich imagination might lead him. The leaders from the South had no such leeway in the sense that their brief was limited to bread and butter issues.

The opening speech by the President of Mexico said everything that the leaders from the South could possibly have said and so there was really nothing new to be said. On the other hand, President Reagan had already touched on the subject in his speech in Philadelphia only four days before the meeting and about which every leader at the meeting had already been briefed. In the absence of anything new to say from both sides, who would begrudge the President of the US for lecturing the poor countries on how to manage their affairs? It was done in a good and friendly spirit and without malice.

In this spirit we can see why Fidel Castro was not invited

to the meeting although he is the current President of the non-aligned countries. Apart from the fact that his security guards could not have got on well with the rest, his alien philosophy and ideology was obviously not suited to the occasion. In any case he is known to be a bad listener and his presence could have stirred up some tension in an otherwise calm atmosphere.

That it was a calm, relaxed and even luxurious gathering no one can dispute. To its credit, the Mexican Government went out of its way to ensure that the guests would be well looked after, comfortably distanced from the madding and hungry crowd.

The feeding arrangements were excellent too, according to reliable sources. Carefully hand-picked chefs were gathered under close scrutiny of the secret police, just in case anybody had any funny ideas. It is reported that both the chefs and the police did well in their respective undertakings, and not a single case of physical upset among the delegates was indicated.

All in all it was a fitting setting to take stock of the situation concerning the hungry people of the world and how to feed them before they perish en masse. It is a sound guiding philosophy that says that if you don't know what good eating is then you have no business to talk about feeding people. The discussion would then be too abstract for any practical purposes.

Poor Willy Brandt must have been stewing in his Survival Report. He it was who had initiated the meeting; who traversed the globe in search of the consensus for the meeting. And now, having got it, hey presto. Reagan takes it over with his messianic vision of the virtues of private enterprise! Brandt's social-democratic notions of salvaging the capitalist world order from total collapse were not even acknowledged by the meeting, let alone accepted as a working document. It is true that it took him and his multinational team more than two years to produce a report which said nothing that was not known before the team was set up. But his efforts could at least have been noted with thanks.

It is known that he spent many a sleepless night nagging himself for having failed to do what he could have done for the poor and hungry countries when he was Chancellor of the mighty and rich West Germany. He was occupied then, to be sure, with his *Ostpolitik* and poverty was not yet pressing enough to threaten the established world order. The meeting could have nevertheless credited him for his born-again spirit.

Edward Heath, his vice-chairman, who is credited with being the hangman of UNCTAD 1 in 1964 as the head of the British delegation, and who has now emerged as a bornagain advocate of the poor, must have equally been disappointed with the meeting, having staked all his future political career on its positive outcome. Now no conservative in Britain who is worth his salt can forgive him for openly advocating ideas which are suspiciously close to those of the Social Democrats. If this will work to the credit of Willy Brandt and his home politics, Heath and Conservatives are definitely the losers.

On the whole, the Spirit of Cancun will be long remembered for establishing a sense of friendship and togetherness. Towards the end of the meeting all the delegates were buddies addressing each other by their first names. Ronald was reassured of Fahd's support of Husni Mubarak who was at home continuing the unfinished job of rounding up the Muslim Muftis. Fahd got his AWACS and Indira her $6.7bn via the IMF. Although the rest went home with nothing except the Spirit, it was no doubt a resounding success as a get-together.

There is a cartoon in the New York Times of Sunday, November 1 which sums up the Spirit of Cancun. The hungry-looking, almost cadaverous delegates from the South are shown approaching enthusiastically their rich counterparts of the North, with bulging bright eyes and empty rice bowls in their hands. They meet, embrace, kiss, and then are photographed together in a splendid unity. Then they part, with the delegates from the South still holding on to their empty bowls, the same hungry looks on their faces.

The Spirit of Unity (Cancun) has at last been established and it is shown in the photograph for all the world, friends and foes, to see. We are all happy together in the FREE WORLD, stagflation, hunger, and all. We shall overcome! Cancun shall live forever!

Non-Alignment in the Post-Gulf War Era
Inqilab, Summer 1991

The Bandung Conference in 1955 brought together for the first time 29 Afro-Asian leaders of the newly liberated countries of the two continents - among them the People's Republic of China which had emerged 6 years earlier from a revolution which had shaken the world. The Conference drew up five principles which would guide these countries future cooperation and struggles. The main objectives of the new movement were anti-imperialism and anti-colonialism and in order to establish good working relations, the conference laid down principles of mutual assistance, of mutual benefits in economic and trade relations, of no foreign military bases in any of the member states, and respect for each other's sovereignty. All this became known as the Spirit of Bandung.

This new Spirit projected the two ex-colonised continents on the world arena for the first time in history as a diplomatic force to contend with. On all important questions, especially that of the liberation of the remaining colonies, they all spoke with one voice and voted as a bloc at the UN meetings and other councils of the world. China was denied its rightful seat at the UN (because the US vetoed the application insisting that the tiny island of Taiwan legitimately represented China) but China's influence in world politics and with liberation movements continued to expand.

The Soviet Union and the USA were, in the meantime, locked in a life-and-death struggle to attain nuclear parity. After exploding the first atomic bombs on Hiroshima and Nagasaki which ended World War II in 1945, the US began to flex its muscles and was bent on using nuclear blackmail to advance its objectives of economic and diplomatic domination of the world. To counter this the Soviet Union in turn embarked on developing nuclear capability and the means of its delivery. The race was on.

Once the Superpowers attained parity in armaments and

means of delivery, the threat of nuclear blackmail receded. Britain, France and China later developed their own independent nuclear capability but because of their limited size they could not pose a threat to world peace or embark on the diplomacy of nuclear blackmail.

The passive approach to diplomacy

As the struggle between the Superpowers continued to gain momentum and the establishment of military pacts and bases continued to spread, the Bandung countries sought to establish a new morality in international politics.This morality emphasised reliance on diplomacy rather than on force as a means of resolving international disputes. To be effective in this approach the Bandung countries had to be seen to be neutral in superpower struggles. Thus the doctrine of "non-alignment" or "positive neutrality", was born. The emphasis was henceforth to be on co-operation and reconciliation, even with imperialism, rather than confrontation.

China backed out of this passive approach to diplomacy, arguing that the relationship between poor countries and the rich was one of exploitation and not a relation of equals. Only vigilance and unrelenting struggle would ensure the survival of the oppressed countries and enable them to develop the capacity to put their countries on a path of genuine progress and national independence. Oppressed countries could not co-exist with imperialism which must be opposed and resisted by every means possible, including force. However, practically all of the "non-aligned" countries were already aligned with the West in all but name. Instead of developing independent national economies, they were all tied as appendages to Western economies, and consequently what scientific and technical development that came our way was of the kind that was designed to serve already developed countries and therefore unsuited to our real development needs. Every effort at development by the "non-aligned" countries, consequently, resulted in impoverishing their economies and their people while enriching Western economies. The more these countries resorted to borrowing from Western banks and governments in order to make up for what had been extracted from their economies to the rich coffers of the West, the more their independence was compromised. Stuck to their diplomacy of "co-operation and reconciliation", they continually gave up not only their national prestige, but in many ways their sovereignty too was gradually being eroded. Diplomacy of "reconciliation and co-operation" became diplomacy of "compromise and capitulation".

Henceforth, poverty became the hallmark of these countries and they came to be known collectively as the "poor countries". Their diplomacy correspondingly made a 180-degree-turn, from that of challenge to that of "accomodation". Without real independence and national prestige the diplomacy of the Bandung Spirit disappeared; instead of being a diplomatic force to be reckoned with as envisaged in Bandung, they became collectively at best a diplomatic nuisance. By the 1970s, "non-aligned" countries' economies became even worse, as Europe and Japan were emerging as new world powers at the expense of Africa and Asia respectively. Cheap African resources, extracted at considerable cost to African people's well-being, supplied Europe's re-industrialisation, and the meagre foreign exchange which went back to the continent was immediately squandered away in the importation of useless manufactured goods, from luxury goods for the elite to trinkets of one kind or another. The same was true for Asia vis-a-vis Japan, with the exception of the so-called Newly Industrialising Countries (NICs) which were reduced to the role of staging centres in Asia for Japanese and US multinational corporations' manufacturing enterprises in the area, utilising Asian cheap labour and market outlets in the region for their products.

The collapse of the Eastern Bloc

The Soviet Bloc in the mean time was being pushed out of the centre of world economic activity. With the "non-aligned" countries firmly siding with the West in everything except the rhetoric of non-alignment, and the US stepping up its economic boycott of socialist countries, the Soviet Bloc could not participate in the dynamic economic development of the 1960s and 1970s that the West was going through.

The nature of the Soviet economic model, handed down from the Stalin era, emphasised heavy industry at the expense of light industry and agriculture - or in Marxist terms emphasised Department I at the expense of Department II. This denied the Soviet economies the benefits of light industries and agriculture; ie., rapid production turnover, profitability, innovation in technologies which serve people's immediate needs, a market for heavy industry and, most important of all, rising standards of living of their people. The Soviet Union, thanks to its massive nuclear arsenal remained a superpower without a superpower economy. The collapse of such an economy was predictable. The Chinese foresaw it way back in 1965 when they pointed out the imbalances inherent in the Soviet model[1]. The success of the counter revolution in the Socialist Bloc was the result of a combination of various factors but the principal one was the economic mess. The "Reformers" made the situation even worse by rushing to adopt and implement the "free market" model in economies which were based fundamentally on diametrically opposite principles and economic laws.

Having been left out of European dynamic development; seeing their standard of living worsening; prompted and encouraged by Western propaganda and intelligence operatives, the East European masses revolted and wanted to be joined to the rest of Europe before the 1992 European economic unification. Unfortunately for them, it is not going to be an easy passage. In all likelihood, Eastern Europe will become the focus of massive exploitation for a long time to come, while Europe will be plunged into a prolonged period of economic and political instability with Germany, the industrial giant of Europe playing a dominant role.

With the virtual collapse of the Eastern Bloc, the Cold War came to an end in favour of the West, and especially the US. The post war bi-polarity in world affairs which to a certain extent worked in favour of "non-aligned" countries, was replaced by a unipolar world dominated and often dictated to by the US. The Soviet Union, the erstwhile Superpower, has been reduced to the status of a by-stander, helplessly witnessing world events take a momentous turn while its diplomats tour Western capitals, from US, Japan and Germany, right down to Spain in search of financial aid.

Nowhere has this pathetic spectacle been more humiliatingly obvious than in the recent Gulf crisis. The US conceived, initiated and executed the war in the Gulf with the virtual connivance of the Soviet Union, inspite of the fact that it was obvious to everybody that America was using the UN to advance its imperialist interests.

Why the Gulf War happened

To understand this phenomena, we must begin by defining what the Gulf War was not about. Anglo-American propaganda kept harping on that the war was being fought on behalf of the United Nations and of the "international community" in order to restore respect for international law, to "punish aggressor Iraq" and to reestablish the "legitimate" rulers of Kuwait to their throne. This was utter rubbish. Before the notorious UN Security Council Resolution 678 (which was interpreted as authorising the Americans and their allies to use force) was rammed through, the Americans had already rushed scores of thousands of their soldiers and equipment to Saudi Arabia to "prevent Iraq from occupying" that country.

In other words, the transfer of massive US forces to Saudi Arabia was a bilateral arrangement between the two countries to defend Saudi Arabia. It had nothing to do with liberating Kuwait, nothing to do with UN resolutions and much less to do with safeguarding international law. Soon after when the event had turned into a bloody war, it was clear that by rushing troops and deadly weapons to the area, the US had initiated the first step to war long before anybody thought of Resolution 678. That is to say US imperialism had made up its mind to fight Iraq with or without UN support.

And if Iraq had been a military lightweight like Grenada or Panama, past experience has shown that the US would have attacked the country without bothering to go to the UN. We can therefore discount the notion that the US was fighting Iraq in order to restore respect for international law. That was not the purpose or motive of this war. In fact the 'International Community', on whose behalf the US was ostensibly fighting this war, cannot trust the US with the task of policing the world when the policeman's own record for breaking international law has long since reached scandalous proportions.

If the US was not fighting to restore international order, then it must have been fighting to safeguard its own global military strategic interests vis-a-vis the other Superpower. Not at all. As we have seen these considerations were relevant during the era of bipolarity in world politics but not now. In a uni-polar world the Middle East has lost its strategic significance militarily.

Well, did Bush kill Iraqis in order to bring about a New World Order, as he has proclaimed? Not on your life! The beyond-the-war rhetoric garbage is the standard stock-in-trade of the imperialists when they enter any predatory war. On the eve of every major imperialist war the world has been bombarded with such high-sounding "visions".

US President Woodrow Wilson entered World War I in 1917 with the declaration that the US intervention in the war would "establish a new world of harmony", democracy, and self-determination, secured by the League of Nations. We know what happened after that war! There was neither harmony, nor democracy or self-determination; only their opposites emerged with the advent of fascism and Nazism.

Franklin Roosevelt, the US President during World War II, entered that war by declaring that out of the ruins of the war would emerge a "concert of great powers, institutionalised in the Security Council, and dedicated to the maintanance of global order and security". Instead throughout the post-World War II era, the US used the UN as an instrument for advancing US foreign policy interests which included bullying third world countries which resisted US domination.

Harry Truman, post-World War II US President, on the eve of the US's war of aggression against the Korean people, declared that his "determination to phase down aggression would set an example that would deter future aggression". John Kennedy too made similar rhetoric to start aggression against the Vietnamese people, and so did Lyndon Johnson in his own Texan style to justify further intensification of this aggression.

The American masses have always been bamboozled into going to war and dying for imperialism with their eyes fixed on the future and not on the torments they inflict in the present.What Bush is saying is not new. The world has heard it before. It is obvious even to a child of ten that Bush could not have been laying the foundations for a "New World Order" by attempting to bombard the Iraqis out of existence - which is what is meant by the American phrase "carpet bombing" by B-52s. In Vietnam they used the phrase "saturation bombing", it meant the same thing: exterminating populations by massive cluster and anti-personnel bombs. That is the task for which the B-52s have been designed and manufactured and that is their "operational purpose" overseas - hitherto used entirely against the people of third world countries.

So what is Bush up to in this US aggression against the Iraqi and Arab people? Is it to ensure Israel's survival? Not even that. Israelis have been taking care of themselves as US surrogates fairly well, as long as Uncle Sam continued to pour in money and sophisticated armaments. They don't need the presence of the paymaster to emphasise the point too vigorously to "embarass our Arab allies".

Has the US been fighting for the Middle East oil then? No, not directly. It is not the fear of who controls the Middle East oil reserves that has sent the US to fight in the Gulf. Whoever controls them will have to sell the oil to the world market; nor is the US seriously concerned with rocketing oil prices since, as an oil-producing country it stands to gain from the price rise.

The US cannot be frightened out of its wits in this way even by the prospect of OPEC coming under the control of

Iraq, for OPEC too must do business with the West to survive since it is their biggest and still expanding market. Also with the Soviet Union entering the world market with unabashed gusto, its vast oil reserves - now at the disposal of its western partners - will counter the power of OPEC to dictate oil prices. No, it is not the fear of who controls the Middle East oil reserves which has sent the US to fight in the Gulf - it is the fear of who controls the money from the oil.

'Dollar hegemony' and Arab radicalism

The real and underlying motive of the war was to preserve the dollar hegemony in the world economy which is being threatened by Iraqi nationalism. It was US imperialism itself which was at stake here, and the US would do anything including the nuclear bombardment of Iraq to ensure its survival. US imperialism has been facilitated not by physical conquest of colonies but by the dominance of the dollar as the international medium of exchange since the end of World War II. The Bretton Woods Conference of 1944 which established the World Bank and the International Monetary Fund (IMF) had ensured the status of the dollar to be "as good as gold", and artificially fixed the price of gold at $35 per ounce to pave the way for the dollar's dominance in the financial and banking system throughout the world outside the socialist bloc.

The US government and US multinationals thoroughly abused this dollar privilege, the former printing many more dollars than the US economy could support in goods and services or in gold reserve and the latter lavishly investing it overseas, mostly in Europe in the aftermath of World War II. The result was that the world was awash with dollars without any equivalent material backing.

In order to prevent this inflationary crisis re-entering the US economy, the then (1972) US President Richard Nixon decided to release gold from the dollar and allow each to find its real value in the market. As financial speculators lost confidence in the dollar panic ensued and the rush to buy gold sent its price rocketing from $35 to $200 almost overnight. (The price of gold now hovers between $350 and $400 per ounce). A year later, after the 1973 Middle East war[2], these financial speculators shifted their dollars from gold into buying oil which promised quick profit. The "unwanted dollar" , ("unwanted" because no government accepted responsibility for it), which until then was known as the Euro-dollar now became the Petro-dollar by virtue of the fact that most of these dollars were now used for speculation in oil purchase and sale. This helped to send the price rocketing as happened earlier with the price of gold. When these dollars came pouring into the Arab Sheikhs' coffers, their backward economies could not absorb them. There were no local industries to invest in and the Sheikhs had no plan for serious industrialisation. So the Sheikhs recycled them back to the West, mostly as dollar reserves. The Kuwaiti Sheikhs, being proteges of Britain, put most of their reserves in Britain and it became the most significant reserve which backs Sterling and the Bank of England internationally. If the Kuwaiti Sheikhs withdraw their money today (current estimate $100 billion) Sterling will immediately collapse as an international currency with devastating consequences to the British economy. But the bigger stake is with the Saudi reserves which is wholly in dollars and under the control of Uncle Sam. (The current estimate of the Arab Sheikhs dollar investments in the West stands at $680 billion). This ensures US dollar domination in the world economy and also helps the US's battered economy. Currently as a result of supply side economics - Reagonomics in the US and Thatcherism in Britain - both countries economies are in a serious recession which can easily slide into slump and then depression. The only hope for survival of both economies is via the Arab Sheikhs' reserves which allow US and UK policy makers room for manoeuvre in the face of fierce challenge from Germany and Japan, the erstwhile enemies of the allies.

For instance the US can get away from its enormous internal and external debt and the balance of payments deficit simply by manipulating interest rates as long as the dollar remains the principal international medium of exchange[3]. Once the dollar loses that status the weakened

US economy will be in the most serious predicament. Its dominant role in the world economy which it enjoyed since the end of World War II will be seriously undermined. The Gulf war in which hundreds of thousands have perished was about preventing this from happening When Bush talks about the New World Order he really means the preservation of the old order dominated by the almighty dollar, and the institutions which have sustained it mostly at the expense of the Third World - the World Bank, IMF, GATT etc. The threat to imperialism posed by Saddam Hussain lay in his challenge to the old order in the Middle East. This imminent threat of Arab radicalism lies in the financial and monetary spheres of imperialism. Production and exchange are two aspects of the struggle for changing relations of production and the establishment of socialist relations. Proponents of Arab radicalism in the Middle East unlike in Asia or Africa can harm dollar hegemony, initially even without changing their own internal relations. They can do this simply by withdrawing their financial and monetary backing to the dollar and sterling and sharpening the contradictions between imperialist countries e.g. Britain and America vs Europe or vs Germany or Japan. If radical Arabism takes over control of the vast petro dollar reserves from the docile and reactionary Sheikhs and transforms it into Petro- Dinar or Petro-Riyal, liberated from the dollar hegemony, US imperialism will face its most direct and immediate threat much more imminent than that posed simply by ideological challenge which is latent and based on long-term projection.

Radical Arabism can, for instance, establish strong links with the rest of the third world with a view to forming worldwide economic relations based on objective economic complementarity of the oppressed countries. It can embark on a massive development of productive forces in the Arab world and form loose economic alliances with Germany or Japan in order to benefit from their technology. This prospect is seen as the worst possible scenario in Washington at a time when these two industrial giants are already challenging the dollar hegemony in their own way even without the help of Arab radicalism.

The future of 'non-alignment'

What should be the position of the "non-aligned" countries in the light of this new and unstable situation? Are they to remain "non-aligned" indefinitely without being clear about non-aligned between whom and whom? Or are they to be termed "South" in contrast to "North" which is the current term for imperialist countries; but south of what, or north of what? Will the new battle cry be for a "New International World Order" and "Debt Forgiveness" or would they utilise this volatile world situation to assert a new agenda for the oppressed countries, which include radical Arab nationalism to influence the course of events in favour of the oppressed? Non-alignment in the post-Gulf War era is certainly dead; it was killed or burnt alive by the US napalm and cluster bombs against Iraqi soldiers, mostly Kurds, for whom the West is now shedding crocodile tears. The shock waves of the aftermath of the Gulf war, the hypocrisy and lies the West resorted to in an attempt to justify their unjust war, should make even the most politically illiterate among the"non-aligned" leaders aware once more that imperialism is alive and shooting. What should the "non-aligned" leaders do now?

Well, in September this year Foreign Ministers of the "non- aligned countries" will be meeting in Accra, Ghana, to prepare the agenda for the summit of their Heads of State and Government, most probably to be held also in Accra. it will be the first post-Gulf War meeting of this kind. In the interests of our own survival and the survival of our future generations this is the time to intensify the struggle, not for the mythical New World Order, but for capturing the political initiative in a world-wide crusade against imperialism. The post-World War II period had offered the historic opportunity in 1955 for Bandung to capture the political initiative to lead the political and diplomatic crusade which helped speed up the liberation struggle of African and Asian countries. That liberation turned out to be a mere juridical independence. What remains to be won is economic, social and cultural independence. Leaders have no longer the excuse that they will be mistaken as pro-Soviet or pro-US. Now they can only be and he seen to be pro-people or anti-people; for the oppressed or against the oppressed. Those who are genuinely for the oppressed people must struggle to turn the Accra meeting into a revival of the Bandung Spirit in our post-Gulf War epoch. Let them come out with a clarion call of the "Accra Spirit". History is in favour of the oppressed, more so now than at any other time in the past era. Seize the Time!

Notes

(1) See Lectures on Political Economy, Peking 1965. The Chinese had rejected the model imposed on them by Soviet experts. They developed their own more relevant socialist model in tune with people's consumer needs in a country with a large peasant population

(2) In the autumn of 1973, Egypt launched an attack across the Suez canal in order to recapture parts of Egyptian lands occupied by Israel in its war of aggression against Egypt in 1967. This became known as the 1973 Middle East war or the Ramadan war or the Yom Kippur war

(3) If the US raises by 1% the interest rate on the dollar all third world countries who transact their international business in dollars will have to pay billions of dollars extra to borrow the now more costly dollar. Similarly in servicing their foreign debt, the interest payments will now be higher. It is like the experience which the British public are going through with a high interest rate on the pound which is causing many bankruptcies- a slump in the construction industry and recession in the economy which at the same time keeps the pound strong. If the British chancellor can bring down inflation via a high interest rate at the expense of the British people so will his American counterpart but in his case he will be trying to stabilise the American economy at the expense of the third world countries.

Third World concern about 'humanitarian' interventions
Pacific News Service, 11 January 1993

Third World countries are concerned about the new US policy of "humanitarian" intervention which they see as a serious post-cold war threat to their newly won sovereignty. As potential victims of this new US posture either as "terrorists", "fundamentalists", "bandits", "looters", "war criminals", and now in the case of China as "cannibals" , or as any other suitably demonising epithet, many Third World leaders and intellectuals are consulting and debating on what actually lies behind this US/Western posture.

The wholly unnecessary massive intervention of more than 20,000 US soldiers in Somalia to counter a handful of looters and gunmen is seen as a pretext seeking to establish a precedent in international law to enable the US to intervene in any Third World country in the future with impunity.

Rakiya Omaar, a respected Somali human rights activist, formerly of Africa Watch, but now fired because of her opposition to the US intervention in her country, wrote recently in the Guardian (in London): "US military intervention in Somalia had followed a gross misrepresentation of the situation in the country". She and her colleague Alex de Waal, also fired, stressed in the article that "three quarters of the country is relatively peaceful, with civil structures in place" ; that the famine was confined to scattered rural pockets, and that "most of the food is not looted" . That Save the Children has distributed 4,000 tons in Mogadishu without loosing a single bag. Other agencies that work closely with Somalia suffer rates of 2-10 %, because they consult closely with Somali elders and humanitarian workers.

In Europe a serious debate is raging among liberals and the political left on the true interpretation of this new US policy. Some see the Somali invasion as a public relations stunt staged by a beaten and discredited president who pardoned those who would have blown the whistle on his role in the Iran-Contra crimes.

Others see the key foreign policy question in 1993 as not

about Saddams and Somalia but about what to do "about the Americans". Is anyone in the world still capable of restraining American power?

Yet others see it as an "imperialist police action" couched in the rhetoric of humanitarianism and human rights and mandated by a cowed and pliant United Nations. They allege that this is a new style of American imperialism, first perfected in the Gulf War.

Those who support the new doctrine of "humanitarian intervention" argue that it is an appropriate response to some of the Third World dictators who shamelessly exploit the doctrine of their inviolability of national sovereignty to shield their domestic persecution from outside sanction.

Third World countries view the UN as the new instrument of US foreign policy. The Secretary General, former Egyptian foreign minister, Boutros Boutros-Ghali, is seen as an agent of the US, who has allowed the White House to dictate the reorganisation of the world body "down to the appointment of its most senior executives".

Sudan is feared to be a potential future target of US "humanitarian" intervention. Already the war in the south of that country, which has been going on intermittently since independence in 1956, is described as a war of "Muslims against Christianity" and the new Sudan leaders as influenced by Muslim "Fundamentalists" and engaged in a "campaign of terror and conquest" of their own country. This is seen as a media image manipulation to create a Third World demon of the west in Sudan's Omar al-Bashir.

He is already said to be receiving "substantial military and economic aid from Iran, including military advisers and troops", and that "thousands of Mujahideen fighters have joined Sudan's jihad against the Christian south". This kind of reporting is usually accompanied by pictures of starving southern Sudaneseas victims of the northern Muslims. All these, it is feared by the Third World are necessary ingredients for a US "humanitarian" invasion in Sudan.

It is a well-known fact in the Third World that since the end of World War Two, every US president from Truman to Bush, has had to have a Third World leader as a demon.

Saddam is still in power - will Clinton create his own demon in Bashir to save Egypt and Algeria from Muslim "fundamentalism", or will the left-over Saddam do, with all his maverick and tricky tendencies?

Africa and the World

After the OAU Summit
Africa Now, August 1981

At no time in its 18-year history has the OAU attracted wider international attention than at the last Nairobi summit. This is due not so much to any significant shift in Africa itself as it is to the international situation which in the last few months has taken a dramatic turn for the worse.

The real reason for international attention on the Summit was parallel developments in the Western world brought about by the new American foreign policy and the victory of the Socialist Party in France. The rest of the world wanted to know Africa's reaction to these very significant shifts.

The reaction at the Summit to Reagan's flirtation with South Africa has, of course, been sharp and almost hostile. What shocked the West was the unanticipated reaction of the so-called moderate African states who, for the first time, took a very strong public position against the US. Whether this was intended for internal consumption to appease the agitated masses who see in Reagan's policy an affront against Africa's dignity we have yet to see; but whatever motivated this strong African stand it had certainly had an impact by its vehemence and intransigence. The masses will no doubt give three cheers for their leaders which they amply deserve.

The result of the French election, however, does not seem to have been given much attention by the African Heads of State; at least no mention of it was made public. Yet any change in France must have considerable impact on Africa in that France is the only Western power which still has decisive influence in Africa. Nearly all French-speaking African countries depend on her for the day-to-day running of their countries. Hardly any of these countries can take any independent economic or diplomatic initiative without the approval of France. Some leaders are maintained in power by the French army; some of these countries are subsidised by the French exchequer; and some leaders have been installed in power by France.

No effort at regional economic integration is conceivable without taking the 'French factor' into account. Most of the national currencies in these countries are linked to the French franc and naturally no independent economic initiative can emanate from such quarters. Which is another way of saying that without France's approval no economic unity in Africa is possible.

The world was therefore rightly awaiting to see Africa's response to the latest events in France. The implications of these events are far-reaching, not only in their significance to Africa but to the rest of the world.

France is using Africa's soil and territorial waters to deploy its forces partly in the service of its NATO allies. The concept of the Rapid Development Force is meaningless without France's African military facility and should Mitterrand decide to close it down the entire arrangement will collapse.

America's publicly expressed concern about the inclusion of Communists in the French Cabinet is not so much due to their possible access to top Western strategic secrets, although that is a possibility. Their main concern is that the Communists may have a decisive influence in the direction of French policy, especially on its neocolonial strategy. For instance, if France decides physically to pull out of Africa who will fill the ensuing 'vacuum'? To the US current thinking, this horrifying move will leave the way open for the Russians, Cubans and possibly, horror of horrors, Gadaffi, to move in, which inevitably will upset the entire Western world strategy.

The emerging contradiction between France and the US will also have a profound effect on Africa, and not necessarily to our advantage either - if, that is, we are caught unawares. The absence of any declared position on this issue by the summit is indicative of. Africa's unpreparedness, which makes our capacity to defend Africa's genuine interests extremely weak to say the least.

The encouraging position-statement on South Africa by the French Socialist Party should not be allowed to lead us into complacency, for it is the tradition of the Western Social Democrats to say one thing when out of power and act differently when in power. Ever since the First World War when they betrayed the world socialist movement and the Second International these parties have consistently been taking opportunistic positions on all major international issues which threatened to undermine imperialism. Their 'national interests' are directly linked with world imperialism which their bourgeois states are obliged to defend.

The people of Africa will follow with interest the contradictory position of President Moi as chairman of the OAU, an anti-imperialist, non aligned organisation, on the one hand and, on the other as the President of Kenya which is reported to have given naval facilities to the US for its Rapid Development Force The RDF is designed to advance the interests of imperialism by suppressing people's revolts in Africa, Asia and Middle East as well as confronting the Soviet Union.

In the coming 12 months till the next summit, but one does not have to be a prophet to predict that we will be confronted with several international crises of Iranian proportions, especially in the neocolonies where the impact of world capitalist economic crises is felt most severely. It is not certain if the OAU will be in a position to face up to the new situation on behalf of the African masses; still all well-meaning people will wish President Moi the best of luck.

The Crowning of Emperor Mitterand
Africa Now, December 1982

Among the people who may, not immodestly, claim to have contributed to the re-convening of 19th OAU summit in Tripoli, is no doubt Monsieur Mitterrand, the Socialist Party President of imperial France. His annual mini-summits in Africa were this year transformed into the African Summit at Kinshasa last September where he was formally crowned as the "economic liberator" of Africa.

Fifty African Heads of State and Government, some of whom had vigorously lobbied to wreck their own OAU summit in Tripoli, trooped to Kinshasa to ensure a resounding victory for the meeting. These leaders were determined to slap Africa in the face and they have done so.

The Western powers, headed by Washington and Paris, were equally determined to make Africans slap Africa. For just before the Nairobi 18th OAU summit these powers, with their divisive and destabilising plans for Africa, started their manoeuvres aimed at frustrating the 19th summit when it became clear that Tripoli might host it Their fear of the summit had nothing to do with the recognition of the Sahara Democratic Republic to full OAU membership. This issue was used to cover up diplomatic skulduggery with far-reaching objectives.

The most important of these objectives is to maintain Africa firmly in the Western sphere of influence and the most important means to ensure this domination is their military presence on the continent, first in the form of the French army and second through the US Rapid Deployment Force, RDF. Two factors that currently undermine these objectives are: the inevitable independence of Namibia under SWAPO and Libya's staunch opposition to RDF.

The question of Namibia's independence is reaching a critical stage and if Africa and the Namibian people succeed in winning their independence without the Cuban withdrawal from Angola, the US will suffer a dual set-back. The first is the destruction of the myth that South Africa will forever maintain the bastion of counter-revolution in Africa, upon which the global strategy is founded. The second myth connected with this this strategy is the so-called Cape Route Doctrine. This myth will evaporate once Namibia attains its independence under SWAPO. The third myth which will also suffer is Chester Crocker's doctrine of strategic minerals. The destruction of these three myths will require a radical change in the global strategy of. the NATO powers which at present it is not in their interests to pursue.

Connected with this strategic thinking is the concern for a possible diplomatic setback in the event of SWAPO winning independence for Namiba without Cuban withdrawal from Angola. This set-back will seriously damage Western "credibility" in the eyes of their allies in Africa.

The second envisaged setback for Western global strategy is the Libyan factor. This country is known for its staunch opposition to the Rapid Deployment Force as well as for disturbing French interests in Chad. With Gadaffi's appointment as chairman of the OAU, he will have a splendid opportunity to conduct his opposition to the RDF in the name of Africa as well as to expose French interference in the internal affairs of Chad.

This fear is one of the causes that led to the West's active involvement in frustrating the earlier OAU summit in September. The objective of RDF is to facilitate the deployment of US marines anywhere in Africa or the Middle East in order to suppress any revolutionary uprisings deemed to be against the vital interests of the West.

By agreeing to act as the Western surrogate in in this strategy Morocco has antagonised every country in the region and it was feared that the Summit in Tripoli would have condemned this strategy and isolated Morocco and the other supporters of the RDF strategy in Africa - Egypt, Sudan, Somalia and Kenya. This would have seriously undermined US credibility and strengthened the anti-RDF countries in the region. So the summit had to be sacrificed.

As soon as it appeared likely at the Nairobi Summit that the next Summit would be held in Tripoli, the US State Department issued a most unusual statement concerning an organisation to which the US does not belong. However, what seems to be an unjustified interference in the internal affairs of the continent was actually intended as a directive to US backers in Africa to act accordingly.

The statement dated June 30th 1981 concluded: "The OAU meeting in Nairobi decided to hold its 1982 Summit at Tripoli, Libya. We note that it is traditional for the OAU to select the host Head of State or Government as it Chairman. If that tradition were followed in 1982, we would look upon it with deep regret since we believe Libya to be a most inappropriate spokesman for the principles of peace and regional stability for which the OAU stands and which we wholeheartedly support". Actually, Libya is one of the most outspoken opponents of the RDF in the region and it is only natural that it would be categorised the US as "a most inappropriate spokesman".

However, US supporters in Africa "got the message" and decided to act accordingly. Nearly nine months after the US statement was issued and hectic arm-twisting diplomacy by the US, her backers in Africa found the SADR pretext at the OAU Council of Ministers meeting in February 1982 in Addis Ababa. Seventeen Foreign Ministers walked out of the meeting in "protest" at the admission of the SADR and ushered in the crisis that led to the abortive summit in Tripoli.

The OAU sunimit has been reconvened but after the brief shock the warning to the people of Africa is clear: African unity is too important to be left to the politicians and diplomats. The OAU must be placed under the firm control of the people by setting up independent "national OAU associations" in all member countries, rather like the UN associations to which the country's representative would be obliged to report regularly and which would be responsible for evaluating their diplomatic actions. otherwise it will remain a vehicle for facilitating foreign interference and ultimately foreign control.

The Dr K/ Mr B dialogue
Africa Now, June 1982

In the late 1960s and early 1970s a group of conservative African leaders - Banda, Houphouet-Boigny, Senghor, and others -were pushing for a "dialogue" between African states and white South Africa. They argued that there would be political and economic advantages from such a dialogue and it might even lead to a lessening of the rigidities of apartheid.

This view was strongly opposed by radical African countries which were led in this campaign by the "Mulungushi Group," comprising Kaunda's Zambia, Nyerere's Tanzania, and Obote's Uganda. They argued that dialogue with the racist regime would legitimise the fascist rule and accord it international respectability.

Last month President Kaunda himself decided (unilaterally, it seems) to go counter to his old position and to have a dialogue with Botha, although the South African position with regard to racism and fascism is no different today than it was when Kaunda led the opposition to dialogue in the 60s and 70s.

So what has changed, it seems, is Dr Kaunda himself and he owes Africa a more plausible explanation of his metamorphosis other than that of the need to free Mandela. While nobody has the right to tell the Zambian people how to conduct their foreign relations, Africa has the right to be told where, in Kaunda's view, Zambia's interests end and Africa's begin, and vice versa.

No doubt such an explanation will be offered soon, knowing Dr Kaunda's commitment to the cause of African dignity and humanity. In the meantime, the following is a dialogue between Dr Kaunda and Mr Botha as seen from abroad:

Mr B: It is encouraging, Mr President, that at last you have recognised the wisdom of having a dialogue with us. You know how much we respect you in this country, although last week my Minister of Defence accused your country of being the centre of communism. I have reprimanded him and he has assured me that it was only a slip of the tongue. I'm sure he was referring to your Second Principle of Humanism, which is communalism, not communism.

Dr K: Well, Comrade Prime Minister, I don't mean to be undiplomatic but actually this is not my first dialogue with your government. You may recall that I met your predecessor Dr Vorster a few years ago and that led to the release of Comrades Nkomo and Mugabe and others. My current mission is to get Comrade Mandela out. As you know, Prime Minister, I am a humanist and I am appealing to your human instincts to release the man. I have come to talk to you because we recognise that you are a de facto power in South Africa. You see, we regard you as Africans - a White tribe, shall we say? I have always argued that you are an independent country and Africa should treat you as such.

Mr B: Yes, Dr Kaunda, I recall that memorable meeting, but look what's happened to Smith now! You are not requesting us to sign our own death warrant, are you? What will the Kaffir - I'm sorry - Mandela do if he comes out? I'll tell you: he will slip out of the country, go to Lusaka or Luanda and lead the terrorists to overthrow us. Do you want us to allow him to do that to us? Come on, Dr Kaunda, let's be serious.

Dr K: Mandela and you are both patriots -Black and White - and with more humanism on your part and more on his part, I'm convinced you can meet halfway. If both of you adhere to my tenth Principle of Humanism, which is Patriotism and Respect, no harm will be done. Remember Brotherhood of Mankind?

Mr B: Okay, Doctor, let's move to the second item. According to BOSS (we now call it National Intelligence Service) reports you are the messenger of the Front Line States to Dr Banda, who would then come to us with the message. Why did you choose to come yourself instead?

Dr K: Inspiration, perhaps. I thought that Banda might not be able to transmit the spirit of the Front Line - second hand and all that. As a matter of fact, even Chester Crocker comes to us first before he goes to Banda. I understand Mr Reagan prefers Humanism to Bandaism, so I decided to come myself.

Mr B: Are the Front Line States behind you on this mission?

Dr K: I don't see why not. They all know that I go by my Fifth Principle of Humanism, which is Self-reliance and Hard Work. I practice what I preach, you know.

Mr B: Third item: Has the Front Line made up its mind whether or not to drive White South Africans into the sea? I'm asking this because BOSS reports suggest that you are not agreed on this issue.

Dr K: Comrade Prime Minister .

Mr B: Please don't call me 'Comrade.'

Dr K: I'm sorry, Prime Minister. I call everybody Comrade in accordance with my Fourth Principle of Humanism, which is Respect for Human Dignity. Comradeship is the highest stage of human dignity. Anyway, I was going to say, nobody wants to drive anybody into the sea. If Mugabe wouldn't drive Smith into the sea, what makes you think we would do that to you?

Mr B: Fourth item. What would MPLA do with Savimbi? BOSS reports suggest that they are willing to cooperate with UNITA minus Savimbi, but we think without Savimbi, there is no UNITA. What do you have to say about that?

Dr K: The Savimbi issue is being handled by France via Senegal, with Portugal as mediator. If you want my opinion, basing myself on my Eleventh Principle of Humanism, which is Reciprocal Obligation, I think MPLA should reciprocate Savimbi and vice versa, and harmony and peace will ensue.

Mr B: Last item: You and Banda met for five days in Malawi during the first week of March, and then you went to Maputo for the Front Line meeting. You don't mean to tell me that you went there for the sole purpose of setting up agricultural commissions.

Dr K: Prime Minister, please don't try to interfere in our internal affairs. Dr Banda actually told me that he supports my Sixth Principle of Humanism, which is, Respect for the Aged and Infirm. I respect him on both counts; that's why I went to see him. And don't you ever suggest that I went there on behalf of the Front Line. Good bye; we'll see you anon, Mr Prime Minister. God Bless Africa!

Portugal's new empire
Africa Now, June 1984

To understand the dramatic change of events in Southern Africa we must go back to the late 60s and early 70s when the armed struggle in the Portuguese colonies was getting better co-ordinated and gaining momentum. Everybody on the other side of the barricade was worried: South Africa was worried that it might lose its cordon sanitaire if the colonies went; Britain was worried that its vast investments and influence in the area via Portugal might be seriously affected; the US was worried that the Soviet Union might gain an upper hand in the region and greater prestige internationally to the detriment of US "credibility"; conservative African leaders were worried that Southern Africa might be too radicalised for comfort.

In Portugal itself, however, a different kind of evaluation was taking shape which combined the situation in both Portugal and the colonies. There was on the one hand the semi-feudal, semi-fascist, petty bourgeois dictatorship at the state level - the Caetanos, Salazars, etc., with the backing of the big landowners, the colonial produce merchants, the settlers and an important faction in the military hierarchy. To these groups, the national stature and economic well-being of Portugal was inseparably linked with her colonial "possessions" and it was virtually impossible even to begin to think about granting them independence. This group had ideological affinity and economic ties with the Boer ruling circles in South Africa.

On the other hand, there were emerging the entrepreneurial classes, the national and comprador bourgeoisie. These classes gained their rapid ascendancy in Portugal in the aftermath of World War 2 and the post-war economic prosperity in Europe. Although Portugal did not enjoy the full benefits of the Marshall Plan of 1947 (because of its poor economic and social infrastructure and undeveloped productive forces) it did initially benefit from US, British, German and French private investments which helped to promote some industrial growth and the evolution and consolidation of the comprador bourgeoisie, with its counterpart, the young proletarians.

The formation of the European Common Market brought about not only prosperity in Europe but also a promise of greater things to come - power, more prosperity, challenge to the superpowers and greater influence internationally. The Portuguese bourgeoisie, coming from a small power, was immediately attracted to this vision of a new Europe initially fostered by de Gaulle of France. They wanted Portugal to be part of this movement since Portugal was linked by geography and trade with Europe.

They argued that to be part of this trend Portugal had to embark on massive large-scale industrialisation and modernisation, to which end two conditions had to obtain: peace in the colonies by granting independence to hand-picked moderates as leaders, as France had done; and the development of conditions to facilitate extraction and utilisation in Portugal of the enormous natural resources, industrial and strategic raw materials from the colonies. At the same time these colonies had to be developed into expanding markets for Portuguese industrial products. In spite of the ups and downs of the preceding years, the Portuguese bourgeoisie still harbours these sentiments and has been waiting for opportunities to implement them.

The country's political leadership at that time, however, viewed Portugal's situation differently. To them Portugal, a small country with hardly any resources of its own, could not hope to play a significant role in Europe's economic and political ventures. On the contrary, they warned, it was likely that they might be swallowed up by the emerging European giant and lose their identity and economic survival as a sovereign state. Hence they must stick to the colonies, come what may, as an imperial power.

These opposing views sharpened the contradiction between the petty-bourgeois political leadership on the one hand and the emerging bourgeoisie on the other. The latter skillfully formed a temporary alliance with the working class, the peasantry, and the middle ranks of the military hierarchy and on April 25, 1974 staged an uprising, initiated by the army, and overthrew the petty-bourgeois (and landlord) political leadership.

However, in the colonies events did not turn out exactly as desired by the metropolitan bourgeoisie. The sudden change of state power had not given them time to prepare the moderate leadership that they had envisaged. In Mozambique and Angola the initiative was captured by FRELIMO and MPLA respectively.

In Portugal itself, in the meantime, the bourgeoisie had not been properly consolidated in the immediate aftermath of the uprising. It found itself in a bitter power struggle against the industrial working class and politically conscious peasants. It was only after intensive covert intervention by the CIA and NATO allies that the left alliance was defeated.

In the former colonies in the meantime, there was massive confusion. The civil war had not completely ended in Angola. The early death of Neto left a huge gap in the MPLA leadership and resulted in a lot of hastily conceived policies and topsy-turvy priorities. South Africa took full advantage of the fiasco and aggravated internal strife.

In Mozambique the leadership proved to be extremely immature and caused a lot of unnecessary internal contradictions, first by branding every leader who had opposed FRELIMO, a traitor and publicly humiliating them to the everlasting anger of their followers. Secondly, they indulged in an adventurist nationalisation spree to the detriment of the economy and great suffering of the people which the South African-backed rebels took advantage of.

In this chaotic situation the Portuguese bourgeoisie, now firmly in power, stepped up its diplomatic offensive directed mainly to its former colonies, to South Africa, and to the US and Britain. The immediate objective was to "stabilise" this area which is so vital to Western interests, and vital also to the long-term objective of serving Portuguese bourgeois interests and those of their backers. A seething diplomatic activity was put in motion at baffling speed. The Portuguese President visited Mozambique and Angola, offering everything from military and economic assistance to the supply of

Imperialism 151

skilled manpower and favourable trade arrangements.

Samora Machel returned the visit to Portugal, and extended it to include Britain of Margaret Thatcher, Britain the traditional mentor of Portugal. No sooner were these diplomatic and state visits over than secret meetings started between South Africa and Angola, jointly sponsored by the US and Portugal. A sort of trilateral diplomatic equation was formed comprising the US, Britain and Portugal as the first element; the two ex-Portuguese colonies as the second; and South Africa as the third. The three-sided discussions were conducted in a highly secretive fashion, so mysteriously secret that many African countries began to be worried as to the possible outcome.

We will not know yet what actually transpired in these not-so-subtle diplomatic manoeuvers, nor will we know yet at whose expense, but the outward manifestations are ominous. A luta continua is discontinued; liberation movements have since been harassed, humiliated and disgraced, being chased from their homes and in the streets like wanted common criminals; proletarian internationalism abandoned; pledges to the OAU and Africa of not trading with South Africa trampled underfoot. In short, a metamorphosis of gigantic proportions has occurred in Southern Africa in which "constructive engagement" has been transformed into a destructive disengagement, Black against Black.

What is even more ominous is the fact that it is becoming increasingly clear that the doors are being left open in all the Portuguese ex-colonies for unimpeded Portuguese plunder, for a renewed and more vigorous intervention of Portuguese capital. When one talks of Portuguese capital one really talks of US, British and West German capital channeled via Portugal.

The front-line states, submerged in their own economic mess, most of it self inflicted, may well begin to ask to be bailed out of the catastrophe by leaving their countries also open to more foreign plunder, since they will be negotiating from position of weakness. The Southern Africa Development Co-ordinating Committee has been rendered redundant. It was intended to be an economic instrument against South Africa (which in reality it never was anyway). It will now very likely be turned into a conduit through which to subjugate and plunder the working masses of Southern Africa.

Thus the strategy of the Portuguese bourgeoisie laid out two decades ago - creating "independent" states in the colonies headed by moderate leadership, *a la* Banda - though it did not succeed then, is now rapidly and alarmingly coming to fruition. Not only will this area become a solid Western sphere of influence, but what is worse, South Africa might well be incorporated in a new guise of "moderation" into a sort of regional defence strategy directed at repressing any movements in the region that are likely to emerge in opposition to this scandalous sell-out. The first victims will of course be the South African exiles whom at one time we used to call freedom fighters but who are now known as "terrorists." Now they are officially characterised by Mozambique not as "liberation fighters" but as fighters for civil rights not for self-determination, since South Africa is said to be de jure and de facto an independent state. The only thing wrong with it is its policy of apartheid.

Swaziland, its secret agreement with South Africa having been exposed two years after signing, has already started hunting them down and where convenient shooting them, as if to emphasise that although the government kept quiet for the last two years it can nevertheless be a ruthless fighter in the interest of its Boer allies.

If the OAU remains silent on this shameless spectacle; if the rest of Africa does not vigorously make its anger known by flooding the streets of its capitals with mass demonstrations protesting against these criminal shootings of kith and kin on behalf of the arch enemy of Africa in return for crumbs of bread, the future of Southern Africa will be doomed to a cycle of violence and more violence and to a greater and more widespread political and economic instability. Those few radicals left in the OAU should give maximum moral and material support to South Africa's gallant fighters.

Africa will be liberated in real terms only when these great sons and daughters of Africa win their true and deserved independence like the rest of us. Radical Africa must not be embarrassed by shouting once again: "*A luta continua!*"

The Struggle for Africa's Mind
Africa Events, November 1984

While Africa is struggling to feed itself and more than half its population is virtually starving, well-fed Europe is engaged in another kind of struggle: the struggle for the "hearts and minds of Africa". Europe's Social Democrats and Christian Democrats are competing against each other to present themselves as the "true friends of Africa." The former, for the first time in the history of their movement, held their annual Socialist International Conference in Africa, at Arusha, Tanzania. Not to be outdone, the Christian Democrats the following month held their international conference in Kampala, Uganda. Why now? After most of Africa gained independence in the 1960s, Europe had no option but to retreat from its vanguard position in the continent. Europe started to lick the moral wounds it inflicted on itself through decades of brutal colonisation. It could not even look at its own hands, dripping with the blood of millions of Africans all the way from Algeria right down to South Africa. Europe's retreat from Africa was also due to the fact that it was still recovering from the ravages of the two World Wars which were fought to shuffle and reshuffle colonial 'possessions' and spheres of influence.

The wars had destroyed almost the entire economic inventory, including a lot of skilled manpower, reducing Europe's erstwhile "Great Powers" to third rate powers. Those harsh post World War II conditions forced Europe to look inwards. The US, now a superpower dominating the entire Western world, was engaged in another preoccupation: the struggle against the socialist camp which from 1945 onwards was rapidly expanding in Europe and Asia.

The US undertook to finance Europe's recovery lest the latter slip into the "Soviet Orbit." For the same reasons, it supported anti-socialist forces in Greece, China, Indo-China and Korea. The US also formed military alliances in its attempt to "roll back" communism and it championed counter-revolutionary wars all over the world. In short, the US overextended itself materially and financially.

In the meantime, Europe rebuilt its economy. But during the recovery, there was an acute ideological struggle within Europe between the Communists and the anti-communists, including the Social Democrats[1], the Christian Democrats, the Conservatives and the Liberals. The split between the Soviet Union and China in the 1960s seriously weakened the communist movement in Europe, its leadership could not understand and much less provide leadership to the workers of a prospering Europe. Euro-communism emerged as a compromise between a weakened communist movement and their need to win over the young European workers who, thanks to the recovery, had a lot more to lose than their chains.

But Euro-communism missed the boat. The bourgeoisie, in the shape of Social Democrats and Christian Democrats, emerged as the leaders of the European workers. The rivalry between the two camps over the minds and hearts of the workers of Europe has intensified since the late 70s. That struggle is now spilling over to the "Third World", especially to Africa - traditionally Europe's sphere of influence.

The European bourgeoisie are frightened by Reagan's cowboy diplomacy which they believe will weaken the influence of the West in Africa. Reagan's policy in South Africa, with its so-called "constructive engagement" is a case in point. To safeguard their "vital interests" in Africa, especially those vast resources hitherto untapped, the European bourgeoisie has thus decided to take matters in their own hands.

In Africa itself, where people are literally perishing from starvation, the fate of the political leaders, most of whom are held directly responsible for this unprecedented disaster, is hanging in the balance. They are being challenged by two forces both of which are not responsive to European pressures. These are Islamic fundamentalism and Marxism. Most political observers believe that these two forces will dominate Africa's politics for the rest of this century and beyond. It is this twin-headed phenomenon that has activated both the Social and Christian Democrats to political and diplomatic offensives in Africa.

What do these two parties stand for? The Social Democrats stand for reforms in their own countries through the setting up of a "Welfare State." With a few honourable exceptions on the Left, the leaders of this movement are quite often indistinguishable from their Christian Democratic opponents, more so in foreign affairs. When the chairman of the Socialist International, Willy Brandt, for example, was the Social Democratic Chancellor of West Germany in the 1970s, he did not depart very much from the policies towards the "Third World" laid down by the first Christian Democrat Chancellor, Dr Adenhauer, immediately after World War II

Because the leaders of the Social Democrats are essentially bourgeois, they almost invariably behave like their conservative opponents - they too are for the maintenance of the 'empah'. "National interests" become paramount at the cost of international obligations. Many anti-colonial thinkers and activists believe that the Social Democrats are worse imperialists than the traditional conservatives; they use the language of liberation and progress but practice the opposite. The most glaring example of this two-faced stance is that of the present President of France, Francois Mitterand, who is said to be more imperial than de Gaulle in France's relations with her ex-colonies in Africa.

The Christian Democratic movement, on the other hand, is a mixture of politics and religion (Catholic). It reflects the political and religious aspirations of the Vatican with the declared objective of fighting communism worldwide and Islam in Africa, where three in every five Africans are Muslims and apparently the number has kept on rising in recent years. Christian Democracy is conservative in outlook, imperial in aspiration and always advances the interests of Europe above everything else.

The Social Democrats have recently been taking a leading role in African diplomacy and even in politics to a certain extent. All declared socialist parties in Africa, from Senegal to Tanzania, are in one way or another connected with and dependent on the European Social Democrats. Hence their international conference in Arusha.

After the US in collusion with South Africa succeeded in frustrating the activities of the 'Contact Group' (US, Canada, France, Britain and West Germany - who were authorised by the UN Security Council to negotiate with South Africa on Namibia's independence), the Social Democrats in Europe decided to take their own initiative, especially since Olaf Palme returned to power in Sweden.

In Arusha, the Social Democrats decided to launch a diplomatic offensive in Africa mostly designed to bring about some accommodation with South Africa. Prime Minister Soares of Portugal, after his spectacular success in mellowing Mozambique and Angola to negotiate with South Africa, was mandated by the conference to coordinate the activities of the Social Democrats in South Africa, especially in dealings with the frontline states. The Social Democrats hope that through the Southern Africa Development Coordinating Conference (SADCC), they can use their influence in the EEC to help develop a wider economic community which may even involve South Africa, once it agrees to leave Namibia. Taking advantage of the possible economic collapse in the region, the Social Democrats also hope to moderate Southern Africa, get rid of the Cubans and Soviet influence, halt Marxist rhetoric and to bring the region firmly under the sphere of influence of the West. With recent developments in the region, it seems their strategy is working!

The Christian Democrats, for their part, were alarmed by the Islamic resurgence in North and West Africa and most recently by Numeiri's introduction of the *sharia* in the hope of harnessing this all-pervading spirit of Islamic momentum in the Muslim world, especially amongst its youth. They have concluded that Islam is rapidly gaining ground. This had persuaded them and other Christian denominations to wage a battle to win the "Heart of Africa". The Kampala conference, like the one in Arusha, was intended to bring the battle closer home.

In a recent Christian conference in Limuru, Kenya, which was attended by the Archbishop of Canterbury, Dr. Runcie, there were only two items on the agenda: refugees in Africa and the spread of Islam in Africa. Similarly in the Lutheran

World Federation Conference held last August in Budapest, the Reverend Sebastian Kolowa of Tanzania openly and eloquently expressed the profound fear of the Christian hierarchy on the spread of Islam and suggested methods to stop it. Already 10 million copies of the Bible are being sent to Africa for free distribution; some are in Swahili but printed in Arabic script. In Tanzania alone some TShs.240m has entered the country for the advancement of Christianity. To facilitate their movement, the Christian missionaries are constructing 14 airfields in the country, much more than the government's own airfields.

We shall no doubt be hearing more of these activities in the immediate future; the most regrettable part of it all is to see some of our governments and political parties being used by these international organisations whose sole objective is to ensure Western domination of Africa

Notes

(1)   This refers of course to the German political party which is not in any way social democratic in the Marxist sense see p3 of The New World Disorder - which way Africa

The Israeli diplomatic offensive
African Concord, 9 October 1986

One of the ironies of Africa's modern political experience is that its most radical leader of late 1950's and early 1960's, Kwame Nkrumah of Ghana, and closest friend of Egypt was also the first leader to open diplomatic, economic and military doors for Israel in post-colonial Africa.It was Nkrumah who started the first black shipping line in Africa (after Garvey in America), the Black Star Line, as a joint enterprise with Israel. From then on, Israel became a respectable ally of the newly independent states, from West to East Africa, and of course, South Africa. George Padmore who was Nkrumah's advisor on relations with African countries was fanatically anti-Arab and very pro-Israel. He regarded Israel as an oppressed Socialist country. He did everything to influence the rest of Africa on his stand on Israel, especially after he visited the country in 1957 and was given a royal welcome. Ghana's prestige and prominence was thus used to advance Israel influence in Africa.

Milene Charles, in his thesis on the Soviet Union and Africa[1], observes that it was the British who helped to promote Israeli influence in Ghana in the first place. "The British had allowed Israel to open a consulate in Accra prior to independence, while Egypt was not even invited to the independence ceremonies. Contrary to the Soviet Union, Israel was bound to succeed quickly in Africa. Africans saw it as a small country, like theirs, successful in modernisation, socialist, and as impressive on the international scene as they wished to become. The Israeli consul in Ghana, Chanan Yavor established contacts with leaders like Kenneth Kaunda, Julius Nyerere and Tom Mboya. Kojo Botsio was known to be the best friend of Israel in Africa. He was greatly impressed by the Israelians during a visit in 1957, as was John Tettegah, the trade union leader, who decided to model Ghana's trade unions on the Israeli Histadrut.

Even after the formation of the OAU in 1963, brought together the Northern African states with sub-Sahara Africa, and the emergence of Ben Bella of Algeria and Nasser of Egypt as the leading force of African liberation struggle, the newly independent countries continue to rely increasingly on Israeli aid. Moshe Dayan the flamboyant Israeli General, was a hero in Africa's military circles, always a guest of honour in many of Africa's independence celebrations. His exploits of the 1967 war with Egypt and Syria were studied with admiration. Israeli military "advisors" were all over Africa, and many intelligence services were either manned or trained by Israeli experts.

On the economic front, Israel's influence was very extensive. In Tanzania, for example, Israeli enterprises dominated tourism, commerce, co-operatives, as well as agriculture. Their "block farms" which were concentrated along Lake Victoria posed a serious strategic threat to countries along the Nile, so much so that Nasser had to express his concern to Nyerere during his visit to Tanzania in 1965.

As Emperor Haile Selassie's influence was growing in Africa after the establishment of the OAU and its headquarters in Addis Ababa, so also grew Israeli influence in Africa. Ethiopia was probably the greatest supporter of Israel in Africa, and her uncompromising stand against the Arabs made her the darling of Israel. They established joint military working relations in the area and shared intelligence operations.The Emperor in his turn succeeded in conveying the impression throughout Africa that the struggle of the Eritrean people for self-determination was actually an Arab plot to dismember his Empire and that in order to fight against this "foreign menace" Ethiopia had to have a close alliance with Israel. He thus not only won Africa's support in his brutal war of repression against the Eritrean people, he was also a key factor in promoting close military co-operation between Israel and African countries.

Practically all the senior cadres of the Ethiopian army, including incidentally the current Head of State, were trained in Israel. The same is true of a number of Africa's heads of state. President Mobutu of Zaire, President Doe of Liberia, Amin of Uganda, and many others, have received some of their military training in Israel. At any of the OAU summits to this day, which are of course overwhelmingly represented by the Generals, many heads of state and government have been in one way or another involved with Israel.It therefore came as a shock, to Israel and the rest of the world, when in 1973 the majority of African states severed diplomatic relations with Israel during her war with Egypt. Also as a result of that war, Arab influence in the world was growing via OPEC; the West was visibly vulnerable; Sadat of Egypt, although virtually defeated in the war front, nevertheless emerged as a hero of the Arab world for having "liberated" the Suez canal and for having destroyed the Bar Lev fortification across the canal. The usually "pragmatic" leaders like Senghor of Senegal, for very sound pragmatic reasons, took a position in favour of Egypt and against Israel, which helped to sway the majority of the OAU member states to support Egypt. Suddenly, Israel, for the first time in her history, found herself completely isolated in Africa with the exception of South Africa and her allies.

In the meantime, however, internally Israel was rapidly moving to the Right and eventually the most extreme Zionist fanatics gained total sway. Sadat, on other hand, having quarrelled with the Soviet Union in a most embarrassingly public fashion, sought to move towards the US for economic and military support. The rest of the Arab world was put completely off balance by Egypt's radical change of policy - Sadat's Camp David negotiations with Israel, his dramatic trip to Jerusalem, the establishment of diplomatic ties with the arch enemy of the Arabs, his policy of Infitah, that is opening up Egypt to massive Western investments, credits, and aid.

Some African countries who had broken off diplomatic relations with Israel in support of Egypt now felt that they could not be more "loyal than the Emperor". In other words, if Egypt the nominal leader of the Arab world, thought it fit to establish diplomatic relations with Israel why should African countries not restore theirs. It was more than a moral question. For quite practical reasons many of these countries, in addition to their earlier attachment to Israel, also had the necessary infrastructure for Israeli economic and security operations in their countries which could rapidly be activated to their advantage, especially at a time when the continent was in a serious economic crisis.

Side by side with these developments, in North Africa Gaddafi was emerging as a power to be reckoned with. His out and out rejection of any compromise with Israel or even with Egypt did not endear him to the West. He suddenly became the object of Western diplomatic offensive on Africa. Gaddafi's own inexperience in the field of diplomatic manoeuvring led to some precipitate and even rash actions on his part which played right into the hands of the West and Israel. His calls for the "second African revolution" frightened the entire conservative camp in Africa which now felt a greater need than ever for Israeli support, especially in the field of security and intelligence.practically every right wing military leader who survived a counter coup attempt, immediately sought solace in Israeli support, inevitably blaming it all on Libya. Their collective anti-Libyan security and intelligence arrangement was and still is almost wholly directed by Israel and funded by the US and the West. Presidents Mobutu of Zaire and Doe of Liberia are said to be the key figures in promoting the re-establishment of diplomatic recognition of Israel in Africa, and both of them are said to be under Israel security guard for 24 hours a day.Their success is staggering. Recently five more countries have followed their lead - Cameroon, Ivory Coast, Malawi, Lesotho and Swaziland; waiting behind them are likely to be Kenya, Togo, Ghana and Gabon, all of whom have already had Israel interest sections in operation. Senegal too is said to be on queue.The total Israeli trade with these countries is now more than 100 million US dollars and is rising steadily, with rapid proliferation of Israeli "technicians". Their trade in the field of military ware is said to be flourishing especially with Zaire, Chad, Gabon, Central Africa Republic and Ethiopia.

The strangest irony of all this is that this development is taking place at a time when Israel is stepping up her relations with South Africa, especially in the field of armaments, including nuclear weapons; at this time of all times when the struggle inside South Africa has taken an insurrectionary turn with Africans, young and old, facing Botha's bullets. In 1976 the then South African Prime Minister Vorster visited Israel and ushered in the era of intensive military co-operation between the two countries and by 1979 South Africa accounted for 35% of Israel's military sales, these include anti-people equipments like missiles, assault rifles, machine guns, pistols and anti-guerrilla control equipment. A Soviet satellite in 1977 photographed a nuclear test site in the Calahari desert, and in 1979 a US satellite registered a double flash of light in the South Atlantic which is associated with a nuclear test. Although the US hushed this up at the time, in 1985 papers released under the Freedom of Information laws showed that a US naval research establishment had concluded that the event was a nuclear test widely believed to be one of the joint South-Africa/Israel ventures.

This association has taken a more serious and ominous turn when the Israelis signed the agreement to participate in the US Star Wars or SDI. This will probably include research into lasers and electronic counter measures; If in the early period of independence most African countries' foreign policies mistakenly regarded the Israeli state as a victim of Arab aggression by the 1970's most of them came to realise that it was in fact a state imposed on and at the expense of the Palestinian people. That the Palestinians have been denied their right to self-determination in their own country in much the same way as the South Africans have been denied their right to self-determination; that Israel was an occupying force on the territory of Palestine just as White South Africans are an occupying force on the territory of Azania; that only a few days after the creation of Israel in 1948 the National Party of South Africa came to power and from that day onwards the two countries developed warm and mutually beneficial relations in spite of the obnoxious policies of apartheid which were being promulgated and implemented at the time which were being opposed by everyone with any sense of human decency.

This awareness became more widespread as more Africans became more and more involved in foreign affairs as Africa gained its independence. The 1960's was the era of

Africa's testing of international relations; the 1970's was the era of maturity. In the former era many diplomatic errors were inadvertently committed by African states, either collectively or individually from their lack of experience. Until independence all foreign relations activities in sub-Sahara Africa were handled by the colonial powers. Only Ethiopia escaped subordination. By the time of the formation of the OAU, experienced Ethiopian diplomats had dominated the diplomatic field and helped to shape Africa's foreign policy posture of the decade.

In the 1970's, the "era of maturity", many African diplomats to their credit, rapidly mastered the art of diplomacy and helped to correct many of the earlier errors or misconceptions. The 1973 Middle East war saw Africa already on the brink of a decisive change in foreign relations and the war hastened the process of de-recognition of the state of Israel. But the reversals of Sadat and the confusions and quarrels within Arab states which precipitated Israeli's invasion of Lebanon in 1982 and the internecine fights among the Palestinians seem to have strengthened the Israeli diplomatic offensive in Africa and revived the pre-1970's misconceptions about the Middle East situation.However, today's Africa of the 1980's and tomorrow's of the 1990's is not the Africa of the 1960's and the danger of repeating the diplomacy of that by-gone decade is quite obvious. The superpowers are facing each other in a most menacing posture; especially when the Western world is increasing coming under the dominance of extreme right-wing governments. Africa contains two of the most dangerous spots that could spark off serious Superpower confrontation - the Horn of Africa with its proximity to Saudi Arabia, the oil reservoir of the Western world; and South Africa, the Cape Route through which the oil-tankers go to the West from the Gulf. A large part of Africa is also part of the Arab world and directly involved in the Middle East confrontation. Moreover, Muslim "fundamentalism" which is engulfing large parts of Africa is threatening to divide Africa on religious grounds. Any religious conflict will be exploited not only by the superpowers, but also by both South Africa and Israel in order to weaken Africa's advance to unity and progress. The last thing, therefore, that Africa needs now is to revert to the policies of the 1960's to face the politics of the 1990's. This is the view expressed by many experienced African diplomats. In this dangerous era each of the three continents of the Third World is an arena of conflict, and need to evolve a diplomatic stance which takes into account both the objective condition of the world situation and the subjective aspirations of the poor countries with all the external and internal tensions that are entailed. The current Israel onslaught on Africa is seen by many African diplomats as an introduction into the diplomatic arena of the continent the ingredients that have all the potential of the spark that starts a prairie fire. It is this fear that concerns not only mature African diplomats but also most of the young generation of African leaders who say they need peace to develop their countries.

Notes

(1) Milene Charles (1980) *The Soviet Union and Africa*, University Press of America Inc.

China and Africa: Can we learn from each other?
Africa Events, July 1987

The United States and the Western world were pushed off balance when the Chinese Prime Minister Chou-en-Lai made his first visit to Africa in early 1964. Until then they were working on the basis of their intelligence that China was totally isolated in Africa and there was nothing to worry about. The visit took place only a few days after the successful Zanzibar Revolution of January 12, and the link between the two events was immediately made after Chou-en-Lai made his famous statement that "Africa was ripe for revolution".

The Western media and governments were now convinced that the Zanzibar revolution was "Chinese inspired"; and that China was out to ferment revolutions all over Africa.

The Soviet Union, an interested party in the global strategic balance, quietly and sometimes loudly supported this US-inspired propaganda. They themselves had embarked a couple of years earlier on a vicious anti-China campaign in Asia and Africa. They now feared that Chou-en-Lai's visit would not only put China on Africa's political and diplomatic arena but would also worsen East/West tension.

It will be recalled that the Soviet Union's foreign policy stance at this moment was based on their theory of "peaceful co-existence" between the two superpowers, and inspired by the so-called "Camp David Spirit" which had emerged after Khruschev's summit meeting with Eisenhower. Chou's visit therefore, was viewed by the Soviet Union as designed to upset the détente.

The joint anti-China propaganda by the two superpowers did succeed in creating a lot of confusion in Africa, especially in the radical countries which were likely to be sympathetic towards China. But it did not succeed in isolating her especially among the masses.

China's socialist revolution was an extension of its own national liberation struggle and consequently there was a very thin dividing line between her nationalism and socialism. This duality of loyalty to the two great movements of the period enabled the Chinese to share more intimately the sentiments and aspirations of Africa's liberation struggles and the struggle for national reconstruction, both of which were Africa's top priority.

The superpowers fear was that this close identity between China and Africa's aspiration might influence in the latter a process towards autonomous and self-sustaining development, leaning neither to the US nor to the Soviet Union. This evolution would deprive the superpowers the political, economic (and yes, even military) clout over these countries. This assessment was actually correct. All Chinese assistance to Africa was indeed designed to make African countries truly self-reliant and self-sustaining. Unfortunately, however, Africa was far from ready for that kind of revolutionary development strategy. Most of its leaders had independence "thrust upon them" without going through the revolutionary experience which is necessary to instil determination and perseverance. Unlike Algeria, and now South Africa and Eritrea, our countries got their independence almost on a silver platter, and we were immediately incorporated into the very system which had first enslaved us and then colonised us.

So the superpowers' worry about Chou's visit also became the concern of a lot of African leaders. Kenyatta cancelled his invitation to Chou-en-Lai after US pressure. Local newspapers in various parts of Africa, most of which were entirely owned and controlled by the West, and some even by the CIA, were full of condemnation of China, of anti-China scare-mongering, describing China as a "God-less monster" and so on. They would appeal to the "African tradition" and would emphasise that the doctrines which guided China's development were "alien" to Africa; or that China wanted to recolonise Africa and send millions of Chinese to settle in Africa to alleviate her population pressure, and so on.

The Zanzibar revolution was singled out by these same forces as an outstanding example of the Chinese penetration into Africa. The Americans went as far as to suggest that the

Chinese wanted to develop Zanzibar as a "showcase" of Chinese socialism in much the same way as the US tried to develop Puerto Rico as their showcase of American capitalism, in order to attract neighbouring countries to come under Chinese domination.

Looking back over the last 20 years or so, therefore, it is clear that the Western fear was not about Communism as such, but rather it was about the economic implications that the Chinese experience offered. Zanzibar in 1964 was the first country in Africa to try to emulate the Chinese experience of developing an integrated and independent national economy which would once and for all deprive the capitalist world system of economic domination and exploitation. And because of this effort to be independent it was targeted for US onslaught.

A secret CIA Memorandum dated 5 February 1964 on the situation in East Africa remarks: "The aura of Communist, particularly Chinese involvement in the......Zanzibar revolt, together with the knowledge of growing communist activity in there own countries, have worried such leaders as Kenyatta, Nyerere and Obote of Uganda. It led to the cancellation of the prospective visit of Chou-en-Lai (to Kenya), has exacerbated relations between Kenyatta and Odinga, and has aroused the governments to some apprehension over the dangers of Communist subversion." It is unfortunate that because of this "apprehension", wholly unjustified and entirely induced by foreign interests, Africa was denied a most splendid opportunity to lead her countries to a promising future. In fact it can now be revealed that this "apprehension" has led many African countries to actually collaborate with the CIA against their own compatriots. For instances, Tanzania is the last country that one could even remotely associate with collusion with the CIA at a time when we were harbouring the OAU Liberation Committee and hosting liberation movements. But the evidence is beginning to emerge that this was indeed the case, uncomfortable as it may sound.

In January 1965. after Zanzibar expelled the notorious US Consul Frank Carlucci (now Reagan's National Security

Advisor and currently advocating the "pre-emptive bombing" or Iran) the US Ambassador to Tanzania was re-called to Washington, the person who temporarily took over, Mr Strong, reported back to Washington on 14 April 1965 that although "Tanzanian complexes re CIA, Congo, etc continue unabated ...day-to-day liaison between CIA representative here and the Government of Union Republic of Tanzania's counterpart has been proceeding normally."

In this kind of atmosphere of dependence even in security matters and actual collusion with imperialism and mutual distrust among political leaders it was impossible for these leaders to take advantage of the Chinese development experience in the interest of our own people.For instance, one of the most important contributions which the Chinese have offered developing countries and which could have led to revolutionising our economies was their identification and analysis of the "*ten major relationships*" which are essential for balanced development and harmonious growth – economically, socially, politically and diplomatically. Characteristically, the slogan for one of these relationships is: Learn from Other Countries. If Africa had been courageous enough to learn from other countries with similar experiences, instead of towing the line as laid out by the World Bank and IMF, we would have a different Africa today. Africa could have learnt from the Chinese experience of transforming a society which like Africa's was predominantly (90%) a peasant society and transforming its peasantry into an asset, unlike, say, India which has allowed its peasantry to remain a liability. In the 1940s, like Africa today, China was almost permanently engulfed in cycles of famine and could only feed its people by massive, and humiliating, international food charity. Even with this charity millions of Chinese died of starvation and malnutrition annually. The situation seemed so helpless that some foreign observers suggested, exactly as they now say of Africa, that it was perhaps God's way of alleviating China's "population explosion".

However, soon after the success of the Chinese Revolution in 1949 the scourge of famine in China disappeared. In less than 40 years, China today is not only feeding itself extremely well, but also enjoys a surplus for export. This achievement (which is almost a miracle) was scored because the new Chinese economic policy was directly linked with the welfare of its people, and not based on attaining some hypothetical statistical data. The policy was geared towards the expansion of the country's productive forces, raising output and the living standards of the people, while constantly stepping up their revolutionary fervour to achieve higher and better results.The first priority was to *feed* the people. To achieve this, they devised policies to defend themselves against natural calamities and they embarked on massive schemes for flood control, taming the rivers, extending irrigation areas, rural electrification, introduction of high yielding grains and advanced animal husbandry. To achieve these targets, very little foreign input was required, everything depended on people's own initiative and ingenuity. Once the peasants were freed from the clutches of the landlords and moneylenders there was no limit to their enthusiasm for production.

African countries certainly could have achieved similar results during the first decade of our independence. But our priorities were not geared towards frontal confrontation with the colonial economic heritage. We did not aim at raising the standards of living of the people by directly attacking the causes of their poverty – we wanted to do it via the medium of the world market with priorities set for us by the World Bank and IMF and the multifarious "aid donors". Our peasants were left to fend for themselves, with only half-hearted, wholly inadequate and inappropriate "extension services", with the result that now 25 years after independence, they are extremely backward in farming, producing only for their own subsistence, with back-breaking effort but very low productivity which does not yield enough to feed themselves all year round.

All our countries without exception are still victims of floods, droughts and of all the natural calamities, because, while we are keen and even pride ourselves in building skyscrapers, modern airports and new cities (which have nothing to do with the welfare of the peasants or of overall development of the country) we are incapable of controlling our own environment. On the contrary, because of our reckless production for "export" we are destroying our environment by overgrazing, deforestation and desertification leading to more droughts and famine. Whereas at independence Africa hardly needed any foreign food aid (only 5% of the total world food aid at the time), today more than 90% of world food aid goes to feed starving Africa with all the attendant humiliation. The callous disregard of the people's welfare is amply revealed by the fact that while our peasants are starving, our production of exportable commodities like coffee, tobacco, tea and luxury flowers continues to flourish. This cruel anomaly was also the story of China prior to October 1949.

In the next 10 years most of African countries' infrastructure will virtually disappear. Roads are already reverting to bush; bridges cannot be repaired; railways are falling to pieces; modern water-supply is virtually non-existent, both in the rural and urban areas. Electricity, where it is available, is irregular and gradually disappearing; telephones don't work – the list is endless. The excuse is: No Foreign Exchange, the magic wand of development. But the truth is that most of the above, if not all of them, do not need any expenditure of foreign exchange to develop and/or maintain. What is missing is the ingenuity of the peasants, skilled manpower and mass enthusiasm for production, all of which are missing due to a wrong order of priorities.

Side by side with the policy of *feeding the people*, China achieved a great leap forward during the first post-revolution decade by adopting the policy of *housing the people*. What we could learn from this policy in China is that housing is not a "welfare project" as most of our countries regard it, but rather it is an essential factor in igniting development. A deliberate policy of housing the people decently would open up a huge vista of development potential – cement industry, lumber and ceramics industries, manufacture of house-building and house-hold equipment, carpentry, civil and mechanical engineering and hundreds of related construction activities which would not only create new material basis for development but also create hundreds of thousands of skilled workers.

A typical example of failure to take advantage of Chinese experience is the Tanzam Railway. When China undertook to construct this massive project it involved training thousands of Tanzanian and Zambian young workers in various aspects of construction industry. They deliberately built a huge repair workshop which could in future be transformed into truck manufacturing industry. However, as soon as the railways project was completed the skilled workers were deproletarised and returned to peasantry because there was nothing for them to do in construction and engineering. And the repair workshop has at best remained just that.

Even the heavy equipment that was used in the construction of the railway has been abandoned. Most of this equipment could be used for earth moving work in flood control activity, construction of canals for irrigation and other heavy tasks. It was offered gratis to Tanzania, but was never accepted or utilised and the Tanzanian people have remained the poorer for that.

The Chinese learnt the value of utilising every type of machinery for their development. This arose principally from their third major policy priority of *clothing the people*. Cotton production was developed greatly as a result of improved agricultural technology. It transformed the peasant producers into highly skilled agricultural workers and managers, and developed techniques in controlling and improving their environment.

The extensive textile industry that followed created massive employment for Chinese peasants and opportunity for learning new skills. It led to increased incomes which has created the basis for the expansion of the home market, a necessary precondition for any self-sustaining development.

When China built the Friendship Textile Mill in Tanzania they started by training young workers in construction skills, in the erection and maintenance of machines, before starting textile production itself. This was designed by the Chinese to train Tanzanians in skills that would enable them to build their own further textile factories without external assistance. However, as soon as the factory was constructed these skilled young people had nothing further to do in their line of training, because no further textile industry was developed or the one or two other textile factories that were built were based on capital intensive techniques designed for advanced industrial economies and could not utilise the existing skills.

These negative examples are also to be seen elsewhere in Africa where leaders were not really interested in the serious tasks of national development which involved sacrificing their material comforts. As experience has shown, many such leaders' ideas of development are about aping the colonial masters and their values – big cars, big houses, and conspicuous consumption - for the elites. They are so brainwashed that they look down upon anything that does not emanate from the US or Europe. They totally reject the doctrine of frugality as alien. For instance, when Nyerere tried to introduce simplicity in the life style of Tanzanian leaders he was resisted tooth-and-nail. He was accused by both his Western critics and local colleagues, of having been indoctrinated by the Chinese and that he was introducing alien culture.

And yet frugality is the essential ingredient for development, capitalist, socialist or any other type. Massive expenditure in consumption, deliberately encouraged by our "trading partners" overseas, has led to the unprecedented indebtedness that eats away more than 60% of our foreign exchange earnings in servicing the debts annually. China, on the other hand, up to the death of Chairman Mao, while achieving magnificent development progress managed at the same time to pay off all external and internal debt obligations contracted by the previous reckless regimes. Frugality plus careful maintainance a proper balance between production and consumption, with production as the Key Link, has enabled the Chinese to achieve this near miracle.

The style of work of Chinese expatriates in Africa was meant to maximise their work effectiveness, as well as to show by example that experts need not be alienated from the people, as is the case in our countries. A senior surgeon or top engineer would live the same mode of life as their junior colleagues, on the basis of the "*three togethers*" – ie Live together, Work together, Eat together.

In contrast to the above style of work, our experience with our own experts, deeply influenced by the colonial heritage, has been - a boss must be seen to be a boss, and act like a boss, in order to instil humility among his or her "subordinates". This attitude has left them open to flattery and corruption, so that today all the bosses bear their own price tags – 10%, 20% and so on.

Mao's China has introduced an epoch in modern history that promised dignity and self-respect for the underdog. Its achievements both in material and spiritual sense has shown the masses of the Third World that there is a way out to their misery and humiliation. It has shown us that a correct world outlook, scientific planning, frugality and a determined people are the essential ingredients for progress towards a brave new world of freedom from the realm of necessity.

Sadly, that epoch has gone. The post-Mao China is reverting back to the ranks of the Third World and there is nothing that Africa can learn from it except to appeal for the so called New International Economic Order and prepare the ground for the so called "South/South" relations whose predictable outcome is for the more advanced to advance more at the expense of the least developed. Africa has missed an historical opportunity which may take several generations of suffering to re-emerge. We have failed to "Seize the Time" to our great cost and to the advantage of imperialism.

Cultural Subversion Through Education
Africa Events, December 1988

The fate of the newly emerging countries was sealed, long before many of them had even achieved their juridical independence. Joseph Jones, the man responsible for the drafting of the Truman Doctrine in 1947, made a fateful recommendation to his superiors which changed the course of history for the developing countries.

Writing to the US Minister of Works only a few weeks before the announcement of the Doctrine (which later came to be dubbed as the "Declaration of the Cold War"), Joseph Jones observed that if post-war Europe and the newly emerging countries were to be left to their own devices, there was a "danger" that they might be tempted at best to develop independent national economies, or "at worst, go into the Soviet orbit". Both possibilities were seen as being against the "vital interests of the US. To prevent this from happening, the US was to devise policies which would henceforth bring all of us, directly or indirectly, under her hegemony.

With Europe, they devised the "Marshall Plan" which transferred billions of dollars and most sophisticated technology to devastated post-war Western Europe. For the rest of us, new economic strategies were devised specifically to suit "developing countries" under a newly created discipline in Economics to be known as "Development Studies". No such "studies" had ever existed before the Second World War.

Side by side with this evolution practically all Western educational institutions of higher learning immediately established departments of "Asian Studies", "African Studies", "Caribbean Studies", etc., inviting scholars from these newly independent countries to participate in the promotion of new "scholars" and "experts" on Asia, Africa, etc. They were assisted by former colonial administrators whose services were no longer needed in the colonies after independence. They were, however, categorised as experts on the "psychology of the native people", utilising the wealth of their experience gained while administering the colonies.

In the meantime, a campaign was launched to re-interpret our national aspirations to conform to what came to be known as the "Western tradition". The concept of "wining hearts and minds" of the newly independent states was then developed into a systematic policy towards these countries.

For reasons which we need not go into in this brief article, most of these new countries blindly accepted this subordinate position and exposed themselves to some of the worst forms of manipulation. One such form of manipulation was via "education."

Lavish scholarships were offered to Asian and African youths who would be flown to the US and Europe where they would be introduced to a new way of life vastly different from the one they came from. They would be made to regard their own mode of living as inferior, culturally backward and unsuited to modern life. They were to be the "elites" who would set the trend for a way of life which would lead to "modernisation." The principal objective of this cultural offensive was to turn these future elites into a sort of cultural "Fifth Column", always subservient to Western values, always cynical about their own national capabilities, always instilling a sense of national defeatism all round with an alarming spiritual despondency.

The "Education" they go through would begin by being informed that the reason why their countries were undeveloped was because the social and cultural institutions in these countries were not conducive to development. It was no use blaming the colonial heritage for distorting their economies and undermining their national pride. Rather, it was their own backward forms which resisted the "progressive" influence of colonialism. In fact, had colonialism been left to its modernising influence much longer than it was allowed to do, the world would have seen less of the miseries that we were witnessing today. This kind of "education" was not exclusively directed to students from the ex-colonies; even students from the host countries who take up "Development Studies" and who aspire to go to the "Third

World" countries as "experts" are also exposed to this indoctrination. In the late 1950s and early 1960s, when independence was seen as inevitable, the strategists for world hegemony selected specific countries for exerting their influence throughout their region. In North Africa it was Tunisia; in West Africa, first Liberia and then the Ivory Coast. In East Africa, Kenya was the target country as a regional influence. Tom Mboya, a Kenyan, who was a most influential pro-Western trade union leader in East Africa, was given the task of offering "scholarships" to potential students, and went as far as arranging their transportation. Planeloads of young Kenyans would be flown to the US almost every month by specially chartered aircraft paid for by George Meany and his right-wing US Labour unions. A trade union school, called Freedom House, was established in Nairobi to train union leaders throughout East Africa with the single purpose of allying them ideologically to the West. US "teachers", who included, as it came to be exposed later, quite an interesting assortment of CIA operatives dominated the school. Milton Obote, who was later to become the President of Uganda, was an active assistant of Mboya in Nairobi during these operations, and may have a lot to tell Africa about the period if he ever decides to write his memoirs.

Through colonialism, the Western bourgeoisie have turned the whole world history into their own history; they shaped the face of the earth to what it is today. Our national histories have been turned into bourgeois world history.

The post-colonial Bandung Conference of African and Asian countries in 1955 was an attempt to reassert ourselves on the world scene; to reclaim our position in history; to re-write it as makers of history, and not as objects to be acted upon; to "take things in our own hands." Alas, it was never to be. The same forces that denied our history have intervened, at a crucial turning point, and turned our independence, which was to be our break with the past, into a cementing tie to a more ruthless and vicious bondage which consolidates the past in a new guise.

We must now create a "New Person of the 21st Century"; freed from the ideological baggage that lulled us throughout the post World War Two era, to carry the banner for a Brave New Africa.

Africa's Interpretation of Soviet Policy Since Perestroika
Africa Contemporary Record - Annual Survey and Documents 1988-89 (Vol.21)

Naturally, there is no single 'Africa's interpretation' of Soviet policy towards the continent, nor can there be. Nevertheless, it is possible to recognize two main interpretations, reflecting the two dominant political trends in Africa, namely, the conservative and radical.

Ever since the era of independence of the 1950s and 1960s Africa became distinguished by these two trends which came to be known, respectively, as the 'Monrovia' and 'Casablanca' groups[1]. The former has always been, at best, suspicious of the Soviet bloc, accusing it of wanting to spread Communism in Africa. This group, dominated mostly by the French-speaking countries, broadly reflected Western views on the whole question of East-West relations, and this was always noticeable in their foreign policy.

The 'Casablanca' group, on the other hand, reflected what might be called the 'Bandung' spirit[2] and came to be known as the 'Non-aligned' position, siding neither with the East nor West, but less friendly with the latter because of its imperialist connections. The Soviet bloc was regarded as the 'strategic ally' by this group, especially in Africa's struggle for liberation.

While in the conservative group the Soviet bloc countries were not always welcome, in the radical countries they enjoyed considerable prestige, and in some cases they even influenced policies. This is especially so in the so-called revolutionary countries which had adopted Marxism-Leninism as the ideology of the State[3].

The Soviet Union for its part devised distinct policies in its dealings with the radical, non-aligned countries. It could not accept them in the 'socialist fraternity' because they were not categorized as Marxist, which would qualify them for that. They were, however, designated a special category which would qualify them for a sort of treatment akin to that of 'favoured-nation'. They were known as countries which had adopted a 'non-capitalist road to development'.

Countries categorized as such usually had 'populist' internal policies, with a strong emphasis on provision for social welfare by the State. Their foreign policy was based mainly on anti-imperialism and anti-colonialism, and they often voted with the Soviet bloc in many of the United Nations' councils. They always entered into trade agreements with the Soviet bloc, although the bulk of their trade still remained with the old colonial masters. Most of their armed forces were trained and equipped by the Soviet Union, including aircraft and heavy weaponry.

All populist countries tended to adopt a modicum of 'planned economy', which mainly consisted in outlining a sort of five-year shopping list and its justification. Such 'planned' economies were not of the kind that could be linked to the Soviet bloc planned economies and, therefore, their relations with the latter were limited to trade rather than to long-term economic ties of the sort common between and among socialist planned economies. This kind of relationship tended to minimize the Soviet bloc's capacity to offer extensive economic assistance because the items needed by receiving countries were usually not provided for in the donor country's plans since they were not included at the time of the drawing up of their respective five-year plans. The Soviet bloc could, of course, offer abundant arms because there was always a surplus of these outside the plans.

When Reagan came to power and introduced his Reagonomics world-wide via the World Bank and the International Monetary Fund (IMF), US intentions became suspect in Africa. Reagonomics hit the continent disastrously and also the US influence in the region. It was further aggravated when his Assistant Secretary of State for Africa, Chester Crocker, developed his policy of so-called 'constructive engagement' in southern Africa, which tipped the US weight on the side of the apartheid regime. Correspondingly, Cuban and Soviet prestige sky-rocketed even higher - the former for sacrificing its nationals in fighting the South Africans; the latter for its diplomatic support and military supplies to Angola.

The tide against South Africa's fortunes which led to the

independence of Namibia, the removal of Botha from that country's Presidency, the appointment of the new President F.W. de Klerk, his On the diplomatic front, however, during the peak of the Cold War this kind of relationship paid off to both parties. The Soviet bloc almost always sided with these countries on major international issues which concerned the latter, e.g., it supported Africa on such questions as economic sanctions against South Africa; the Palestinian cause; national liberation movements; and the demand for the establishment of a 'New International Economic Order'. In turn, the radical countries would side with the Soviet bloc on most of its diplomatic skirmishes against the West.

The Soviet Union's diplomatic objective of isolating the US coincided with Africa's grievance against the latter. The total preoccupation of the US with global priorities in its foreign policy and its apparent insensitivity to regional concerns tended to alienate most African countries, to the advantage of the Soviet Union. Throughout the Nixon-Kissinger era, and during most of Carter's Administration, Africa featured very insignificantly in US policy initiatives. This has been described by US Africanists as the era of 'benign neglect' towards Africa. As a result, the US always found itself identified with some of the most discredited leaders in Africa, while the Soviet Union was constantly on the side of the angels.

It was not until Cuba and the Soviet Union sent soldiers and massive military supplies to Angola in 1975 in response to the Angolan Government's distress call for assistance against the South African military invasion of Angola that the US was forced to abandon its policy of indifference. It was both too late to prevent Soviet bloc entrenchment in this strategically important area, and, the US once again, sided with Africa's arch-enemy-the apartheid regime of South Africa.

Introduction of liberalization policies which led to the release of Nelson Mandela and, finally, the unbanning of political parties, were a direct result of the stunning defeat which the South African Defence Force suffered in February 1988 at Cuito Cuanavale. For the first time South Africa's air superiority was effectively matched by the combined Cuban-Angolan air and military operations which led to the South

African army being outmanoeuvred, outflanked, and ultimately encircled. They were left with only a corridor to enable the troops to effect an 'honourable withdrawal'. This defeat reduced US prestige and enhanced Cuba's, and by extension the Soviet Union's, subsequently increasing their influence not only in Angola but throughout the frontline states. The negotiations that followed between the two superpowers over the withdrawal of the Cuban troops from Angola and independence for Namibia saw the Soviet Union negotiating from a position of strength, a position of victors with the total support of Africa, radical and conservative.

This escalating Soviet prestige, however, was marred only by its involvement in the Ethiopian wars especially that against the delayed decolonization struggle of the Eritrean people. Here Soviet policy has been exposed as unprincipled, opportunistic, even cynical The Soviet Union had been supporting the Eritrean cause ever since that country was forced by the UN into a 'federation' with Ethiopia in 1952. And when the Eritreans embarked on the armed struggle after the Ethiopian Emperor, Haile Selassie decided to abrogate the UN resolution on federation and forcefully annexed Eritrea in 1962, the Soviet Union gave the Eritreans full diplomatic and moral support.

However, soon after the Emperor was overthrown in 1974, and when the new regime later declared itself as Marxist-Leninist, the Soviet Union not only abandoned the Eritreans, but also sent massive arms and military 'advisers to help Ethiopian troops in their attempt to crush the Eritreans. They even declared the Eritrean struggle as being 'objectively pro-imperialist' since it was now fighting the 'revolutionary, anti-imperialist' regime of the new Ethiopian leader, Col. Mengistu Haile-Mariam. Many Africans saw this sudden shift of loyalty on the part of the Soviet Union as dishonest and cynical, and this sent its prestige plummeting in most parts of Africa. Even in the radical countries such as Mozambique, the Soviet about-turn on Eritrea was viewed as betrayal. The late Samora Machel, then President of Mozambique, openly supported the Eritrean struggle, thus by implication, criticizing the Soviet Union. Cuba too, whose army was fighting alongside the Ethiopian army against the Somali invasion of the Ogaden in the mid-1970s, refused to allow its troops to be used against the Eritreans. Soviet influence in the conservative African countries has been very minimal, consisting of some trade relations here and there but hardly anything else. These countries often voted against the Soviet Union at the UN on most of the major international issues and have been reluctant to respond to any Soviet overtures, even if at times these were accompanied with aid offers. Soviet diplomatic offensives in these countries were often described in private by the local elites as uncouth, in contrast with the more subtle, confident, and urbane Western diplomatic approaches.

In both the radical and conservative African countries the ruling elites preferred to 'do business' with their Western counterparts despite untiring attempts from the Soviet bloc to have a share in the trade. This is because the long-established business channels in these countries were towards the West, especially to the colonial 'mother country'. Secondly, the structure of production in these countries has not been changed even after independence, and the economies consequently have remained colonial in character, with very limited room for manoeuvre. Thirdly, the shipping lines which carried goods and commodities to and from these countries to Europe and elsewhere were wholly monopolized by Western shipping 'conferences' making it impossible for the Soviet bloc shipping companies to penetrate. At best they were given the status of 'tolerated outsiders' which enabled them to carry some cargo peripherally.

All this was, of course, in line with the Western strategy of isolating the Soviet bloc from the world economy. The effectiveness of this strategy has not only led to serious strains in the Soviet bloc's economies but also effectively kept them out of touch with modern technology in light industries and communications, the two essential stimulants in a modern economy. *Perestroika* and the resultant upheavals which have been shaking the Soviet bloc since the Autumn of 1989 are seen in radical Africa as a direct result of the economic stagnation which had ensued from this isolation. Eastern Europeans whose economies were tied to the Soviet Union were now looking towards Western Europe and were mesmerized by its consumerist prosperity. *Perestroika* gave them the timely opportunity to opt out of the Soviet orbit and join their Western kith and kin before the 1992 European Single Market shut them out.

The impact of these European uprisings on Africa have been immediate and stunning. The one-party states in both conservative and radical countries came under fire and the ruling elites in these countries were immediately put on the defensive. The people's complacency on which the ruling elites had flourished since independence turned into a pro-democracy militancy. Mass demonstrations in the streets of most major African cities and students' strikes spread throughout the continent, from Abidjan in Cote d'Ivoire to Lusaka in Zambia, all demanding democratic reforms in their countries. All presidents in the one-party states were obliged to assure their citizenry that sooner or later the system, which was admittedly archaic, irrelevant, and oppressive, would give way to a more open, competitive, and pluralist regime.

The radical one-party regimes, which have been justifying their rule on socialist principles of 'democratic centralism' and emulating the Soviet bloc practice of governing, found themselves without any theoretical justification, and they soon resorted to the old argument that, because of 'tribalism', Africa was not yet ready for a pluralist democracy. This argument was not only rejected by the masses but it was also taken as an insult to Africa's prestige. The leaders who resorted to such an argument were seen to be ready to denigrate the dignity of the African simply in order to continue to remain in power.

The conservative one-party regimes which justified their system on 'cultural' grounds, i.e., that Africans could only be governed by a strong chief, as in Kenya and Zaire, were challenged to provide evidence of this on a nation-state level; they were accused of "counting backwards" instead of forwards: they were said to be resorting to the colonialists' argument which sought to justify colonization. President Mobutu of Zaire immediately succumbed, ordered immediate dissolution of his ruling party, and appointed a caretaker president who would oversee the transfer to a multiparty democracy in one year.

President Moi of Kenya, meanwhile, was fighting a rearguard action to preserve the one-party system and the status quo which was being challenged by some very respected senior politicians and ex-cabinet Ministers[4]. Their demand was for the abrogation of the 1982 Constitution which established the one-party rule, and they called for a general election in 1990. The beleaguered President reacted harshly and, ironically, accused his critics of being dictators and tribalists.

The interpretation of *Perestroika* in other words, had one meaning to the ruling elites and another to ordinary people. The rulers have been emphasizing that what was happening in the Soviet Union and Eastern Europe had nothing to do with Africa because Africa was being guided by different values. Even socialism in Africa, in the words of President Kaunda, was based on African traditions and Christian humanism.

The ordinary people's interpretation of *Perestroika*, on the other hand, could be summed up as follows: *Perestroika* meant that the democratic rights of the people which were denied them since independence should now be restored unconditionally, otherwise the upheavals in Eastern Europe, which were the direct result of implementing *Perestroika* in the Soviet Union, could have a spill-over effect in Africa on a much wider scale. The moral from Eastern Europe was that it was possible for the State to deny people their basic human rights temporarily, but suddenly the people would become aware of what they were missing and would rise up to demand the restoration of their rights. And that moment of realization everywhere was now.

On the economic front, too, there were different interpretations of the implications of *Perestroika*. Among African leaders there was concern that in response to 'democratization' in the Soviet bloc, the West would shift most of its aid from Africa to Eastern Europe. Western investors, too, would now be more inclined to go East since the existing economic infrastructure and skilled manpower available there would ensure a greater return on capital than in Africa. This concern was eloquently expressed by African delegates to the IMF Governors' meeting in Washington which opened on 7 May 1990. These delegates also expressed their concern that even the IMF and its sister organization, the World Bank, might be inclined to follow the new trend at the expense of Africa.

Radical African economists and politicians, however, take a different view. To them the diversion of attention away from Africa by aid donors might be a blessing in disguise. According to this view, most of the aid destined for Africa did not reach its intended targets. A large portion of it would remain in the donor country as payments to the inflated aid-bureaucracies; some would go to the supplying companies, in the case of 'tied-aid', and most of the rest would go to the bureaucracies of the host countries. Only a tiny bit would be left to trickle down to where it was intended.

The same is true of the loans. Most of the foreign debts that were incurred by African countries (current estimate $260 bn) were used either to pay for arms or for useless, unproductive, and wholly unnecessary projects, and to fatten the foreign bank accounts of contracting officials. Africa, in this view would have been much better off without this kind of aid and credit in that it would have developed a more self-reliant approach to development.

On the diplomatic front, the positive outcome of *Perestroika* and the end of the cold war was to save the continent from continuing to remain one of the areas for the diplomatic manoeuvres of the superpowers. By taking the initiative to work jointly in seeking peaceful solutions to regional conflicts in Africa, the superpowers have opened up a huge vista of hope for the continent, which has been plagued with such conflicts. Already these conflicts have turned Africa into a continent of refugees. Of the 12m refugees world-wide 4.5m were in Africa[5].

There is a prospect of peace in Angola and Mozambique, now that Namibia is independent. South Africa itself is on the way to ending apartheid. This turn of events is thanks to the favourable international situation ushered in by *Perestroika*.

In the Horn of Africa too, the Soviet Union is said to have given notice to Ethiopia that it was not going to renew the agreement on arms supply. This is likely to force the Ethiopian Government to take seriously the peace negotiations with the Eritreans started by the former US President, Jimmy Carter. It may also pave the way to a peaceful solution in Sudan where the Government is fighting southern Sudanese led by the Sudan People's Liberation Army (SPLA). The latter have been relying on support from Ethiopia, but if Mengistu is on a peaceful path he may persuade the SPLA to go for a peaceful solution.

The possible ending of internal conflicts is thus the positive effect of *Perestroika* in Africa. Its negative side is that *Perestroika* has opened the way for some of the most reactionary, right-wing, and neo-fascist elements in Europe to emerge. The newly 'liberated' Poland, Hungary, and Romania have adopted policies inimical to African interests. For instance, they are now inviting investments from the racist regime of South Africa they are strengthening trade links with them; and they are encouraging their citizens to emigrate to South Africa, thereby blocking the way to the emergence of Black skilled workers needed in the expanding industrial and mineral enterprises.

African students on scholarships in the Soviet bloc are 'encouraged' to return to their respective countries. Some who were stranded at the height of the uprisings before they had been settled down by the old regime were sent home and their embassies had to foot the bill. Until *Perestroika*, Africans in Eastern Europe were treated honourably as 'strategic allies' in the struggle against imperialism. They now face the same hostility and even racism which has now become common in the rest of Europe in the wake of the emerging 'national fronts' and 'neo-fascist' movements.

When Gorbachev talked of working for a 'common European home' on his visit to Finland towards the end of 1989, many African leaders were astounded, They recalled that, the century before the Russian Revolution of 1917, Europe, dominated by the enterprising bourgeoisie, wreaked havoc on Africa. They took out of Africa its able-bodied youth into slavery in the 'new world'; they carved up and colonized the entire continent among themselves; and they diverted its economy to serve exclusively for the production and consumption needs of Europe; they robbed it of its history and its culture; and reduced the people of that rich continent to the poorest of the world.

The Russian revolution divided that Europe ideologically and paved the way for Africa's independence. Africa succeeded in effectively exploiting East-West rivalry, which led not only to independence, but also to economic benefits from both sides. But now, Gorbachev has brought all that to an end by his new policies of *Perestroika* and consequently robbed Africa of its most reliable diplomatic clout. Weakened by bleak economic prospects and an unbearable foreign debt, Africa is thus facing this formidable 'common European home' from a position of extreme weakness and limited room for manoeuvre. It has no external allies strong enough to counterbalance Europe, and its continental unity is extremely fragile and unreliable.

The chances of individual African countries forming alliances outside the continent are limited due to the concentration of political power in the one-party state system, which is the dominant form of government in the continent. Every political action in the circumstances is directly linked to the State, and all alliances automatically became State-to-State alliances. This precludes any affiliation with like-minded political parties or movements in Europe, which is the only possible way of challenging the drift there to right extremism. On the other hand, a ruling party in Africa cannot form alliances with the parties in opposition in any country in Europe without creating diplomatic crises in relations between the countries concerned.

Perestroika has presented Africa with both its positive and negative aspects. It is a challenge such as the continent has never faced since independence. Internally there are confrontations almost everywhere between the rulers who have jealously amassed both power and wealth and are reluctant to give way, on the one hand, and the mass of the impoverished people without rights or security, on the other.

Externally the continent is confronted with a rapidly reunifying Europe to which it was first tied by colonial bondages and now bound to it by the many 'Lome Conventions' which have brought all African countries under its economic patronage. It is difficult to predict how the continent will come out of this dilemma, just as it is difficult to foresee what the post-*Perestroika* world will look like ten years from now. *Perestroika* has ushered in an epoch of uncertainty which is both challenging and exciting, especially to the emerging and energetic peoples of Africa. The next century is the century of Africa irrespective of how the continent resolves its dilemma.

Notes

(1) The Monrovia group consisted of the 20 states which attended the Monrovia conference in Liberia on 8 May 1961 primarily to oppose Nkrumah's PanAfricanism. These were Congo (Braizaville), Cote d'Ivoire, Senegal. Mauritania, Upper Volta, Niger, Benin, Chad, Gabon, the Central African Republic, Cameroon, Madagascar Liberia, Nigeria, Somalia Sierra Leone, Togo, and Ethiopia (with Tunisia and Libya as observers) The Casablanca group consisted of the seven states which were identified with radical, anti-imperialist policies which had attended an earlier conference initiated by Morocco and took place in Casablanca in January 1961. These were Morocco, Egypt, Ghana, Guinea, Mali, Libya (later defected to the Monrovia group) and the Algerian Provisional Government. These two groups later combined to form the Organization of African Unity in 1963.

(2) The Bandung spirit arose out of the Bandung conference in Indonesia in 1955 which was attended by 29 African and Asian countries to cement Afro-Asian solidarity in economic, political, and cultural fields. All the 'giants' of the two continents took part, e.g., Nehru of India, Nasser of Egypt. Nkrumah of Ghana, Chou en Lai of China, Sukarno of Indonesia, U Nu of Burma, and others. The 'Spirit of Bandung' is derived from their joint stand on anti-colonialism, non-alignment, opposition to military blocs, non-interference in the internal affairs of member states, and fraternal consultation. It marked the beginning of political principles which guided the world outlook and diplomacy of many Third World countries

(3) Out-and-out Marxist-Leninist states in Africa came into being after the victory of the Mozambican and Angolan revolution in 1975. following the collapse of the Portuguese colonialism after the 1974 revolution in Portugal. Both these countries immediately declared their adherence to the doctrine, formed close affinity with the Soviet bloc, and adopted centrally planned economies as the strategy for their development. Other African countries to follow that model were Benin, Congo, and Ethiopia

(4) Guardian, 7 May 1990. "On 8 May 1990, two former Cabinet Ministers, Kenneth Matiba and Charles Rubia, called for a multiparty democracy in Kenya and were promptly declared subversive, tribalist, and foreign agents by the ruling authorities. But their call was popularly received by the people and the agitation for pluralist democracy continued until it culminated in mass demonstrations and police violence on the week ending 8-10 July. Ten people were reported shot dead by the police and many injured."

(5) UN High Commissioner for Refugees (UNHCR) Report to the UN, 2 August 1988. Africa counted between 3.5m and 4m refugees by the end of 1987. Although voluntary repatriation movements were under way towards Chad, Ethiopia, Uganda. and Zimbabwe, 1988 also proved to be an unfortunate year with over 800,000 new refugees. mainly from Burundi, Mozambique, Somalia, and Sudan. At present between 4m and 4.5m refugees are living in various pans of the continent, which is a large number on a world scale of 12m, according to the UNHCR Report to the 43rd session of the General Assembly. Doc. A43/12, 2 August 1988. (See 'Human Rights in Africa', *Netherland Quarterly of Human Rights,* Vol. 7, 1989.)

From Political Commissar to Presidency
Africa Events, August 1985

The Soviet Union's evolution to the status of a superpower occurred almost simultaneously with the maturity of Africa's struggle for national independency, and her foreign policy was shaped as Africa, Asia and Latin America were becoming major targets of neoocolonialism.

As the Soviet Union and the US were locked in a life and death struggle of manouvering for strategic positions worldwide, two parallel and contending forces were also emerging internationally in which the two superpowers automatically found themselves involved:

In the case of the US, the development and spread of multinational corporations helped to fuel her diplomacy. In the Soviet Union's case, the revolutionary struggles in the underdeveloped countries tended to supplement the evolution of her foreign policy strategy and tactics.

Andrei Gromyko, the new President of the Union of Soviet Socialist Republics, was by and large the skillful helmsman of Soviet diplomacy throughout this exciting and momentous era.

Africa's relations with the Soviet Union went through critical ups-and-downs beginning from the mid-1950s when the struggle for independence was gaining momentum. Nasser dominated North African politics, including Sudan and the Middle-East. Nkrumah dominated the rest of Africa as his Conventional People's Party demonstrated in concrete terms the unlimited strength of a "mass party". In Kenya, Kenyatta was being accused, falsely as turned out, by the British colonialists of being the leader of Mau Mau with strong pro-Soviet leanings. Western presence in Africa was being challenged from every corner of the continent as the British and French were palpably losing grasp of their old colonies. As with Reagan today, there was then a communist phantasmagoria behind all these events as viewed from the imperialist quarters.

America then, anxious to "fill the vacuum" in order to pre-empt Soviet advance into Africa, blundered its way into

Africa's political arena with its CIA money and its diplomacy of deception. US self-confidence had just been shattered by Soviet attainment of nuclear parity with the explosion of its first A-Bomb on 22 September 1949; followed by its H-Bomb in November 1955 (US exploded its own in May 1956); by Soviet introduction of the Inter-Continental Ballistic Missiles (ICBM) in August 1957, but most spectacular of all, by the Soviet Union sending the first satelite into space by ICBM rocket engines on 4 October 1957.

Soviet prestige in Africa, already high by its support of Nasser in Egypt during and after the "Suez crisis" in 1956, now received a bigger boost. But more importantly, the Soviet Union throughout the liberation struggles took an anti-colonial stand by extending not only a hand of friendship and diplomatic support but also material, military and educational support to the newly emerging countries. When the US entered African politics it was thus in a position of weakness, morally at least. Andrei Gromyko has been associated with most of these achievement of Soviet foreign policy as it became increasingly global.

In the US these Soviet successes were interpreted as America's defeats. To counter their impact on the rest of the world the US mounted massive propaganda and smear campaigns against the Soviet Union (the "Russians" as they called them), first under Truman and Eisenhower and then under J.F. Kennedy ("a friend of Africa" as described by some simplistic African leaders). The UN instead of being a forum for international good-will and understanding among nations was turned into an instrument of US propaganda and a means of embarrassing the Soviet Union - Professor Inis L.Clauder, Kennedy's Assistant Secretary of State for International Organisation Affairs, openly confessed that "the bulk of our policy with regards to the UN has been directed towards enhancing its usability as a Western instrument". Other US goals in the UN, he said, had "always been secondary to our general commitment to theextraction of the fullest possible political value from the organisation as a buttress to the Western position in the global struggle (against the Soviet Union, of course).

The US plunged the world into unprecedented international tension in order to justify to the American people massive expenditure on armaments at the behest of what General Eisenhower described as the US "Military Industrial Complex". The Cold War officially declared by the Truman Doctrine of 1947, now reached its peak.

In their subjectively stepped up paranoia the US and her Western allies' view of Africa was that as soon as independence was achieved the whole continent would be occupied by "the Russian Communists" who were presumably hiding behind every mango tree waiting for the occasion. To a certain extent they succeeded in putting this childish fear into most of our politically underdeveloped leaders with some tragic results. A lot of these leaders had already developed vested interests (e.g. CIA money in Swiss banks) in anti-Sovietism.

Although Nkrumah had a progressive foreign policy stance, the man in charge of Ghana's African policy until his death in September 1959 was none other than George Padmore, who was so pathologically anti-Soviet that at times he was prepared to advance the CIA's anti-Soviet propaganda in Africa.

Most anti-Soviet African leaders concentrated their attack where the Soviet Union was most vulnerable - the economic front. Although it had established under Khrushchev in 1957 a Council of Ministers' "Committee for Foreign Economic Relations", the Soviet Union's internal economic system of Planned Economy precluded any possibility of spontaneous aid other than military aid. This was interpreted by its detractors to mean that the Soviet Union preferred to offer "guns instead of butter".

But the real and objective reason is quite clear. As a superpower engaged in a global struggle against the other superpower, the Soviet Union had and still has to keep up with advanced technology in armaments, if only to maintain parity with the other superpower As a result there are always arms available in abundance which are no longer useful to a superpower but very useful to a newly independent country.

On the other hand, however, you cannot simply go to

Moscow with your shopping list of economic aid and find them waiting for you, as in Western countries; and the reason is equally clear. Whereas in the West these countries are based on a "free market economy" and always saddled with the crisis of over-production, in the Soviet Union production and consumption are proportionately balanced under planned economy and therefore there is no unwanted surplus to give away. Any significant aid to a foreign country must be taken into account well in advance of the Plan so that resources can be allocated accordingly. There is thus no spontaneous economic assistance except on exceptional and emergency situations, and then at the expense of other projects.

This difference between the Western and Socialist economies has been used by the former as an anti-Soviet propaganda weapon to show the superiority of their system. The anti-Soviet elements in Africa deliberately or otherwise swallowed this propaganda hook, line and sinker and they have been echoing it quite vigorously

The other means of frustrating Soviet aid to Africa is through foreign expatriates in our government, mostly from the West. Political heads of departments would successfully negotiate an aid agreement with the Soviet Union but its implementation would be obstructed for years by the expatriates (and their local lackeys of course) on one pretext or another, and by the time they give the go-ahead the agreement would be no longer valid or the projects no longer relevant, and the whole process of renegotiation would have to start all over again at the political level, and so on *ad infinitum.*

Any foreign ministry subjected to these kinds of obstruction and rebuffs is bound to lose its patience and give up, but not the Soviet Union under Gromyko (and incidentally the same can be said of China under Chou en Lai, who was effectively the foreign minister). Not because Gromyko is a saint but because he understood one significant fact of international life, namely that, as a foreign minister of a superpower you cannot afford to be petty or even seem to be petty.

The reason why America's multifarious Secretaries of State almost all fell by the wayside of world politics while Gromyko endured is because they were petty - petty in their outlook, petty in their assessment of world affairs and petty in their response to unanticipated international events or turning-points.

For its part, the Soviet Union made several blunders in their policies towards Africa. Of course none of the two superpowers can have an exclusively regional policy outside of its global dimension; nor can they embark on a policy without taking into account what the other superpower is up to. Consequenty whatever policy initiative one superpower takes in one part of the world is bound to affect its policy on another part. Moreover, that policy, if it is significant, is bound to be responded to by the other superpower in another part. For instance, Soviet intervention in Afghanistan was a response to President Carter's establishment of the Rapid Deployment Force, extending all the way from the US via North Africa to the Persian Gulf. By their extended activities spanning the entire globe and beyond, the two superpowers often tend to he either ignorant of or insensitive to local situations and often end in blunders.

But as both have to deal with Africa and African states they must at least have some knowledge of Africa, if their relations with the region are to be effective. Unfortunately, both of them are at a disadvantage because their knowledge of the region ~leaves much to be desired. The reason is historical. Both the British and the French who colonised Africa almost completely for more than a century (with the Belgians, Italians and Portuguese here and there) had isolated Russia (and the US) from Africa, first against the Tsarist imperialism during the shameless 'scramble' for Africa of the last century and then against the USSR of the 1917 October Revolution.

Consequently, when African countries one by one began to gain their independence Soviet knowlege of these countries was extremely fragmentary. For example, when Congo (Zaire) stormed into independence in 1960 the only contact the Soviet Union had with that country was through. a Czechoslavakian trade representative who was so ill-informed about what was going on in the country that he gave the Kremlin a completely wrong picture of the situation when Lumumba requested Soviet military assistance a few weeks before he was arrested and assassinated by Tshombe.

Soviet policies on Angola and the Horn of Africa are inconsistent: in the former it is principled and revolutionary, but in the latter it is not. Moscow brought the Sino-Soviet dispute into Africa and helped to split the liberation movements with damaging consequences. A lot of the current internal conflicts in African states can be traced to this dispute.

But its economic relations with African countries could have been on a sounder footing inspite of the above mentioned constraints.It could have paid more attention to to regional manors and sensitivities to its own advantage instead of being exclusively global in its approach. It could have helped the evolution of socialist thinking from within instead of ramming it in from above and from outside.

Compared to the US which has interfered in African affairs to the point of instructing our leaders how to handle their countries, Soviet errors are not serious. They can be rectified. Now that Gromyko, whose diplomatic skills could make bad policies look good, is gone there is ample opportunity, indeed a need, to correct some of these errors. We have a vague idea of what are Soviet Union's vital interests, but we also know that a stable and prosperous Africa is the strongest and most viable arsenal against imperialism we can ever have. This must be part of her new regional policies on Africa as well as part of her own national interest considerations. Goodbye Mr Gromyko, the Foreign Mister, and welcome Mr Gromyko, the President of the Union of Soviet Socialist Republics.

DEMOCRACY

Obscenities of Preventive Detention
New African, November 1980

Among the many afflictions that the people of underdeveloped countries suffer from is the denial of human rights. Most of these countries are ruled by despotic and tyrannical regimes. The people are deprived of the basic human necessities by a combination of a chaotic international economic order to which they are subjected and bad economic management at home. On the economic front they see no hope of any improvement; hunger and malnutrition are no longer a shock to them; both have become constant facts of life.

In addition to these sufferings the people are subjected to degrading treatment. They live permanently under regimes which deny them everything that ordinary human beings elsewhere take for granted. One of the instruments these regimes employ in their repression is the PDA (Preventive Detention Act). This law gives the rulers unlimited powers with devastating consequences for the people.

Our function as fighters for human justice is to find ways and means of taming this overwhelming power of the state over our defenceless citizenry. This depressing situation has become the daily routine of ordinary people and as most of our countries are under authoritarian regimes the people have no means of expressing their resentment or of organised resistance. Most of these countries are "stable" and the leaders often enjoy international respectability. Liberia is a recent case in point. It was described as the most stable country in Africa.

However, when the people had an opportunity to express their opinion they expressed it in a most unpleasant manner. This reaction of the people, too, is degrading, but it is a reaction of a desperate people. If we cannot condone it, we can at least understand its inherent causes.

Unlimited powers in the hands of the state, which cannot be subjected to people's supervision and intrusion, inexorably leads to repression irrespective of the will of the holders who wield such powers.

In his essay, The Taming of Power, Bertrand Russell quotes the following anecdote: "In passing by the side of Mount Thai, Confucius came on a woman who was weeping bitterly by a grave. The Master... sent Tze-lu to question her. 'Your wailing,' said he, 'is that of one who has suffered sorrow on sorrow.' She replied: 'That is so. Once my husband's father was killed here by a tiger. My husband was also killed, and now my son has died in the same way.' The Master said: 'Why do you not leave the place?' The answer was 'There is no oppressive government here'. The Master then said: 'Remember this, my children: Oppressive government is more terrible than tigers'."

The immediate struggle for democratic rights in the emerging countries is about "ensuring that government shall be less terrible than tigers."

The short, post-colonial history of emerging countries has been one long, sad spectacle of naked misuse of power by the people in authority. In some cases governments can be compared with the worst despots history. This malady is slowly spreading even to the most enlightened parts of Africa. It is frightening, partly because of the corruptive influence which this misuse of power has on both the leaders and the led; and partly because the denial of people's democratic liberties often demoralises the population and as often leads to the development of a destructive disposition to economic and social development.

It has been shown that the misuse of power by an oppressive regime not only demoralises the community, but also reduces it to infantilism - symptoms of which are irresponsibility, alcoholism, laziness, corruption, lying, petty theft, Uriah Heepish humility - all of which are becoming widespread in our own experience. These symptoms, it is interesting to note, were also common among the inmates of Nazi concentration camps. A people reduced to such levels can hardly he useful material for developing self-reliant, self-sustaining, independent economies, the lack of which already undermines our national self-respect.

The inarticulate sometimes express their frustrations by saying that things were much better under the colonial

regime. In a very important sense they are wrong. The struggle for independence was fought on two principles:
* That, as alien powers, the colonialists had no right to impose their rule on us;
* That such a rule had impoverished us through economic exploitation and denied us our basic human rights by depriving us of our democratic liberties; their tendency towards arbitrary exercise of power obstructed our development as self-respecting human beings.

The attainment of juridical independence automatically satisfied the first principle. This was a basic human right which was denied us: the right to rule ourselves. Nobody under any circumstances can deny a people this right. To say that we were better off when we were denied this right is just plain rubbish.

Whether the attainment of independence satisfied the second principle is another question. It is now clear that the economic strategies adopted by nearly all ex-colonial countries have failed decisively to alter the colonial structure of the oppressive state machine as well as that of our economies. Some economists argue that the "progress" we have registered since independence was a normal development process which would have taken place in any case, with or without independence. As long as people are alive, they will always improve their living conditions one way or another. This progress, according to these economists, is wholly spontaneous. They point out that in many respects we have not done so well at all, considering the enormous and rapid development which the advanced industrialised countries have achieved in the two decades of our independence.

They also point out that the still colonised countries in Africa have registered much greater economic gains during the period than their independent counterparts. This, of course, is not intended to justify colonialism. What they are saying is that our independence should not be assessed by what we have achieved, which is not much, but rather by what could have been achieved, taking into account the mass enthusiasm at independence which could have been directed towards the restructuring of our economies and set the people on the road to independent development.

On the economic front, therefore, the question whether our independence has initiated any decisive boost to development is open to debate. On the democratic front, however, the picture is quite different. Here, as was noted earlier, a lot of our countries have actually regressed, and their governments have not been "less terrible than tigers." There are only very few exceptions to this degenerating trend. In most countries the following practices are quite common: arbitrary arrests of citizens; disrespect for the writ of Habeas Corpus; imprisonment without trial; denial of freedom of movement; the "pass" laws (hated in South Africa); organised and systematic police brutality; domination of government by secret police; mass arrests and detention; concentration camps; physical and mental torture of prisoners; executions, which have now become an accepted form of public entertainment.

In the colonial days when the governing authority resorted to some of these undemocratic and totalitarian measures it would first declare a "state of emergency" which would last for days, weeks, or months (in Kenya it lasted for almost 10 years). But as soon as the 'emergency' was over, the democratic liberties of the people would be restored; at any rate, those liberties which people enjoyed prior to the 'emergency.' Not so with the majority of our governments. Nearly all of our independent states have given themselves these emergency (i.e. totalitarian) powers, for as long as they are in power, under the obnoxious law known as the Preventive Detention Act, an all-purpose legal instrument for repression, which lawyers describe as a 'bad law.' Initiated by Adolf Hitler in Europe, PDA spread across ex-colonial countries like prairie fire. It gave heads of state and gover nment extraordinary power over life and liberty; and through the exercise of this law they try to control and direct the political behaviour of the population.

Under this 'law' a citizen is hounded out of his house, usually during the early hours of the morning (most likely 2 a.m.) in the best tradition of the Gestapo. His house is ransacked by the invading armed police who expropriate anything they fancy. Then the citizen is hauled to prison where he remains for weeks, months, or years without being told the reason for his imprisonment.

The prisons are usually manned by guards who tend to be enthusiastic about their total power over their victims. In addition to enjoying unlimited powers they quite often misuse them. Thus although technically a citizen detained under FDA is supposed to be a civil prisoner, these powerful gentlemen are above such legal frills. To them, as soon as a citizen enters the prison gates he is as good as a convict and is dealt with accordingly. At this point the bewildered citizen comes face to face with the coercive apparatus of his government. He is often beaten up, locked up in solitary confinement, denied food for the first day or two (because his ration has not yet been allocated by the authorities!); stripped naked, and generally subjected to all kinds of degrading treatment designed to undermine his self-respect.

The food is poor and the manner it is dished out is enough to put the newly arrived citizen off food for several weeks. Public health is almost non-existent, and the citizen is often exposed, and as often falls victim to, all sorts of communicable diseases. A mere clinical assistant is in charge of dispensing treatment and only rarely does a qualified doctor visit the prison, often too late to save the patient. On the whole such prisons are very inefficiently run - and inefficiency is tantamount to tyranny, because prisoners go without food, without water or without medicine, for several days as result.

The citizen is subjected to all these humiliations, let it be repeated, without even being told why he is there. Suddenly and often mysteriously he may be released after several months or years of incarceration. In many emerging countries thousands of citizens are thus daily exposed to such brutalities no matter whether they break the law or not. It just depends on what the secret police think the citizen is up to, or when the political leadership consider such imprisonment necessary in order to keep themselves in power. PDA is often handled by the secret police, who are as a rule cruel, crude, and rough.

Prisoners under PDA often end up mentally deranged or, at best develop extreme depressive maladies which last for the rest of their lives. A convict prisoner at least knows his crimes and knows the date of his release. A prisoner under PDA knows neither; which makes his situation much worse than that of the convict. The reason for the psychological damage to a detained person is obvious: men and women usually get distressed and are eventually afflicted psychologically when they suffer undeservedly or see transgressors, in this case the secret police, escape punishment.

What was intended by the legal drafters of the Act to be a preventive law has been turned into a punitive law. Preventive Detention Act is now "preventive" only in theory. In practice it is Punitive Detention. Resort to use of this law by unscrupulous politicians (and their scruples tend to diminish in exact proportion as the sense of their political insecurity heightens - this is the law of the struggle for power in conditions of moral and economic underdevelopment) is increasingly becoming an important political weapon; it has become a vital instrument for maintaining in power unpopular and tyrannical leaders whose usefulness has long been exhausted. In their hands PDA is an enabling law, to break all the laws; it is the paralegal instrument for survival.

In the early days of independence PDA was justified on two grounds. Firstly, since most countries attained independence at different times, those that got theirs earlier were confronted with the possibility of agents being infiltrated into their countries from neighbouring countries not yet independent. The ordinary process of the law was seen to be too cumbersome to deal effectively with such emergency situations, because agents could freely enter any one of the independent countries with legitimate traveling documents and without breaking any laws of the country concerned. At the same time most of the police force was wholly dependent on foreign, ex-colonial officers some of whom were not too happy about our independence. The powers of detention were, therefore, felt to be necessary to defend the young states before the damage was done.

Secondly (and this was also the argument to justify the

establishment of a one-party state system in many countries), since the colonial rule was notorious for its policies of "divide and rule," there was a threat to the peaceful evolution to a homogeneous nation, and therefore it was felt necessary for a young state to arm itself with sufficient preemptive powers to forestall any such disruptive developments. If these arguments were valid at the time, they are no longer tenable politically and much less so morally. If insecurity still exists after nearly 20 years of independence, it cannot any longer be blamed on external forces; and if it emanates from internal forces then it is an admission of the leadership's own political and administrative failure.

In any case, in many instances governments are overthrown in spite of (or probably because of) the existence of the PDA. In other words, PDA has ceased to serve the function originally intended. On the other hand, if ethnic loyalties still exist after so many years of independence, again it is an admission of the leadership's political failure. If they solved the problem of ethnic loyalty the Act is redundant. Only one African country came to this conclusion. Sudan rescinded the act in 1973, although the authorities proceeded to imprison students and other political activists with the same arbitrariness as if PDA were still in force.

So when the inarticulate say that colonialism was better, it is only a crude way of saying that the people are not yet free and that our political and administrative practices have blocked the way to freedom. Understandably, leaders are always very sensitive when this question is raised, and they react very harshly. But as long as repressions continue people are bound to ask such questions, what else do they have to compare things with?

It is a sad reflection on the leaders especially the liberal and radical ones, that they still have this law on their statute books while claiming to leading the. struggle for human rights and dignity. Nothing dehumanises and degrades a person more than this 'law'. It makes him degraded and insecure in his own country; it is in fact an insult to human dignity, especially when the leaders then claim that we are not yet ready for full democratic liberties.

The story is even worse with the more extreme cases, especially the military regimes or the insecure civil governments. Here is where you would rather 'face the tiger'. No political or any democratic rights of any sort are tolerated by the leadership except those sanctioned by them. What they call democracy here would be called despotic dictatorship elsewhere. Under these regimes the leaders speak only one language - the language of force. Almost without exception such leaders are politically illiterate, and they make havoc of our national image internationally. They meddle in world affairs with the meticulousness of a bull in a china shop and are much worse in their handling of internal affairs. Whereas under the generals, governments are straightforward military, under weak 'civilian' leadership governments are run by secret police. To the citizen both have the same effect - suppression of the citizenry. To these governments the people are nothing; they are only faceless tatterdemalion crowds who are there to be manipulated and forced to do whatever the regime wants.

The danger in this situation is not just that there is a denial of civil liberties, or arbitrariness which accompanies such solitary use of power. The serious danger is a lasting one; the perpetuation of the kind of established disorder which is slowly tending to become universal in our countries. The following characteristics are common in nearly all such types of governments: leaders are increasingly isolated from the people and reality, and they live in a world of their own delusion, which forces them to actions which are irrational and often damaging to the country and people. They then subvert the very machinery of government by covering it in a web of secrecy and more secrecy, until secrecy itself becomes a system of government.

At this point of disorder, leaders begin to confuse the distinction between their private wishes and their national duties. They invent reasons and ethical justification for doing what they should not have done, and for leaving undone what their duty obliges them to do. From here they degenerate to gradual moral deterioration until at last they cease to have any sense of respect for others' rights and by the same token they lose their own freedoms as well. They rarely appear in public as before, scared of the people's wrath for which they are themselves responsible. Naked violence begins to be introduced into the system of government, with the secret police being allowed extraordinary powers to trample on people's liberties as they please. With this state of affairs we find ourselves in a preordained descent into the realm of politics without morality. It is at this level that absolute power corrupts.

To the people, a state of established disorder is a state of no law and no rights. Injustice is taken for granted; it is seen as a constant element rather than a shocking intrusion into people's existence. Those in power demand from the people only unilateral, in place of mutual, respect; the respect of inferiors for superiors, rather than respect between equals. To such leaders the people are only part of their estate, and in such an estate the masters are insensitive to appeals for justice; to them justice is whatever is useful to maintain themselves in power. Their ideal is to govern with a minimum of dissent and the maximum of domination. They regard themselves as demigods.

Anybody honest enough to refuse to acknowledge them as such is a criminal and he is punished accordingly, mostly through the use of PDA. The country in the meantime moves by desultory stages nearer and nearer disaster. In the end such regimes reduce the entire population to the economic level of beggars and the political level of convicts.

Giving the Left a bad name
Africa Now, September 1983

The overthrow of Major Jean Baptiste Ouedraogo by Captain Thomas Sankara in the latest Upper Volta coup is an excellent example of a progressive faction of the military taking over power from an old, pro-establishment and pro-status quo military leadership When Ouedraogo plotted with France and the US last April to undermine the army's left-wing faction he at once created conditions for his own overthrow.

The radical left in the modern African army (going back as far as Nasser's "Young Officers") is generally more serious, more relevant, more energetic and better equipped to take over power than their older colleagues who are associated with the discredited ruling clique and the status quo. Since they are young, they are more willingly acceptable in this continent of the young.

But, as a rule after taking over power, these young officers, untrained in the affairs of the civil society, the state or its management, often tend to be overwhelmed by what they have landed themselves in and, as a result, they retreat to the same, safe, old and humdrum practice of the status quo which they had earlier sworn to upset. The recent example of this about-turn betrayal is that of Master Sergeant Doe of Liberia who started off as an anti-corruption radical but has now emerged as one of the most corrupt leaders in Africa.

Doe is probably an unfortunate example of a dishonest, unimaginative and unpatriotic military upstart of lumpen origins and, therefore, cannot be universalised as a "type." But other young officers of more patriotic bent have also landed themselves in at least some confusion if not in utter opportunism.

Nasser once told us that, after taking over power in Egypt in 1952, the young officers, sitting at their first Cabinet meeting, looked at each other and asked themselves: "What do we do next?" No one had any idea and eventually one of them said: "Why don't we dig up from the old files projects that were promised by King Farouk (whom they had just overthrown) but never implemented, present these to the people and then proceed to implement them?" "Brilliant," said Nasser and from then on followed the policies that later came to be known as Nasserism. Nasser was a very intelligent and honest patriot and therefore even his style of muddling-through had the appearance of honesty to the Egyptian public. However, hardly three years after his death, his successor, Sadat the renegade, succeeded in degenerating into the most discredited internal and external policies in complete reversal of Nasser's, and yet the Egyptian people went along with him. Sadat, incidentally, was himself one of the "Young Officers" of 1952.

In other words, it is not enough to be progressive and radical; you must also have correct, well defined and - which is more important - workable policies which will bring about significant and progressive changes and lead to the economic, social and cultural well-being of the people. This is all the more important for the radical leadership which also declares itself "socialist." Socialism is not a localised sentiment or eccentricity; it is a universal doctrine and part of the international class struggle and therefore all actions of such a declared socialist country are subject to international scrutiny and appraisal. In other words, no socialist leadership can be protected by the "noninterference in our internal affairs" blanket.

Since socialism represents the highest ideals of humanism, to be accepted it must in practice be seen to be upholding those ideals. This is not the same thing as the idealism or even the humanism of pursuing dream worlds or of a simplistic "brotherhood of mankind." It is the idealism and humanism of realism not of illusions; of liberation not of repression; of humankind taking control and direction of its own history instead of remaining the victims of history; of abolition of imperialism in all its manifestations; and, in our case, of making Africa a strong and unified continent of socialist commonwealth.

We would expect from Captain Thomas Sankara, who has declared his coup to be a socialist one, a decisive departure from the ones we have so far experienced in Africa.

This is because many people in the continent have become extremely skeptical of all brands of such declared socialism. The Marxism-Leninism of Ethiopia, for instance, has proved to be the most cruel, the most repressive and the most imperialistic of the leftist governments in Africa. Its anti-imperialism is not consistent, sometimes running with the hare and at other times hunting with the hounds. Its land reform is commendable but its pursuit of imperialistic ambitions in Eritrea is universally condemned. Its class struggle is suspect after having exterminated some of the most excellent leaders of the proletariat in Africa, especially the trade union and youth leaders. Its erroneous political and economic strategies have strengthened rather than weakened the counterrevolutionaries.

The Marxism-Leninism of Mozambique is no better; its economic policies are so wishy-washy that nearly 10 years after liberation it is still dependent on South Africa. It has not only re-imposed the death penalty but deepened this degradation by making public executions a fun-fair spectacle. Friends of that country's liberation are saddened by the fact that it seems to be heading nowhere except into the chaos of economic disaster and thus playing into the hands of South Africa and its counter-revolutionary stooges.

Captain Thomas Sankara will do well to learn from these inexcusable follies if he is serious about his socialism. He must learn that our greatest asset is the people and he must handle them with utmost respect. Repression must be struck out of his vocabulary and he must try to evoke from them the positive rather than the negative. Repression of poverty-stricken and defenceless citizens is the easiest thing to do in our countries, but its consequences are the most difficult to contain once the people begin to hit back.

He might also try to avoid giving the impression, which many of the so-called socialist countries in Africa do give, that they appear in practice to have more in common with fascism than socialism; that they have been attracted more by the repressive aspect of the state rather than by its liberating aspect; or of being anti-imperialist in words and colluding with it in practice.

Democracy

Socialists in power cannot afford to make too many mistakes and it does not absolve them by making public self-criticism and admissions about the mistakes. A single mistake by the state means disaster for millions of citizens and ruin to large sectors of the economy; a mere public admission of the obvious will never satisfy anybody and it gives more ammunition to the enemies of socialism.

Socialists are not merely attempting to upset the internal status quo but also challenge the entire world system of repression and exploitation, not by arguing with it but by taking concrete measures to ensure uncoupling themselves from it. This is not an easy task, especially now when the Western world is virtually governed by a desperate lunatic fringe of the extreme right. Notice, if you please, the unwarranted attacks on Gadaffi whose only crime is that he dares to challenge the mighty of this unjust world. Notice also how many stooges in Africa have been mobilised to do the dirty work of imperialism's anti-Gadaffi campaign, on the one hand, and the utter silence of the progressive countries on the subject, on the other.

Actually, in the current Chad crisis the progressive countries have come out rather disgracefully and all the diplomatic and propaganda initiative was captured by the right-wing conservative countries. While most of Africa has already dismissed the latter as incurable surrogates of the West and it is no longer shocking to see them prostrating and humiliating themselves for mere crumbs, Africa expected a firm and disciplined stand from the progressives.

It was the latter who, since independence took upon themselves (quite rightly) the task of standing up for Africa dignity, the exponents of what is just, honest and noble, the fighters against injustice and humiliation; it is these countries that one looked up to in times of crises like these, but instead there has been utter silence while France and the US are sending in troops and material to slaughter and maim sons and daughters of Chad with the connivance of Hissen Habre and his ilk. They are mute when Mobutu and Nimeiri are joining in the slaughter to appease their paymasters.

The most these progressive countries have done so far

is to appeal rather half-heartedly for "foreign countries to quit Chad," in a manner that would make one think Goukouni Woddeye was himself one of the foreigners. This current tragedy was, in fact partly precipitated by the OAU and the progressive countries when they decided to "recognize" Hissen Habre after he was installed at N'djamena by foreign arms and foreign mercenaries and by abandoning Goukouni Woddeye whose family and himself have been carrying the struggle for the freedom of the Chadian people long before Gadaffi was born and Habre was serving the French colonialists as a district officer.

Although patriotism is beginning to lose its meaning in Africa as leaders become more and more "pragmatic" and therefore saleable, progressive leaders cannot afford to abandon it. It is a hazardous option in the short run but in the long term it is infinitely rewarding and honourable. But a patriot is judged, not only by his or her stand against foreign interference, but also by their stand against injustice to their people and their respect for human rights in their own country. This is more so when the patriot also describes him or herself as a socialist.

To be a socialist in Africa carries a special responsibility, especially on the question of human rights. Africa is a continent which has suffered the worst violations of human rights, all the way from slavery and colonialism up to neo-colonialism. Its people are being humiliated, not only in South Africa's apartheid, but also in the most advanced bourgeois democracies in Europe and North America. The dignity of the continent cannot be upheld by the sell-outs who have traditionally enriched themselves by perpetuating that humiliation. Socialists must, therefore, be in the vanguard of the struggle for human rights in Africa.

However, what we see in practice is very disappointing. Instead of being the advanced fighters in safeguarding those rights, they tend to be the arch violators as soon as they are in power. Witness the sad spectacle in Zimbabwe and the attacks on the opposition by a most ruthless ethnic army in the name of socialism and anti-imperialism - indeed, with the army having been trained by socialists. It is no use arguing in defence that the Mobutus are doing worse; socialists are judged by standards which are much, much higher than those of the Mobutus.

It is no argument either, to say that socialists take greater care of the people on the welfare front. To argue that civil and political rights are not the only rights that should be taken into account or that economic, social and cultural rights are primary and others secondary is to miss the whole point about human rights.

Similarly, to argue that in a poor country the priority should be given to the elimination of poverty, ignorance and disease rather than to civil political rights such as freedom to elect your leaders or the rights that protect a citizen from arbitrary arrest and imprisonment, is to misrepresent the whole case about human rights. This is definitely not a socialist argument and those who advance it are obviously more interested in holding on to state power than in advancing the true welfare of the people.

In December 1966, the United Nations adopted two Covenants of great significance: one "On Civil and Political Rights" and the other "On Economic, Social and Cultural Rights." The world body did not favour one over the other - both are equally important and they complement each other. The one on political and civil rights was directed at the colonialists, particularly at Britain, France, Portugal and South Africa who still hung on to colonies in Africa where the arbitrary use of state power was common. Is it not ridiculous that those same victims of colonialism should now, not only adopt the very policies that oppressed them, but also invent justifications for this?

There was a time in Africa when the progressives were actually leading the politics of the continent and all the major diplomatic and economic initiatives were taken directly or indirectly by them. When one talked of leadership one talked of progressive leadership. The conservative countries, especially the French-speaking ones who reluctantly went into independence, had to toe the line if they were to enjoy any credibility in their own countries. The OAU and its liberation committee, the formation of the "Group of 77" at

UNCTAD I, and so on - all these were the initiatives of the progressive African countries. But in the late 70s the progressives lost the initiative and found themselves on the defensive. The conservatives took over, to the detriment of the African masses. The progressives henceforth ceased to act; they only reacted to others' initiatives.

Why? The reason is simply: in the absence of any lasting and viable ideology which reflects the present and future realities of Africa or the lack of any concrete and workable policies based on a clear and realistic theory that will deliver positive results - reality itself confronts you rudely. It shatters your self-confidence, your credibility vanishes and you are left with only vacuous rhetoric which evokes only nostalgia and self-pity. This is unfortunate because at no time has the need for decisive, clear-headed and progressive leadership been more urgent than now.

Captain Thomas Sankara may not fill this leadership gap but he can be instrumental in reviving that post-colonial enthusiasm which most people had hoped would be rekindled by Zimbabwe but was not; the enthusiasm that cleared bushes, built thousands of miles of modern roads, that dug canals on the basis of free labour and the spirit of nation-building.

It is not too late, believe it or not. The people are ready; all they need is honesty, commitment, genuine progressive policies and a clear sense of direction from those who claim to lead them. They want a leadership that will not oppress them, that will identify with them, a leadership that will not rob them and mislead them.

Captain Thomas Sankara will do well to ponder on all this and, being the latest socialist aspirant, try to set new standards to be emulated by future socialists which would make other socialists elsewhere proud of socialism in Africa.

Leader knows best
Africa Events, March 1985

It is not possible to formulate a general theory that can categorically show that either a one-party or a multi-party system is necessarily democratic under any circumstances and for all time. Experiences in democracy have been mostly in the form of 'representative government' or 'parliamentary democracy' and all the debates that have been raging over the subject since the last century have not yet fully answered the question: What is the best system that ensures full democratic rights to the people?

Thus the subject is not only complex and inexhaustible, it is also virtually open-ended and cannot be tackled satisfactorily in one or two articles. The purpose of this one therefore is not to raise and answer all the questions on the topic, but rather to keep talking about democracy (or the lack of it) instead of remaining silent.

This is essential in view of the many threats to democracy by the power-seekers who exploit our ignorance to strengthen their hold on state power and political domination. Since independence Africa has witnessed a proliferation of one-party states in both the "radical" and "conservative" countries. You have on the one hand the liberal humanists or the magnanimous despots who mean well but always err - and err in good faith. On the other hand you have the African version of the so-called "Asiatic despot" - ruthless, brutal, oppressive, they generally use the wealth of their country to enrich themselves or their families and relatives.

Both camps defend the one-party system as the only state form suitable for Africa. In the first case they argue that it is the most effective democratic form compared to multi-party systems or the "Westminster model". In the second case they don't even bother to argue their case; they simply assert that it is the best system to fight against the "enemies of the state" or "dictators" - that is any patriot who challenges their robbery of the national wealth

In many instances it is difficult to distinguish the first from the second. In either case there is the dominant "top-person-in-authority" with unlimited state and political powers, surrounded by hand-picked sycophants who represent nobody except themselves and the interests and welfare of the person they serve. There is "the party" whose bureaucracy is appointed and directed by the top person in state power, a bureaucracy whose relation with the population is as a superior. The latter humbly begs, the former magnanimously delivers, if he sees fit. The secret police pervades every section of political and social life, with the army visibly or invisibly as the final arbiter.

The top bureaucracy of the state is also hand-picked by the top person in authority, not necessarily on the basis of merit but essentially on the basis of loyalty. As it is impossible for the top person to be sure of the loyalty of all his appointees, he tends to follow the rule of thumb by trusting only people of his own ilk or from his own area whose survival in their appointments is intimately linked with his own; if he goes, they go too.

These "trustees" (to use the unfortunate term of the prison system) are generally put in charge of the "sensitive" areas of the state power, the army, the secret police, the prison system, the judiciary, the financial institutions, economic establishment, the party hierarchy and so on. Because of their links with the "top person in authority," they are very powerful; indeed they are more powerful than the formal appointees of the state apparatus like cabinet ministers and senior civil servants.

In this arrangement, the top person in authority has a secret way of maintaining contact with these trustees, usually through an intermediary like the "private secretary" of the top person in authority or a Minister of State for Presidential Affairs or Minister Without Portfolio. These transmit personal instructions from the top-person-authority to the trustees.

Thus in the one-party state as a rule there are two or three "governments within government" There is the formal government with all the paraphernalia of the state -the Head

Democracy 217

of State, his Cabinet, Parliament, the judiciary, the army, police and prisons.

Then there is the invisible Secret Service, generally known as "Security" which keeps everyone high enough in government under constant surveillance, except of course the top person himself.

Then there is the secret Secret Service (or SS II) which is known only to the top person in power and a few of his aides, whose task is to spy on the formal Secret Service (or SS I) and to counter-check on the latter's secret reports. They are directly under the top-person-in-authority to whom they report and from whom they receive their instruction.

Then there is the Presidential Secret Service (or SS III) manned by a handful of highly trained, ruthless loyalists who generally come from the President's own home village or his own blood relatives and are known only to him and to no one else, nor are they answerable to any one else but him. They are even authorised to kill and get away with it. They consist of elements from the army and civilians who are given specialised training by a select foreign government entrusted to maintain absolute secrecy. These are so powerful that it is said that even the top-person himself is scared of them. Only their absolute loyalty to him ensures his survival

Then there is the government of the "Presidential Palace" or the "State House", the all powerful state functionaries close to the top person in power, who can and do dictate orders with presidential authority. They are usually a clique of people renowned for their fierce loyalty because they have no other qualification or political history to be where they are.

Because of their enormous power and the fact that they are accountable to nobody except the top person himself, they tend to be extremely tyrannical and very corrupt. They interfere in government departments, issue orders often contrary to laid down policies, terrorise other government functionaries into submitting to their whimsical instructions, and do all this in the name of the President.

There is then the party bureaucracy, which in a country

which adheres to the system of the "supremacy of the party" is really supreme. It dictates policies, interprets them in its own light, claims the right to interfere in government activities and can order the arrest and detention of citizens in the name of the party. They harrass constituency members of parliament and always claim to be the "real government". This bureaucracy is generally demagogic but otherwise politically illiterate. Most of them owe their position to the top person in power or to one of his trusted aides.

When it holds its periodic elections after every five years and puts two candidates in every constituency, and when the electorate vote into parliament one of the two (they differ only in personality not in the policy of the party they both represent). the system is hailed as democratic and the people's choice. As if to emphasise the democratic nature of the system, there will be a presidential election, contested, as a rule. This is usually the same top person in authority who is always elected by not less than 97.3% or some such fictitious figure always above 90%. Anything less will tarnish the presidential image

If democracy is the rule of the majority, this is certainly not. If it is about the expansion and protection of individual liberties, this is not. If it is about the protection of the minority and civil liberties, this is definitely not. If it is about political competition, this is not. If on the other hand the one-party state is about transition to some higher social order then this is far from it.. If it is for Africa, it obviously is so; but certainly not for the political and economic development of the African people.

Our short history since independence has shown that the one party-state has now become the major problem which has resulted in the serious economic and political crisis we are going through. It is an obstacle to our development and to our liberty and freedom. It must be scrapped from our system of government.

Uganda's Lesson in democracy
South, October 1986

The political and economic crisis that has gripped Africa in recent years is of the classical kind in social evolution in which the "old is dying and the new cannot be born". Two decades of post-colonial experience and the eruption of "unmanageable poverty", in which hundreds of thousands of poor peasants are left to suffer the most agonising death by starvation while their political leaders are engaged in other preoccupations, has led to profound disillusionment with the post-colonial political tradition: the people "no longer believe what they used to believe".

Nowhere has this revulsion against the old been more dramatically revealed than in South Africa where, against all odds, the youth have taken over the townships on their own initiative and through their own organisation, independent of the old political tradition, black or white.

Recent events in Uganda and the maturation of the Eritrean situation in the Horn of Africa reflect the same revulsion and/or revolution which is sweeping the continent. The Ugandan example has captured that mood at a critical moment, and the tide of the National Resistance Movement rose simultaneously with that of general resentment, so that most Ugandan youth - and not only Ugandans - could identify easily with the movement and give it undivided support.

This has achieved an African near miracle. For the first time in modern African history, ordinary young men and women (26 of them to begin with) organised into a resistance movement against a formidable militaristic dictatorship, gradually amassing popular support until they defeated not only the Obote state but the military establishment which sustained it. This is no mean achievement in a continent in which the military is supreme, overthrowing established civilian governments or eachother on a regular basis, and in the process making havoc of the social and economic bases of our societies - while the masses are reduced to passive bystanders.

What has made the Ugandan experience so popular throughout Africa is the fact that not only has the revolution succeeded in overthrowing an oppressive military dictatorship heavily backed by foreign governments, but it has set itself the immediate task of restoring democracy and reconstructing the economic foundation to correspond to it. By the same token, it has put the "question of democracy" and national economy on the African agenda in such a compelling way that no African government can ignore it and get away with it.

In most parts of Africa the saddest experience is the destruction of democracy: the denial of the right of a people to participate in the making of decisions affecting their lives; the right to freely elect their representatives to the councils of the nation and to recall them when necessary, the right to utilise their latent human and natural resources without interference; and the supreme right essential for human survival - the right to engage in productive activity.

And the economic objectives that necessitated this arrant destruction of democracy proved not only unattainable but actually led to a cesspool of graft, fraud and corruption from which there appears to be no way out.

So when the new Ugandan revolutionary government set its new objectives: in politics, democracy; in economics, the provision of food, clothing and shelter for the people - those outside Uganda took note, for in effect it has set a new direction for the entire continent to emulate; it marks a decisive departure from the old colonial and post-colonial path.

Africa has up to now been experimental with democracy, if not altogether suspicious of it. Stability was regarded as primary and democracy secondary, and therefore the establishment of law and order was given the highest priority. Like the colonialists before them, the new leaders believed Africans were not yet ready for democracy. President Kwame Nkrumah of Ghana was the first to introduce the one-party state in Africa, in his case in the name of "socialism" and "African democracy". And to make his "transition to socialism" more effective, he enacted the preventive detention laws which empowered him to lock up any "troublemaker" indefinitely, without recourse to the courts. This mode of government became so attractive to the new elites of emerging Africa that it set a pattern for practically all the newly independent states; all abrogating the existing constitution and establishing a one-party constitution; all in the name of either socialism, African democracy, or African tradition or authenticity. But whatever it was called, in effect the system denied practically all basic civil rights.

It is ironic that colonial rulers went to great lengths to establish independent constitutions which departed significantly from the dictatorial rule they had practised hitherto, but as soon as they went away the new governments reintroduced administrations as restrictive as colonial government, for exactly the same reasons that the colonialists had invoked for their rule - namely, that Africa was not yet ready for democracy, or the Westminster model. The state structure never changed either; it remained intact with its district and regional commissioners and other officers, only now manned by local elites with powers of arbitrary arrest and detention in the name of the president.

The military saw the system as having prepared the ground to their advantage: if societies must be ruled by brute force, who is better qualified to do so than the army? Military takeovers became as regular as the proliferation of one-party states. Even in those states which are not formally under the military, they still have a decisive say in major matters of state. The military constitutes the core of political life in the continent today. The institution is notoriously corrupt, because it is the biggest spender. It is also virtually autonomous. Presidents in Africa can rule forever without the people's consent; but they cannot rule for one day without the consent of the military.

Most of our "economic partners" in the West, who themselves cannot live for one day under this system, nevertheless condone this deliberate destruction of democracy, not only because of colonial prejudice but because it is good for business. A repressive state machine allows no rights to the workers - neither the right to organise independently nor the right to withdraw their labour, both of which obstruct foreign accumulation of capital. In other words, in many instances there is a coincidence of interest between our ruling elites and our foreign economic partners : the former repress and the latter exploit, for the benefit of both and at the expense of the people.

This African reality of the last two decades has culminated in the worst economic experience of our history. It has reduced the masses to the depths of human suffering and degradation, televised to the world.

This reality, however, has also invoked the most profound rethinking about our past, present and future. "Whither Africa?" has become the most urgent question in the continent. Even President Julius Nyerere, one of the earliest advocates of the one-party state, was recently reported as expressing doubts about the functional usefulness of the system. Above all, the dramatic victory of the people over the military establishment in Uganda and the new vista it has opened have attracted widespread attention.

We can learn several lessons from this experience and its potential as a pathfinder to democratic and economic reorganisation of our societies.

It is not enough to reject the old without creatively constructing conditions for the new direction, otherwise we will end up in an impasse. The direction that must evolve must take into account the concrete African situation, which cannot adequately be confined to the well-trodden but often misguided capitalist or socialist metaphors, useful as these may be as guidelines.

The Ugandan experience, which broadly summarises African reality, shows us that a people's own leadership, to be successful, must be founded on a broad democratic alliance of various social groups, and must draw its strength from free expression and initiative among these groups; from retaining their identity; and from their contributions reflecting their own interests. This will ensure a democratic evolution in which vast numbers participate in decision-making, and which in turn will ensure full control of their lives. For unlike the one-party system, popular democracy, which is the basis of people's own leadership, can be realised only by recognising the coexistence of many and varied interests within the nation. In other words, the colonial state we inherited has not been smashed by the one-party system; on the contrary, it has consolidated it, when the real need of a free people is a democratic united front to bring about first, the essential unity of state and nation; and second, the restructuring of the colonial system to enable the majority to take an active role in political and economic life.

The replacement of the colonial state will not only restore our democratic rights but will also give us a new insight into our economic reality and the way to change it. The economies that form the foundation of our societies are not our economies in the real sense; they are an extension of the metropolitan economies. This is so because our countries were annexed to the European capitalist economy for more than a century, and as a result, they have evolved in a specific, historically determined way, with a definite mode of production which principally served the production and consumption needs of that economy that had annexed them. Consequently, they have subordinated their production to the metropolitan markets, which siphon off almost all their economic surplus, leaving hardly anything for the national accumulation essential for extended reproduction.

To understand it well enough to change it therefore, this situation needs to be looked into in the context of its own reality, and not from outside. The process must begin by raising the most fundamental question: how to change this situation in order to bring about conditions for economic formation that will ensure steady development of economic and political well-being. And the guideline to a realistic answer must begin with the recognition that ultimately the solution is internal since, as we know, external causes are only the condition of change, while internal causes remain the basis of change. Only a free people can be the effective agents for changing the base, and only by changing the base can conditions be created for the new to be born - the establishment of a lasting and genuine democratic system.

The Right to Demand Freedoms
Index on Censorship, 4 April, 1992[1]

"Democracy" is not a new thing in colonial and post-colonial Africa. Throughout the colonial struggle the principal demand of the anti-colonial movements was for the restoration of the right of the majority to rule themselves. This was a uniquely democratic demand.

Secondly, the liberation movements themselves were all organised on democratic principles, as their party constitutions testify. They were all based on the "democratic centralism" principle of a minority abiding by the majority decision. This principle was later subverted by the Soviet Union and the former socialist countries of Eastern Europe when they elevated it from the realm of political parties to that of state power. And so did the so-called "progressive" African countries who after attaining independence adopted the Soviet state model.

Thirdly, all "Independence Constitutions", whether negotiated with the British, the French or other colonial powers, were based on democratic principles which provided for parliamentary elections, the separation of state powers between the executive, elected parliament and the judiciary; a free press, plus freedom of association.

In other words, not only was there a commitment to formal democracy, but the machinery for a democratic process was carefully instituted. Furthermore, thanks to the democratic traditions of the liberation movements noted above, the people already had a fairly long experience in democratic practice when independence came. That is to day, Africans do not need to be lectured to by the "born-again" democrats on the merits of democracy.

And who are these new advocates who express so much passion on the rights of Africans to democracy and human rights? Who are these people who have suddenly become so fanatical about these rights for Africa to the cruel extent of making their aid conditional upon restoration of democracy and human rights in Africa? They are none other than the same old apologists of human rights violations in Africa! Practically all Western governments, as well as the Soviet bloc, and the multilateral institutions, not only tolerated but in many cases actually collaborated with the local ruling elites in instituting authoritarian systems which denied hundreds of millions of African citizens their basic human democratic rights. They all encouraged "strong, decisive and authoritative" governments in Africa with whom they could "do business". They even alleged, and were supported by academic justifications from their sycophantic institutions of learning, that democracy was "culturally alien to Africa"; that the one-party state was the most suitable system for this "tribally divided" continent, and so on, and so forth.

Many Africans now wonder, why is it that these same forces have suddenly turned into ardent advocates of democracy for Africa. Is it because of their love for the Africans? If it is, why now, and so belatedly? Where were they when the Bandas, the Mobutus, the Mois, and the military dictators of all brands, were killing, maiming, imprisoning and banishing millions of innocent Africans? Were they not, throughout that gory history, in collaboration with these same tormentors of Africa, responsible for addling the continent with an unbearable debt burden of $3000 billion to be paid, not by the corrupt leaders who have contracted these "odious debts", as Patricia Adams[2] calls them in her book of the same title, but by the unsuspecting toiling and starving masses of Africa? Are they not to this day manoeuvring to keep in power the arch violator of human rights, Mobutu Seseku of Zaire, in spite of the wishes of the people, on the argument that any alternative to his cruel rule will be chaos? One can go on and on about these conflicting Western positions between then and now, but the question is, so we as Africans need democracy now, in spite of this apparent hypocritical posture of the born-again democrats?

The masses of Africa, of course, needed democracy at the dawn of their independence, and more so now. And the reason is obvious: it accumulates millions of dollars in personal wealth by exploiting their people and their national wealth in collusion with the IMF and the World Bank, and international money lenders. It was the lack of democracy that has enabled these people to reduce Africa to its current status of Least Developed Continent which needs external assistance just to survive, in spite of its enormous natural resources and hard-working people. All the gains that have been achieved by the sweat and efforts of the people in the last three decades of independence have gone to enrich our foreign "trading partners" and a tiny minority of local elites, while at the same time reducing Africa from a surplus food producing continent to one condemned to perennial famine and mass starvation.

The other question is: What do Africans make of this new posture of the born-again democrats? Well, the consensus among many Africans is that this posture by the West is really strategic, and has nothing to do with humanitarian concern for African people. Imperialism, according to this view, is alive and kicking, and, since the "cold war has been won", it is seeking new allies and a rearrangement of forces necessary for the "new world order". The current, "post-Yalta" trend in international situation seems to suggest the emergence of a new "pattern" with a scenario which will make it necessary to relegate the former Soviet bloc to the status of a "third world" proper, in competition with the newly industrialising countries (NICs) of South East Asia, and possibly India. For at least two of three decades to come these countries are likely to constitute a third tier of the world capitalist order, whose industries, based on cheap labour will produce for the consumption and production needs of the "post industrial West", dominated by US/Japan/Germany (or more properly by the dominance of the Dollar, the Yen and the Mark) which will gain the status of the "first" world, competing among themselves for the domination of Europe and possibly China, who together will constitute the "second" world. Africa, according to this scenario, and most of the rest of Asia, the Middle-east, and large parts of Latin America, are to remain a "democratic" source of cheap energy and primary raw materials, attaining the new status of "fourth" world, amenable to the whimsical dictates of the IMF and the World Bank, and a new type of "democratic" leadership who would be willing to sacrifice their national sovereignty and subject their people to massive exploitation by foreign capital in the name of "free market" principle of comparative advantage.

The way to prevent this harrowing "new world order" from ever becoming a reality, according to this view, is for Africa to strictly observe the following "rules", as it were: First, do not allow yourself to be hoodwinked by "formal" democracy, but instead ensure that any democratic reform must be, what scholars call, "substantial" democracy; that is, an institutionalised democratic process, which, among other things, empowers the people not only to elect their rulers, at both central and local authority levels, but also to kick them out of office if they cease to work for people's needs.

Secondly, it is essential not to confuse democracy and free market necessarily to mean a "free market economy", as the advocates of the "new world order" would want us to do. All of Latin America, except Cuba, is operating on the basis of a free market economy, but they are far from being democratic. And, on the other hand, a planned economy is not necessarily a negation of democracy.

Thirdly, strive, step by step, to change the structure of the economy from its colonial orientation, which is the source of Africa's massive exploitation, to a truly national and independent economy. (There is already a model for this strategy of liberating and democratising the national economy away from the IMF's conditionality, and the World Bank's "structural adjustment programme", both of which are designed to perpetuate the colonial economy instead of liberating it).

Fourthly, there must be a free press. Free, that is, from the control of the media barons, both local and foreign. A free press is the best guarding of people's democratic rights. Ideally, it should be owned by the people either as co-operatives, trade unions, local popular authorities, or by a combination of the press technicians, journalists and private financier(s), and democratically controlled. Fifthly, establish as a matter of top priority, popular institutions against human rights violations, as well as instruments for seeking redress.

These "rules" are only tentative and a lot more work needs to be done by way of research and case by case study. It is in order to facilitate this kind of work that the International Institute for Democracy and Human Rights in Africa has been established in London in collaboration with popular democratic movements in Africa[3]. Its purpose is twofold: To promote genuine democratic struggles where these are already in motion; and to help devise sound development strategies for the newly won democracies in order to put them on a sound and relevant development track. All well-meaning people and democrats are welcome to contribute their views and visions on this worthy cause.

National Liberation

Eritrea: its present is the remote future of others
Africa Events, October 1985

What the Ethiopian regime refers to as "bandits" are in fact Eritrean revolutionaries who have liberated their country - more than 80% of it - by means of armed struggle. I have just spent two weeks in the liberated areas, including the recently captured and recaptured town of Barentu. And I am not ashamed to admit that I have been overwhelmed by what I saw. Living, working and eating with these staunch revolutionaries I am tempted to echo the famous quote: "I have seen the future - of Africa - and it works"[1].

This is not an easy statement to make after so many political, social and economic shocks that we went through in post-independence Africa. Who can be enthusiastic in the midst of the political chaos of military coups and counter-coups and the economic pains of bankrupted and heavily indebted nations? Of the humiliating and degrading experiences of dependence on the very imperialism that cost Africa lives and hardships to be rid of? Of the pathetic calls of despair for a dream-world of failed politicians known as the New International Economic Order? But experiences with liberated Eritreans give you confidence in the capacity of the African masses to take history in their own hands during the challenging journey from the realm of necessity to the realm of freedom.

Where in Africa today would you see doctors, engineers, mechanics, technicians, all of world standards, inspired enough to flock back home enthusiastically from foreign universities and institutions of learning to serve their country - without pay? Where in Africa would you see a mature community minus the pompous party functionaries, insensitive bureaucrats and over-indulged diplomats? In short, it is a unique experience of the absence of the exploited or exploiters, of true equality between man and woman, experience of witnessing normal human beings free from hang-ups, engaged in an honourable stuggle to liberate the rest of their country on the basis of self-reliance and independent of external power.

This armed struggle is the longest in Africa, now in its 25th year. It is the most ignored by the African states who conveniently regard it as an "internal affair" of Ethiopia in which no member of the OAU can "interfere"; it has been protected from international scrutiny by the notorious resolution of the 1964 OAU Summit in Cairo which ensured a permanently divided Africa by recognising the boundaries inherited from colonialism as intangible and sacrosanct. Although Tanzania, the architect of this resolution which guarantees and rationalises Africa's balkanisation, did not feel bound by it when she, together with Zambia and other countries, decided to recognise Biafra it 1969, allegedly after pressure from the Vatican.

However, the same resolution should in fact strengthen the ease for recognition of Eritrea for the simple reason that its boundaries were set by the Italian colonialists in 1889 and the Eritrean nation as we know it today evolved within those same boundaries They are the very boundaries which separate it from Ethiopia. But unfortunately, one of the saddest shortcomings of the OAU is that its members are bound by the last century imperialist-induced norms of classical international law which ignores peoples and their rights and deals only with relations between states, and consequently, in the myopic eyes of the OAU, Eritreans do not exist.

Sooner or later, though, the world will have to acknowledge that the Eritrean question is not a secessionist struggle; it is a liberation struggle against Ethiopian colonialism as authentic as the Namibian struggle against South Africa, the only difference being that Ethiopia is a Third World colonial power and a member of the OAU and South Africa is neither.

Namibia was a German colony and was given to South Africa to administer after the defeat of the Germans in the first World War. Eritrea was an Italian colony and was given to Imperial Ethiopia to administer after the defeat of the Italians in the Second World War. And after a brief period of UN imposed "federation" with Ethiopia, the Emperor of that Imperial country decided unilaterally to annex Eritrea and made it part of his empire on 14 November 1962. In the proclamation to this effect, the Emperor ordered that "... Eritrea, which continues to constitute an integral part of the Empire of Ethiopia, is hereby wholly integrated into the unitary system of administration of Our Empire..." and that Eritrea would thus be governed by the feudal Emperor and his feudal laws of the Empire.

Annexation

The Emperor's argument for his singularly predatory act, apart from fictitious claim to history, was that Ethiopia was a landlocked country which needed an outlet to the sea and a "front gate to the world". This argument is as untenable as, for instance, Malawi annexing Mozambique on the pretext that it needs an outlet to the sea. The Emperor, however, got away with it because he had powerful supporters at the UN. The western powers, with whom the Emperor had allied himself, were interested in Ethiopia's occupation of Eritrea. John Foster Dulles, the outspoken US Secretary of State, way back in 1952, addressing the UN Security Council had this to say: "From the point of view of justice, the opinions of the Eritrean people must receive consideration. Nevertheless, the strategic interest of the United States in the Red Sea basin and consideration of security and world peace make it necessary that the country had to be linked with our ally, Ethiopia."

At the time of annexation in 1962, there were hectic diplomatic moves and arm-twisting going on among independent African Countries in the effort to establish what later became the Organisation of African Unity. The tug-of-war was between the 'Casablanca Group' and the 'Monrovia Group', the first radical, the second conservative. The radicals, headed by Nkrumah, were ready to go to any length to get the organisation set up, while the conservatives were hesitant and slow moving. The Emperor cunningly made himself indispensable by taking a neutral position between the two groups. He mediated between them and even offered Addis Ababa as the centre for the first summit and eventual headquarters of the organisation. He at once became the respected father-figure and it was thus bad manners and undiplomatic to raise awkward questions about his Empire. The radicals, traditionally fighters against injustice in Africa and elsewhere, conveniently overlooked the Eritrean issue for the greater cause of African unity.

The Emperor took advantage of this diplomatic retreat by the radicals and of the fact that, as the host of the first summit, he chaired the conference and from his vantage position, he shrewdly inserted in the newly-drafted Charter the clause for "non-interference in the internal affairs of a member state." Henceforth, Eritrea became an internal affair of Ethiopia, whatever the three-and-a half million Eritreans think about it.

Most of the countries which voted to perpetuate this injustice knew nothing about the history of the Eritrean people and cared less. But by this time, however, the Eritreans had already taken up arms to defend their inalienable right to self-determination, OAU or no OAU.

In this determination, they realised that they would have to depend entirely on their own effort and ingenuity, having been abandoned by both the UN and the OAU. They proceeded to create "facts" to bring forth the Eritrean reality through intensified armed struggle. This was no easy task considering the military might of Imperial Ethiopia - it was being backed militarily by the US which made sure that their client state was one of the best equipped in Africa.

Furthermore, soon after his diplomatic victory at the first OAU Summit in 1963, the Emperor in that same year turned to Israel for additional military assistance which included training of their predatory army. One of the cadres to benefit from this training was of course Mengistu Haile Mariam, the present leader of Ethiopia. The card which the Emperor played to win Israeli support was the "Arab menace": that the Arab states were out to dismember Ethiopia; that the Eritrean struggle was in fact only a terrorist activity engineered by a handful of bandits paid for by Arab reactionary rulers; and that His Imperial Majesty was ready to offer a rear-base for the Israeli army in their fight against Egypt and other Arab States and so on.

To the Americans and the West, the cunning little Emperor presented the Eritrean struggle as a communist-instigated rebellion whose purpose was to advance Soviet influence and hegemony in the Horn of Africa. The Soviet Union at that time did indeed support the Eritrean struggle, but not, as we understood it then, to advance her influence but to abide by the Leninist major principle of upholding the "right to self-determination of the colonised people up to and including secession." The Emperor got his unlimited military ware from the US on the basis of this Soviet card. But the Eritreans made it quite clear at the time that although they enjoyed Soviet moral, diplomatic and material support, and that they did share socialist aspirations, they were not fighting the Emperor in order to bring in the Soviets or anybody else. States have permanent interests, never permanent friends or enemies.

History has proved them right. As soon as His Imperial Majesty was overthrown in Ethiopia and the army took over, the Soviets immediately shifted their allegiance to the new regime. When Mengistu emerged as the leader of the so-called "military left", after eliminating the anti-imperialist forces such as EPRP and progressive trade union leaders, and allied himself with the Soviet Union and declared himself the leader of a Marxist-Leninist military vanguard, the socialist camp began to regard the Eritrean revolution as "objectively reactionary" (in the famous Stalinist principle) because it opposed Mengistu who was anti-imperialist. And the Soviet Union now took over as the supplier of unlimited arms and ammunition in place of the US and Israel.

Like emperor, like heir

Many sympathisers of the Mengistu take-over, including many progressive Ethiopians, had hoped that he would now take advantage of the favourable political situation to resolve the Eritrean question politically rather than militarily. That as a Marxist-Leninist, he would accept it as a colonial question first of all, and secondly handle it on the principle of the right to self-determination.

He, of course, did neither. Instead, he first silenced all progressive Ethiopians and the traditional anti-imperialist elements, consolidated himself firmly in power and then he not only refused to seek political solution to the problem, he actually denied the existence of the Eritrean problem. Like the Emperor before him, he defined the Eritrean struggle merely as a "group of dissidents willing to sell out the interests of the Eritrean people to the highest bidder."

With this definition and Soviet backing, Mengistu intensified the military option, the war of conquest, and proved himself to be more ruthless than the Emperor himself. His army now with the combined resources of both the US and the Soviet Union at its disposal, he was certain he would march to victory over the "bandits" in a matter of months if not weeks. A Soviet-Ethiopian offensive of 1978 on Asmara and other major towns (from which the Eritrean fighters chose to withdraw strategically) gave Mengistu a false hope to confirm his prediction of easy victory.

So, what has happened to the prediction? A string of disasters, the major one being the Red Star offensive of 1981 in which the Ethiopian army suffered almost unbearable losses in equipment which went to strengthen the Eritrean arsenal. From then on, the Eritreans have been scoring spectacular victories - the blowing up of 33 planes at Asmara airport, the conquest of Tessane; the battles of Toghombia and Molki and Sahel in which the Ethiopian deputy commander Col. Girmma Tessema was captured together with 3000 soldiers. The most spectacular victory, however, was the capture of Barentu on 7 July this year. This was a well fortified garrison which had never been occupied by the Eritreans, even at the height of their near-total domination of Eritrea prior to 1978.

Its capture has confirmed the total isolation of the Ethiopian army even in the still occupied Eritrea. This spectacular Eritrean offensive which lasted only 19 hours was organised and mobilised for weeks in the area but not a word escaped to the Ethiopian intelligence and they were caught completely by surprise at considerable cost in men and material. In mid-August, however, the Ethiopians recaptured it after the withdrawal of the Eritrean combatants.

Armed at prayer

All these military and civil activities have afforded the Eritreans enormous experience in every field - social, economic, political, military and so on and has given them a lot of confidence. This sense of being on top of things is visible throughout the liberated areas, whether in factories, in hospitals, in laboratories. It is visible among the nomads, the peasants and the urban dwellers. For instance, when the daily Ethiopian MIG sorties thunder overhead, people go about their daily routine unruffled. I'll never forget the sight of some Muslim nomads saying their evening prayer with their submachine guns besides them. When the Ethiopian MIGs threateningly passed overhead, the Eritreans continued with their prayers, quite in the open, as if nothing was happening.

This calm confidence goes on in spite of ruthless air raids on civilians. Arriving at refugee camp H.50 at Elmat ten hours after it was bombarded with napalm, the whole atmosphere was reeking of the lethal bombs as 70-year old Meksa Karar Mohamed Satak was put on a stretcher crying in agony with both her legs broken. Others had already been taken to the hospital with more serious injuries. But in all of them, the injured and the hungry, there was a look of determination and confidence. This is the most important asset which will ensure their eventual victory.

It is clear that even with the current massive counter offensive by the Ethiopians, with the most sophisticated Soviet weaponry, this issue cannot be won by military force. The Aniericans have learnt this lesson in Vietnam with bitter memories. And Mengistu and his Soviet backers must face the obvious fact that the solution to the problem can only be found through political means, not by war. If Mengistu is a genuine revolutionary as he claims to be, he must accept the fact that the Eritrean question is a colonial question, a national question and its solution is through acknowledging the revolutionary principle of the "right to self-determination up to and including secession." The Eritreans have already proved that they cannot be ruled by force. Remember the old revolutionary dictum: No country can be free if it denies the freedom of others.

A costly war

The war is already costing his regime more than it can earn. One MIG sortie costs the Ethiopian people $13,000 and the 20 sorties or so a day which patrol, harass and bomb Eritrean nomads and peasants is costing them more than a quarter million US dollars per day. And this is only one and least costly item of the war. The cost of keeping more than five divisions of unproductive soldiers with advanced and sophisticated weapons in an unwinnable war is astronomical. For a country in which millions of its people are permanently threatened with starvation, the war option verges on the criminal. The only beneficiaries in this war are the arms suppliers.

If Mengistu continues with his dream victory, Africa must not go along with it. Individual African states, as well as the OAU, must rethink their position on the issue. The Eritreans have already created facts and reality more solidly and permanently than ever before, and we must never allow ourselves to be bamboozled again as we were by His Imperial Majesty in 1963. That year it was an African Imperial stance that caught us; this time it is a "proletarian revolutionary" stance that is presented to us to achieve the same colonial objective. We must be wise and reject both. **Eritrea must be free**, should be Africa's slogan which corresponds with Africa's reality.

The Future That Works
Africa Events, November 1985

They cleave to life most tenaciously those prone to lose it any time. Eritreans do so to the last woman and man. They do it creatively. And given the odds, they do it daringly. Eritrea is a nation at war. It has been at war for the last quarter century. And has known virtually no peace under either Africa's arch-emperor Haile Selassie or under his super-lumpen successor Mengistu Haile Mariam. Its range of external enemies includes both ideological extremes - from the Soviet Union to the United States. Sometimes together, sometimes separately, the weaponry of both these superpowers have sought to pound Eritreans to extinction. And ubiquitous Israel has always stood by to lend a helpful surrogate's hand, completing the siege and compounding the odds. But after every round of sorties, Eritrea has risen up, robust and defiant. Testifying to peace-ridden Africa that peace is no alibi for backwardness aud lethargic resignation to outsiders' dictates.

Orotta - to use the hackneyed phrase - is a model town amongst Eritrea's many model towns. It lies in the north, 200 miles from the Red Sea and about 100 miles from the Sudanese border. One reaches it by a circuitous route that's a concession to war and the policy of neighbours letting neighbours live.

The visit coincided with torrential downpours of rain. Rivers overflooded as a result. They were temperamental. Overwhelmingly disruptive for one hour and gone the next - very much like the Dodoma rivers in dustbowl Tanzania in their spasmodic fury aud their subsidence.

We spent the night on high ground besides the river bank, waiting for the flood to ebb away. It was one of the few nights that I will remember for its Animal Farm quality - without the pigs! We went to sleep to the groans of goats, the cluck-cluck of hens, the wailing of dogs and the vigilant munching of camels.

In the morning the rivers were as turbulent as ever.

Hence a captured Soviet truck replayed the old legend of Noah's Ark and the Floods. It ferried us across - all of us God's creatures, men and mammals, and man's crafts. The Customs and Immigration checks were normal. Normal that is because they are untainted with dash-demanding officials as is the case elsewhere where dashing is customary.

Past the gates, past the desultory nomads, past the picturesque graveyards lie the POW's camps. They run along 5-6 kms. Captured Ethiopian soldiers are held there. One had a battle hetween curiosity and principles A visit to the camps was suggested but firmly and courteously declined. A visit to a murderers' den waging an unjust war was just unthinkable.

Under a variety of camouflage, life went on as it should. Petrol stations and auto- repair garages dotted the way. The amazing thing is that in Eritrea life begins when dusk sets in. Daylight makes them vulnerable to lethal air attacks.

It was night when Orotta came into view. Its environs had begun to buzz with activity. Floodlights flared, as heavy road making equipment trundled out to working sites on mountain sides, scooping, levelling, gravelling desparately needed, all-the-year round roads.

The guest house that awaited us was Alice-in-wonderland, having been carved out of the flanks of a hill, and supplied with all modern comforts and facilities. To the Eritreans' credit everything worked efficiently and one did not need to go to bed prayerfully that the morrow may bring working taps in the bathroom and responsive flush in the toilet. The hotel foyer was full of international personages - some brought by aid agencies, some journalists, and some just hooked to the place out of altruism and the thrill of creating something viable out of so much man-made debris.

The hospital complex lay down the valley spread over 6kms - easily the most extensive hospital in the world, and the most all-purpose. Eritreans have here all manner of physicians. Surgeons operate the most complicated cases in movable theatres. They can be shifted to an emergency location almost at will, and can be moved out of harm's way at the hoot of the siren.

Such is the Eritreans' versatility that even containers have been put to productive use. Instead of ferrying goods, in Eritrea containers serve as laboratories, complete with windows, doors, plumbing and electricity supply.

Nerayo Tekle Michael is not a character out of a thousand-and-one nights fable. Of medium height, slightly on the plump side, easily tipping the scales at 160 pounds, Nerayo is packed with the energy required for the demanding job of Eritrea's public health co-ordinator.

Nerayo had a lucrative and prestigious job as a leading paediatrician in Addis Ababa, but the pull of the homeland at war proved irresistible to him.

It was a fraught homecoming. The professional order awaiting him was tall. The colonial heritage in the field of health was burdensome, For one thing it was urban oriented. Nomads and rural dwellers were completely outside its range.

In the wake of the 1978 offensive, as war casualties piled up, the exodus of trained doctors swelled. Foreign specialists and general practitioners cut and run and the indigenes followed suit.

Nerayo had to develop a strategy that would not only cope with Eritrea's myriad health problems and needs, but also prevent an outbreak of ills well beyond his nation's meagre resources..

His team and himself came up with what can roughly be described as a four-point assault:

* Barefoot doctors.
* Universal health education that took in city and rural dwellers without forgetting the nomads.
* Mobile clinics that could surive the ravages of war.
* Doctors and auxiliary staff that were at one with patients and fully equipped morally to withstand the strain of sustained hostilities.

A complement of 60 physicians and surgeons work with Nerayo. They tackle assignments as complicated as bypass surgery and treatment of napalmed victims.

Orotta health complex has its own indigenous pharmaceutical department. This produces a whole range of day-to-day medicines including anti-biotics The emphasis here is on sulphur-based rather than penicilin-derived antibiotics.

Skin-transplantation, plastic surgery, bone-setting are also part of the services rendered. Traditional bone-setters as much as traditional medicine complement modern expertise.

The disabled administer the rehabilitation clinic in Port Sudan which finishes off the health assembly line. There cripples who elsewhere may be given up for useless dependents are given a new confidence to deal with their changed circumstances and new techniques to overcome their phvsical disabilities. More important they are taught how to help others do the same.

Eritrea looks forward to universal primary health care for the entire liberation area come the next five years.

After Liberia, Eritrea is perhaps the only other nation on the continent which does not have its own currency. Its business community make do with Sudanese money as well as Ethiopian money. Otherwise it manages on a barter system exchanging equivalents.

Indeed the tatter or reward in kind has taken root so much that Eritrean officials take time to adapt when they go shopping abroad. Upon taking goods off super-market shelves they must always consciously remind themselves that they are not at home after all. For at home, the norm is long established that each will get according to his need, no matter his status. This institution caters for essentials only.

Human resources and skills are put to maximum use. and the old adage, a change is as good as a rest, translated to maximum productive result. Thus a driver for a week is a bare foot doctor for three days, a combatant for another week and a construction worker for another week. Eritrean cadres are motivated by only one commitment: give to society the best of your potential.

The Shadow of Iran - Apartheid Power can no longer control Black townships
Pacific News Service, 25 July 1985

South Africa's declaration of a State of Emergency can do nothing to control the black townships, now the focal point for black insurrection. Instead it is a sure indication that white rule has never been under greater threat than now.

Behind the State of Emergency is a plan to first encircle the black townships, then install a military administration and finally arrest all grassroots leaders.

It is, of course, possible to encircle the townships with tanks and machine guns, and even to cut off electricity and water. But the young people -- who are effectively leading their own struggle -- have already made provision for such eventualities, preparing for alternative supplies of essentials. Prolonged boycotts of white goods in some regions testify to the high level of their organization.

According to one recently-released black leader interviewed here, the young people in the insurrectionary townships have created a vast underground network of communications. Travel routes have been set up to work at night. Coded messages are relayed in many ways - through the playing of special songs and tapes, for instance.

The woman burned to death as an informer before the television cameras apparently identified one such song to the authorities. When police came into the township at night and sang the song, five youths appeared, believing it was a signal to gather. All five were shot down.

Nor can the township people become confused by a lack of leaders. As recent events have shown, as soon as one group of leaders is arrested, a new leadership takes over to maintain the momentum. This classic revolutionary tactic - absent in the major uprisings in Sharpeville in 1959 and in Soweto in 1976 - has baffled even the most seasoned white leaders.

In addition, South Africa cannot afford to keep the townships in a state of siege for long. It cuts off the black labour on which the whole system depends. Moreover, it frightens off investors because business cannot function under conditions of prolonged martial law.

Finally, the government simply does not have the requisite physical resources to sustain such extensive use of military force. South Africa must station a large part of its army on the borders of Mozambique, Botswana, Zimbabwe and Angola, and an even larger force in Namibia where SWAPO guerrillas are now on the offensive.

The situation will deteriorate further once the black labour unions join the township uprisings, as they almost certainly will, by declaring a general strike in the factories and mines, In that event, the tables will be turned, and it will be the white regime which will be in a state of siege.

One frightening prospect is that, although the uprisings are well organized and coordinated at the local level, there is no central, national direction. This could mean that spontaneous moves, if they continue, will get out of hand and lead to a horrible free-for-all racial conflagration.

The situation resembles that of Iran in 1978, when the entire repressive establishment collapsed as a result of spontaneous mass insurrection. But Khomeini did have a modicum of nationwide organization through the mosques.

And unlike Khomeini, Bishop Tutu, now an acknowledged spokesman of African people, denounces violence. For that reason, he can only mediate between contending forces; he cannot lead one against the other.

In the circumstances, the human cost is likely to be much higher and the uprising more protracted than in Iran.

It is this harrowing possibility that has prompted the EEC foreign ministers to demand the immediate dismantling of apartheid, especially its key elements - such as the pass laws, forced removals, and detention without trial. They have also demanded common citizenship for all South Africans, an immediate end to the state of emergency and unconditional release from prison of African National Congress leader Nelson Mandela and his colleagues.

European states, especially Britain, may have been moved - after so many years of pusillanimous neutrality - by humanitarianism, but they also have large economic stakes in South Africa, which are seriously threatened by the uprising.

It is likely that South Africa's leaders will release Mandela as soon as they can find a pretext which lets them avoid the appearance of yielding to the pressure of popular violence. In the last few months Mandela has emerged not only as a leader of the ANC but as a national leader. He may now be the key figure who will determine whether the situation is resolved in a relatively peaceful fashion or through bloody revolution.

Who are the good guys in Rwanda?
Pacific News Service, May 6 1994

The Western media have presented the Rwanda situation as a mindless bloodletting, with Hutus savagely massacring Tutsis merely out of tribal hate.

Now, as a rebel movement made up largely of Tutsis is on the verge of taking over the country, the United Nations and the Clinton administration are urging the dispatch of foreign troops to prevent an even greater bloodletting from occurring.

Yet the Rwandan emergency is far from being some primitive eruption of Africans unable to rule themselves. It is a political war rooted in 20 years of tyranny by a military regime backed by death squads. And any effort by U.N.- or U.S.-sponsored outside forces designed to thwart its overthrow in the name of saving civilian lives would in fact be a neocolonialist intervention aimed at propping up the status quo.

While depicted by the West as a spontaneous uprising, the so-called Tutsi rebels are actually members of a 20-year-old political opposition movement - the Rwandese Patriotic Front, which is the only organized and disciplined force committed to and capable of bringing peace and security to a country that has long known neither.

Originally made up of exiled Tutsis, the front leadership is now primarily Hutu, and the areas under its control (approximately two thirds of Rwanda) are characterized by ethnic harmony. Defectors from the Rwanda military regime, sickened by the ethnic carnage of recent weeks, have begun joining the front in droves.

Faced with the growing strength of the front following the April 6 plane crash that killed Major Gen. Juvenal Habyarimanan, the Rwanda regime sought to avert its downfall by inciting an interethnic war. But the subsequent slaughter of half a million Tutsis, far from being a race war, was guided throughout by one single political aim on the part of the military regime: to eliminate not only all opposition leaders, both Tutsi and Hutu, but an entire middle class - civil servants, businessmen, teachers, clergy - who could hold the country together under a new Rwandese Patriotic Front-led government. Today there is hardly a Tutsi still alive in the capital of Kigali.

Ironically, among the very powers now intent on rescuing the Rwandese from themselves are some who have armed and supported a military regime that tortured, raped, killed and forced into exile nearly 2 million Rwandese long before the recent carnage. Most notable of these is France, but also included are Belgium, Zaire, South Africa's former apartheid regime and Egypt. Cairo has long been suspicious of the RPF's links with Sudan which it regards as an enemy.

Only two days before the plane crash on April 6, the vice president of the Rwandese Patriotic Front, Patrick Mazimhaka, told the 7th Pan African Congress meeting in Kampala, Uganda, that the intention of the front was to restore peace and order in the country and to disarm the government's death squads. The meeting was attended by delegates from all over Africa who applauded the announcement.

In a country where the only political ideology has been that of promoting one ethnic group over another, the front promotes a vision of national unity that calls for the introduction of democracy, security for all people irrespective of their ethnicity, the abolition of the notorious passes based on ethnic identity, and the resettlement of Rwandese refugees living in exile.

As of now, the front's fighters are well on their way to total liberation of their country. The murderous militia are fleeing in disarray, some escaping to Tanzania as refugees. In those border areas with Tanzania where the front has consolidated its position, ensuring security, the flight of refugees has slowed down.

Surprisingly, instead of supporting this gradual return to stability, the U.N. High Commission for Refugees is reported to be calling for the front to "allow" more refugees to cross the border to Tanzania.

Even more surprising, U.N. Secretary General Boutros Boutros-Ghali is urging the Security Council to send in U.N. peacekeeping forces to "restore order." This is echoed belatedly by President Clinton with his offer to pay for African peacekeeping forces to do the job. It would be criminal and only further undermine the prestige of the United Nations were it to be seen as working toward reestablishing the status quo when the Rwandese themselves are well on the way to solving, once and for all, a 20-year problem of marauding death squads.

South Africa, April 1995 –
Do the fundamentals remain the same?
(Notes during a visit to South Africa)

The wage and welfare gap in South Africa is well known on a theoretical basis by most serious students of the South African situation. But no amount of reading and discussion can prepare one adequately for the reality on the ground. It is when confronted directly with this social and economic phenomenon in its geographic context that the full force of it strikes home.

The sheer scale of the poverty and the marginalisation of the poor in a society which displays often ostentatious wealth is mind boggling. South Africa is not a miracle in the making. It is a society in which much has changed but in which all the fundamentals remain the same.

The change - and it is one that should not be underestimated -has been in the deracialising of a deeply divided society. But the legacy of the racial divisions, most obvious in the widely segregated residential areas, perpetuates in fact what in law no longer exists.

This makes for a volatile social base. Especially because of the greater levels of confidence among the dispossessed resulting from the changes that have occurred. But these changes, combined with climatic factors, have also seen a huge influx of rural migrants into the segregated areas on the fringes of towns and cities.

The massive sprawl of shacks outside Cape Town provides perhaps the most graphic illustration of this phenomenon. It is a stark illustration of the magnitude of the problem and a warning to any government.

Only slightly less evident than these distortions to the social fabric of South Africa is the damage done to the economy by the system of apartheid. I would contend that this system contained many aspects which had more in common with feudalism than with modern, free enterprise capitalism.

The logic of the market dictates that capital be accumulated and invested to widen, deepen and make more efficient the economic base. Yet South Africa, a country with a long history of massive and profitable minerals extraction has a negligible manufacturing base. At the same time it has an extremely high level of expenditure on luxury items by the managerial elite.

Much accumulated capital has apparently been lavished on mansions, tennis courts, swimming pools and luxury items with high import content. This is counter-productive in terms of economic development.

To me, this is one of the obvious contradictions in this most powerful of African states. It is evidence of an attitude - a culture - which had, and has, much more in common with the attitudes of minor aristocracy in a feudal state than with a modem industrial society.

Talk of entrepreneurship is widespread, but the rhetoric fails to match the reality. Even by the standards they profess, most members of South Africa's still largely racially-based elite fail. Their attitudes amount to the antithesis of the free enterprise ethic.

That this managerial aristocracy is also still largely racially based merely complicates the problem. The vast mass of the poor are mainly black while the elite remains largely white.

Any government which continues to support this state of affairs will inevitably incur the wrath of the vast mass of the poor and dispossessed. This will have racial overtones, but it will fundamentally be a matter of the have-nots rising up against the haves.

In such a situation, subtle reforms and tinkering with the system will not be enough. South Africa is a case for radical policies. Anything less will merely perpetuate and even exacerbate the problems.

But such answers and probable or possible solutions should not be dictated from outside. It is not for self-styled experts, be they individuals or the representatives of nation states or international institutions such as the International Monetary Fund, to provide direction.

Many will, of course, take it upon themselves to spell out answers for South Africa. And some, such as the IMF, may eventually be in the position to be able to exert pressure to gain compliance with the courses of action they have deemed appropriate. On the basis of African experience, this would be a sad day for South Africa. At the moment the country is still able to preserve - if it wishes - a high degree of independence from such international meddling.

But time is running out. President Nelson Mandela said last month that there would be visible development over the coming year. There will need to be concrete evidence of redistribution sooner rather than later. But it is difficult to see how this will be possible without much more radical and decisive steps than have so far been taken.

MARXIST THEORY

Introduction to the 'University of Dar es Salaam Debate on Class, State & Imperialism'

Here is a vigorous, sometimes too vigorous, discussion on what are probably the most burning questions of the day - imperialism, finance capital, monopoly capitalism, neo-colonialism, and classes in the neocolonies. For the most part these questions have either been ignored in Africa or subjected to a rather simplistic and therefore misleading investigation by the opinion leaders who have themselves already developed vested interests in neo-colonialism and the status quo. For let it be said at once that the advocates of "third worldism" have now become shameless apologists of neocolonialism, which is a direct offspring of the dominance of finance capital in the entire capitalist world, developed and underdeveloped.

It is heartening that this excellent discussion by some of the finest brains in East Africa should have occurred at this moment when all of us need a clearer understanding of what is taking place under our very noses. Significant changes in our societies are occurring now and it needs a clear analysis which subjects them to serious scrutiny in order to bring out into the open their underlying causes and tendencies.

This is what these essays have succeeded in doing. Social change, like changes in the human body, occur slowly and unseen until they reach their maturity and reveal themselves with a bang. This maturation is known as the aggregate of objective conditions or, to use modern Marxist parlance, the conjuncture. Marxism is first of all about understanding these changes by observing them in their nascent form to prepare ourselves for organising subjective initiative to coincide with the *conjuncture*, for the second task of Marxism is to change the world.

These essays are showing us these invisible changes through a penetrating analysis employing the well-tried and tested methodology of dialectical and historical materialism. This is the most reliable way of uncovering the hidden links that tie together the seemingly unrelated phenomena and thereby helps us to see reality as it exists in the real world. Dialectical materialism which was first discovered and utilized by Marx and Engels in their investigations and studies has proved itself to be the only philosophy that answered all the questions which troubled orthodox philosophy throughout history, especially the most fundamental and critical question: what is the law of the motion and development of the universe? The correct answer to this question has developed into the Marxist philosophy.

This philosophy has discovered the most cardinal law, which guides all objective life; i.e., the law of the unity of opposites. According to this universal law, all objective things have two opposite tendencies, which are independent, and at the same time struggle against each other. This unity and struggle determines the life of things and pushes their development forward. This law, consequently, is the Marxist world outlook as well as methodology. Marx himself made all his important discoveries by utilizing this methodology. In discussing these important discoveries, such as the law of the *tendency for the rate of profit to fall*, Marx pointed out "this inner and necessary connection between two seeming contradictions."

As a *world outlook*, this philosophy therefore regards all things as the unity of opposites in accordance with the law of self-movement and development of objective things.

As a *methodology* it uses this law as the dialectical method of analysis in order to *know* and *change* the world.

On the basis of this law, Marxism developed the theory of the evolution of classes through struggle and leaps. It showed the evolution of the working class from being a class in-itself, i.e., the original identity of the hidden, underdeveloped conditions within things, to that of a class-for-itself, i.e., the coming into the open of the distinction and separation of these hidden and latent elements which is the starting point of their struggle and contradiction.

Prior to Marx, the basis of philosophy was the formal logical method but this proved to be totally inadequate and unsatisfactory as a way of understanding the real world. As a rule, we formulate our language logically but the real, objective world does not behave logically. This important fact was overlooked, sometimes deliberately, by orthodox philosophy and resulted in confusing *language* with *reality*. Herein lies their problem of understanding the world clearly. This is the first point to remember in reading these essays.

The second point worth remembering is that as Marxism sees process and development through the struggle of opposites and contradictory forces it traces decisive historical conflicts and changes to roots in the mode of production. These are known as the class struggles. Behind these struggles lie the essential economic relations. These are the most important elements which are isolated and analysed through abstraction. Earlier philosophers could not see the economic basis of contradictions and they resorted to logical illusions of the illogical world.

Thus, contradictions, class struggle, modes of production, the economic base and its superstructure are the stuff of Marxist investigation and analysis. These are the substance of the essays contained in this volume.

The theme of the essays can probably be broken down to four main subthemes: classes in the neocolonies; imperialism and the national question; the relationship between the economic base and the superstructure; and neocolonialism.

In an introduction of this nature, it is impossible to deal with each of the points raised or with each writer's position. To attempt to do that will require a whole new book. Thus, only major issues will be dealt with, those which are likely to be of more practical value in our on-going struggle.

Classes in Neo-Colonies

There seems to be some misunderstanding on the question of the national bourgeoisie. One writer argues that there is no national bourgeoisie in neocolonies because under the imperialist world order they cannot accomplish the national bourgeois revolution due to the dominance of monopoly capital and their subservience to it. Here the argument confuses the existence of the national bourgeoisie with its capacity to lead or accomplish national bourgeois revolution.

That they exist there is no doubt. Their capital is "national" in the sense that it has been accumulated within the neocolony concerned and it continued to appropriate surplus value generated by the workers under its employment, e.g., small soap manufacturers, etc.

Distinction must be made between these small (not petty) and the big bourgeoisie. The latter, like Madhvanis in East Africa, of course, derive the capital from, and are therefore linked and tied to, imperialist finance capital. The small bourgeoisie has contradictions with imperialism because it impedes its expansion. The big bourgeoisie on the other hand is in harmony with imperialism because it is its final recourse. But neither of them can accomplish the national bourgeois revolution because, in the former case, it functions in the wrong historical epoch, and in the latter case it is subservient to imperialist finance capital and consequently it cannot revolt against itself. Historically, the bourgeoisie is a dying force.

Our small national bourgeoisie is not the same class as the petty bourgeoisie because of their respective position in production, and this position is not determined by wealth. A petty-bourgeois, say a successful auctioneer, may be wealthier than a small manufacturer but because of his position in production i.e. appropriating no direct surplus value, the former will still remain petty-bourgeois and the latter full bourgeois. Wealth is not a Marxist criterion of class.

Again, it is important to distinguish between the existence of the national bourgeoisie and the *national capital* in the neo-colonies. National capital is the capital which constitutes the basis of the political economy of a country. In the neocolony this capital, through loans, grants, aid, foreign investments, etc. is a part of imperialist finance capital and to that extent it is not national.

If, say, a national marketing board or a milling corporation borrows from the World Bank to purchase agricultural commodities from the peasants, the board or the corporation becomes an agent of imperialist finance capital by introducing it into the country

The entire business operations of the board or corporation are thus subjected to finance capital. It appropriates surplus value in milling, ginning, textile mills, etc. on behalf of finance capital and it plunders peasants commodities through "exchange" on behalf of that same capital. This capital is not national; it is a part of the imperialist finance capital.

Our small national bourgeois, on the other hand, can conduct his business with or without recourse to this capital. An excolony which cuts off links with the capitalist world order, as in North Korea, China, or Vietnam, can still have a role for its national bourgeoisie although it cannot play a leading revolutionary one as did its counterpart before the October Revolution. Its non-revolutionary role in this case is not due to its being subservient to the imperialist finance capital but because this is no longer the epoch of the bourgeoisie; this is the epoch of the proletariat.

There are thus two types of the national bourgeoisie: the small one, which generates and accumulates capital without recourse to finance capital; and the big bourgeoisie whose capital is part of imperialist finance capital. This bourgeoisie must not be confused with the comprador capitalist who is exclusively in the service of, and an agent for imperialist finance capital and cannot survive after cutting off links with imperialism.

Analysis of classes in the neocolonies is one of the most difficult studies in Marxism and it is thus no accident that most of the discussions in these essays are centred on the subject. African countries were annexed to European capitalist economy and they have evolved in a specific, historically determined way, in a definite mode of production which serves external interests.

Their economies have been penetrated by external capital from metropolitan economies and they suffer the pernicious subordination to those markets which siphon off their economic surpluses leaving hardly anything for internal accumulation. In a normal, noncolonial development, accumulation of capital leads to a situation where one class becomes economically dominant and constitutes the "civil society". Its economic strength leads it naturally, by either revolution or stealth, to take over the reins of power, i.e. the state. At this stage it constitutes the "political society", or the superstructure (This is not the "civil society" and the "political society" of John Locke)

In other words, the social organization evolving directly out of production and commerce forms the basis of the state and its ideology. They establish institutions for the mutual guarantee of their property and interests, and for further facilitating and strengthening their economic dominance, in this instance the economic base is said to be determining the superstructure.

In colonized countries, this evolution did not take place because the dominant economic force remained the colonial power, and the economies remained only as extensions of the metropolitan economies. The normal development of classes was interrupted and economic groupings gravitated towards metropolitan interests. Our history ceased to be national history; we became part of bourgeois world history.

When independence came, those who took over state power from the colonialists were the intellectuals of mostly peasant origin - son of a chief, of a parish pastor, of a rural school teacher, of a successful rich peasant - and their economic and social base, i.e., class origin, is consequently peasant. How then does this ruling stratum constitute a class independent of the peasantry? Obviously, there is a problem here.

In countries where the land is privately owned and the peasants are already involved in commercial, or commodity production class struggle develops between the peasants and the landlords. The peasants are forced to pay in cash or in kind for the use of the means of production - the land - which has been appropriated by the landlord. Here we can see the essential but conflicting economic relations between the peasant and the landlord, the latter exploiting the former through his ownership of the means of production.

In the least developed countries where the vast majority of the peasants are not involved in commodity production and have not yet developed independent class interest the struggle may appear in individual form. For the vast majority the struggle is against nature because the peasants are still in the "realm of necessity." The struggle here is for survival and not yet for conflicting commercial, i.e. economic interests. Where the land is communally owned, even if the peasants have advanced sufficiently to be involved in commodity production, their struggle will not be over the means of production because the landlord class does not exist. In this situation, their struggle will take a different form. It will be a struggle against the forces that intercept and deny them the realization of the full return for their toil-the middlemen i.e. produce merchants, the money lenders, marketing boards, marketing cooperatives and so on. Again, we see here conflicting economic relations between the peasant and the middlemen, the latter plundering the former through a predatory relationship.

In both of these economic relations, the ultimate beneficiary is imperialist finance capital. However, some local groupings who facilitate this operation also benefit. These include, in addition to the national bourgeoisie, state bureaucrats, managers of private and state economic institutions, the emerging millionaires who take advantage of the economic chaos to enrich themselves, and so on. How do we classify these groups?

Some comrades in these essays, Shivji, for instance, suggest that this is in fact a new class and it is formed from the state level downward; they first take over state power and then develop an economic base through their control of economic enterprises, banks, corporations, whether private or public, and the comrades call these the "bureaucratic bourgeoisie".

Other comrades, Nabudere and others, reject this proposition and say that since these managers of neocolonies are nothing but agents of imperialist finance capital they cannot constitute an independent class, and that the economically dominant class still remains the world bourgeoisie. Here again the question arises: can there be an international ruling class, a class outside the nation-state?

There are difficulties in accepting either of these propositions. To accept the first one is to accept the logical rather than dialectical standpoint. We have seen above that classes are first formed at the economic level, the "civil society", before they reach the state level. To assume otherwise is to put Marxism upside down. We shall return to this problem when we discuss the relationship between the economic base and the superstructure.

The second proposition is also difficult to accept. The proletariat cannot lead the revolution against an unseen, abstract "international ruling class." It must have an identifiable, local and existing class to marshal its forces against.

Imperialism and The National Question

On this extremely important subject too, there seems to be some misunderstanding. Do our countries constitute a nation in the Marxian sense? Stalin's famous definition of a nation is that a nation is a "historically constituted, stable community of people, formed on the basis of a common language, territory, economic life, and psychological make-up manifested in a common culture."

For historically determined reasons African nationalism comprises more than the above definition. In Asia there is no Asian nationalism: there is Chinese nationalism, Vietnamese, Japanese, Indian, Iranian nationalism, etc. There is no European nationalism either, only French, British, German, etc. In the US there are nationalisms within the artificial US nationalism.

In Africa, on the other hand, there is no Nigerian, Kenyan, or Tanzanian nationalism; they are subordinated to the stronger and more overriding one-African nationalism.

The reason is clear. Unlike any other continent, an African wherever he or she may be is categorized by his or her Africanness, his or her colour. This peculiarity has not been introduced by the Africans themselves but it has been imposed on them by the long and terrible recent history of slavery, the color-bar, segregation and now *apartheid*. It is part of an African's consciousness, his psychology, and his identity. We constitute a "nation" not by territory or common language but by our physical characteristics. That is why, unlike Pan-Helenism, Pan-Slavakism before it, Pan-Africanism has a much stronger appeal to all black people of African descent the world over.

The discussion on the subject in these essays is about the economies and politics of separate nation-states and consequently it is not comprehensive enough to include the currently most burning question of African nationalism. Practically all the contributors of these essays seem to be aware of this question but none seems to be prepared to discuss it at length. The reason is obvious: Marxist politics is about the class struggle; its economics is about social relations of production; there is no room for nationalism. The national question is discussed as a part of the general problem of the proletarian revolution, as a part of the problem of the dictatorship of the proletariat. Herein lies the difficulty which Marxists are confronted with in dealing with the phenomenon of African nationalism.

Some comrades, Nabudere and others, argue that since our countries are dominated by imperialist finance capital they do not constitute separate political economies independent of imperialism. Consequently, our struggle is essentially an anti-imperialist struggle and not exclusively a class struggle confined to each country or "nation". It is a struggle by the whole people against "national oppression". Our "national" bourgeoisie, or whatever we call it, is also oppressed by imperialism and therefore has the chance to join the popular united front against imperialism in the period of the "new democratic revolution."

The opposing comrades, Mamdani *et al*, argue that although imperialism is the main enemy it remains an external force and we must first identify the internal force which oppresses the people, on its own behalf and on behalf of the external imperialism; otherwise we shall be disarming the working class ideologically and allow their oppressors to shelter in the camp of the people.

Here we see nationalism as the preponderant consideration in the first case and the class struggle within a nation in the second.

Current developments in Africa show one interesting characteristic. Whereas African Marxist intellectuals tend to be reluctant to categorize fellow-Africans as the enemy, the new generation of African working class tends to be less so inhibited. The reason is that in general the intellectuals come from the same stratum as those who now comprise the "ruling class", whether these are in politics or business. They share the same background, they went to the same schools, and they shared the same passion against colonialism and racial oppression, and so on. It is inconceivable for the intellectuals to think of them as their enemies, until, perhaps, when they send them to detention camps or subject them to personal or political humiliation.

The gradually emerging African working class and the ubiquitous lumpen proletariat, especially the younger generation who have no direct experience of colonial oppression, although they are constantly reminded about it by the political leaders-in schools, party meetings, etc. who desperately wish to establish their legitimacy, appraise their situation differently.

It is true that they are not as articulate as the intellectuals but they express their disenchantment with their rulers by other means-through action. While their industrial action is still at the level of "economism", being still a class-in-itself, their enthusiastic response to the Master Sergeant Does and Lt. Rawlings speaks louder than words.

In other words it is difficult for an African intellectual to be objective on this question and the only valid test as to what is primary in our circumstances between anti-imperialism and class antagonism is through the inarticulate expression of the working class, and to some extent, the poor peasants, and by the observations of those not directly involved in this nationalism.

In discussing this question in the essays, some ambiguity has crept in which needs to be clarified. This is in connection with the definition of the "New Democratic Revolution". One gets the impression that some comrades consider any form of a united front as new democratic, provided it is anti-imperialist. To clarify this question to the general reader we should bear the following in mind:

New Democracy

(a) The establishment of the New Democracy does not come prior to but after a successful socialist revolution.

(b) New Democracy is not any kind of united front; it is of a specific kind. It is a united front in which the proletariat has already led a successful socialist revolution, smashed the oppressive state machine, and established its own democratic dictatorship in alliance with other oppressed classes and "nationalities" or "national minorities." This is a prelude to and a first step towards the dictatorship of the proletariat.

(c) New Democracy is a necessary transitional phase only in countries where the productive forces have not been fully developed and the existing relations of production have not yet become a fetter to their development. In other words, in advanced capitalist countries there is no need for New Democracy phase after the socialist revolution.

Anti-Imperialist United Front

(a) The anti-imperialist united front is not the same thing as New Democracy.

(b) This united front must be under the leadership of the proletarian party otherwise it cannot be revolutionary.

(c) It is anti-imperialist and its ultimate objective is social revolution, not just liberation.

Thus we have two kinds of united fronts: first, the anti-imperialist united front which will lead the struggle to socialist revolutions; and second, the united front under the New Democracy which will lead the struggle for laying the foundations of socialist construction. It is also anti-imperialist in essence. Both the united fronts are under the firm leadership of the proletariat.

This clarification is important for devising political strategy and tactics, i.e., the General Line.

Relationship Between The Economic Base and The Superstructure

This discussion is inevitably linked with the above discussion on classes. Does the economic base - the Civil Society - determine the superstructure all the time, or does the superstructure- the "political society" or the state - on certain occasions determine the base? We have seen above the difficulty of resolving this question from the non-dialectical standpoint. Many Marxists are not clear on this question and there are a lot of disagreements around it. Those who support the contention that the superstructure does under certain conditions determine the economic base go by the authority of Chairman Mao who asserted that "politics" does determine the economic base under certain conditions.

Mao, of course, consistently urged "putting politics in command", i.e., the class struggle comes first, then economics and finally the superstructure. This is a revolutionary strategy whereby in order to win the economic struggle the masses must first strive to win the political struggle, establish a proletarian economic base after which the abolition of the ideological foundation of feudalism and capitalism, i.e., the superstructure will follow as a natural consequence of victory in the political and economic struggles. These are the "certain conditions" under which politics determine the economic base.

Conversely, when revisionism takes over state power in a socialist society they depart from the principle of the law of planned and proportional development, reintroduce competition and the law of value, and eventually the change in the superstructure will follow automatically to correspond with the new capitalist economic base. This is the process by which capitalist restoration is achieved. It does not mean that the proletariat has changed to capitalist. It only means that owing to some mistakes by the proletariat, at party and state levels, the remnants of the bourgeoisie have temporarily won an upper hand in the ongoing class struggle and seek to establish an economic base which will determine a capitalist superstructure.

However, this is not the same thing as saying that the superstructure can determine the economic base. Under our condition of neocolonialism the "bureaucratic bourgeoisie" do not "determine" the economic base; they merely carry forward the peasant mode of production to the capitalist relations, which is its logical destination. Left to itself the peasantry gravitates towards capitalism and not socialism; peasants are inherently capitalists. Only proletarian intervention and under its leadership can the peasants move towards socialism.

In other words, Mao's statement is not inconsistent with the dialectical principle that the economic base in the final analysis determines the superstructure, and not vice versa.

Neo-Colonialism

Another important issue in these essays is how and why does the gap between advanced capitalist countries and neocolonies continue to widen? Why are these neocolonies permanently subordinated to the capitalist world order?

We know that this is achieved by the huge transfer of value, i.e. wealth, from the neocolonies to the metropolitan countries. The question is: how is it achieved? Is it through "unequal exchange" or through the "exploitation" of the peasants? First, let us be quite clear that exploitation does not take place at the point of exchange because at this level no new value is created - it is only transferred from one party to another. It can take the form of legalized looting or plunder which we call "trade". There can never be equal or unequal exchange between commodities of the subjugator and the subjugated, and the law of equivalents cannot operate under the circumstances. Our exchange with imperialism is not determined by market mechanism or by the law of demand and supply, and consequently prices neither gravitate towards nor deviate from their value. These laws operate only within a single economy or between economies of more or less equal development where the "cost" of labour, or variable capital, roughly corresponds.

Exploitation takes place only at the level of production

where new value is created. In our case the developed capitalist countries exploit the surplus value created by the workers in mines, industries, as well as by agricultural workers, as distinct from commodity producing peasants in much the same way as they exploit "their" workers at home. The cheap labour in neocolonies helps to create a colossal return to the capital so invested. For instance, in developed capitalist countries the average return to capital is about 5% while in our countries it ranges from 40%, to 200% as in gold mining and petroleum. Thus, the huge transfer of wealth from the neocolonies to the metropolitan countries takes place through the exploitation of our workers and the looting of our peasants.

Why we allow this to happen is another question. The politicians and bureaucrats in underdeveloped countries who supervise this exploitation and plunder are not themselves underdeveloped. They enjoy as high a standard of living as their counterparts in the developed capitalist countries; and through bribery and corruption, some enjoy even higher standards. They have therefore developed a vested interest in the system which they are reluctant to change, whatever they say to the contrary.

There is also emerging a new group of local millionaires who benefit from this exploitation and plunder of their people by their foreign masters; they also take advantage of the economic chaos which the system has brought about. Both groups are developing material bases for reproducing themselves as a class whose vested interest is inextricably bound to neocolonialism.

We cannot discuss neocolonialism without touching on the controversial question of "three worlds". Comrades have raised this issue in the essays but for some reason they did not go into it in a thoroughgoing way. Are there "three worlds" in this world of ours? The Chinese say there are, and they have categorised them as follows: First World is the Superpowers- i.e., US and USSR; Second World - Eastern and Western Europe, Japan, Canada, Australia, New Zealand; and Third World- the rest of us. They have also a thesis to support this division.

Briefly this thesis is as follows: since the advent of revisionism and capitalist restoration in the Soviet Union that country has now become a social-imperialist power, as vicious as US imperialism. And because they are new in the game, they tend to be more ruthless than US imperialism. The Soviet Union and the US have divided the world between themselves, each having its own hegemony over their respective spheres. They also struggle between themselves to expand their respective hegemony at the expense of the other.

Although they struggle between themselves, these superpowers unite in their world domination. This quest for Soviet-US condominium has created contradictions between them on the one hand and the rest of the world on the other. In spite of the fact that the Soviet Union and the US respectively share ideological affinity with Eastern and Western Europe the national interests of the latter group of countries force them to resist condominium. Thus, the interests of these European countries and Japan - the Second World - resisting superpower hegemony and those of the neocolonies - the Third World - coincide, although there may be secondary contradictions between the Second and Third Worlds.

Socialists, according to this thesis, must support the national governments in the Second and Third Worlds in their objective contradiction with the superpowers even if the leaders of some of these countries are despotic, reactionary, and repressive, or subjectively pro-imperialists.

This thesis has been elevated to a theory by the Chinese Communist Party since the death of Chairman Mao who is said to be the originator of the theory.

As a result of pursuing this theory in diplomatic practice, the new Chinese leaders have often found themselves in some awkward situations, the most dramatic ones being Iran and Angola. It has also resulted in China joining the World Bank and IMF; the leading organs of imperialist finance capital. All this has created a lot of confusion among Marxists the world over.

For instance, it is impossible for an Iranian Marxist, revisionist or otherwise, to support the Shah when the entire population of the country rejected him. It is equally impossible for an African Marxist to support Savimbi of Angola who is in shameless collusion with the South African fascists to dismember his country. Or to support Mobutu of Zaire or leaders like him.

Until the death of Chou-en Lai and Chairman Mao the Chinese government pursued this policy of "three worlds" only tactically. It was not elevated to a theory or strategy. They found it a useful guide with which to conduct a revolutionary diplomacy. Marxists found no difficulty in supporting this tactical guide at the time because it was accompanied by an important injunction, which guided it from getting out of hand and turning it into an opportunistic diplomacy.

The injunction was that: countries want independence, nations want liberation; people want revolution. The last one - people want revolution - is the guiding principle and it is the main link of the whole injunction.

Where there was a clash between the socialist and imperialist camps the Chinese supported the socialist camp, as in Korea, Vietnam, and Sihanouk's Campuchea. Where there was a clash between Europe or Japan and the USA, they supported Europe and Japan. Where there was a clash between the imperialist camp - USA, Europe, Japan - and the colonial and neocolonial countries, they supported the latter. Where there was a clash between a reactionary ruling class and the people in the neocolonies they supported the people. The support for the people also extended to supporting the people in the US, Europe, Japan when they clashed with their governments. (Incidentally, the idea of the Third World came into being with the advent of the Cold War in the 1950s. The two worlds were then the Capitalist camp and the Socialist camp and the Third World was comprised of the so-called non-aligned countries. No Marxist accepted this obviously propagandistic categorization at the time on the ground that there are only two ideologically opposing systems in the world and we are either in the one or the other, capitalist or socialist. But now both capitalist and socialist countries try to woo these countries to support their respective positions in international issues, the reason being that these non-aligned countries on many issues have a block vote at the UN)

The "theory of three worlds" as interpreted by the present Chinese leaders and its practical consequences has thus become a very controversial question among Marxists.

Among the most outspoken critics of this theory are the Albanian Community Party leaders who have gone out of their way to attack not only the theory itself but to accuse Chairman Mao of having been more of a petty-bourgeois nationalist than a communist.

In these essays, all the comrades seem implicitly to accept the categorization of the three worlds. For instance, one group asserts that winning concessions from the imperialists by the neocolonies is objectively a victory for the Third World and a defeat for the imperialists. The other group concludes that such concessions are actually a decoy designed to entrap neocolonies more firmly in the imperialist camp and thereby facilitate more intensive exploitation and plunder at this stage of the development of finance capital. The Lome 1 and 11 Conventions are said by the first group to be a victory for the African, Caribbean and Pacific (ACP) countries; while the second group regard it as a victory for the US and Japanese monopolies on the grounds that it is their capital which owns the factories in the neocolonies whose products will now be exported to the European Economic Community with lesser restrictions.

The first group seems to view the world as a gigantic balance sheet whereby a plus on neocolonies means a minus on the imperialists. But in the era of the IMF, World Bank, multinational corporations, free trade zones and finance capital under which the entire capitalist world, including the neocolonies which comprise the OECD (Organization for Economic Co-operation and Development) the balance sheet view of the world seems to be unrealistic. Such a balancing can be relevant only in evaluating the gains and losses between the socialist camp and imperialism.

Conclusion

Finally, what is the purpose of these essays? They originate in response to the publication of three most important books to come out of Fast Africa. One of these is Issa Shivji's Class Struggles in Tanzania, one is Dan Nabudere's The Political Economy of Imperialism, and third is Politics and Class Formation in Uganda by Mahmood Mamdani. These books have inspired a lot of thinking among East African intellectuals [unfortunately they could not reach the masses because they are written in English] and especially among those with Marxist inclinations.

The purpose of these essays is obvious; Marxists do not engage in debates just for the fun of it as in school debates. Their principal task is to change the world. Their debates are about the correct understanding of the world around us. Once this world is understood then the task is to outline policies, which will guide their struggle- to draw up the general line. This is arrived at by concrete analysis of the concrete situation in any given area. To do this they use the dialectical methodology, which is universally applicable, and they relate it to their concrete situation.

The second point in Marxist debate is about state power: who controls it, what class interests does it serve, what is the role of the proletariat, and so on. If the state is the most important instrument in the class struggle how can the proletariat achieve state power - spontaneously? or through conscious, organized leadership? And having attained state power how should they use it in continuing the class struggle from that level?

The essays are limited to the first part only and have not touched on the second at all. This is unfortunate, especially when they are being published for the general readership. The most burning issue in people's minds at this crucial moment is: what shall we do to extricate ourselves from the horrifying situation in which Africa finds itself? Without tackling this question there is a danger that the essays might be dismissed as irrelevant and will be relegated to academic circles only. This will be a tragedy because the work which has gone into this debate would then be a wasted effort.

How do Marxists view the problem of extricating ourselves from our horrifying experience of hunger and misery? Marxists assert that to change the situation the proletariat must struggle to win state power first of all, and to do this it must organize itself under the leadership of the vanguard party. The party then trains its cadres as "professional revolutionaries" who carry out the day to day political work, to agitate and propagate. In other words, to take up issues which affect the masses and struggle for their resolution, and at the same time to educate the masses by raising the class consciousness of the working class and political consciousness of the masses. And also to train other cadres at the lower levels of the organization - the factory level, farm level, street and village levels, etc.

The cadres at both higher and lower levels develop a style of work, which wins over people's confidence in their leadership. They do not lord it over the people but on the contrary constantly learn from them, because people may be ignorant but they are not stupid. The cadres learn what the people want, feel, aspire to, and so on as they are conveyed to them in a disjointed, sometimes incoherent and fragmnented manner. They then analyse these feelings and aspirations, synthesize them in a coherent manner and formulate policies, which reflect them. This style of work is known as *from the people and back to the people.*

This form of organization is the surest way of leading to state power. After winning state power the proletariat is then faced with the task of establishing their own state machine on the basis of democratic dictatorship of the proletariat in alliance with the popular forces-the peasants, petty bourgeois intellectuals, oppressed minorities, etc. under their own leadership. This is the stage of the New Democracy.

Then comes the most important task of the administration of the country, which is distinct from the political task of organizing state power. The basis of socialist administration is socialist accounting and control during the complex period of the transition from capitalist domination.

The economic task is more difficult than that of winning state power and it begins by organizing it slowly, systematically and cautiously. The principal aim of such organization is the rapid development of the productive forces without which the country will be plunged into permanent and profound economic and political crises.

The aim is to improve as soon as possible the well-being of the majority of the people, in our case the peasants, through increased production of material goods. This will in turn expand industrial production and the growth of the proletariat. The practical meaning of the worker/peasant alliance is for the proletarian state to help the small peasant develop their productive forces with state assistance. Without this development the worker peasant alliance will break up and the peasants will go over to capitalism.

This assistance is based on the peasant's personal incentive during the whole period of the new democracy. If the peasants' condition is not improved, if agriculture does notfiourish, then industrialization will not take place and the proletariat will not grow-they will in fact be a declassed proletariat as industrialization stagnates. Thus the industrial strategy must be linked with the development of agriculture and vice versa.

Every important branch of the economy during this period of the new democracy is built on the basis of personal incentive-collective discussion but individual responsibility. Meetings and discussions are encouraged among the people in order to remind themselves of their overall revolutionary tasks summing up experience setting new targets and so on, but at the same time learning to distinguish between what is appropriate for meetings from what is appropriate for administration, for production and for achieving new targets.

All this effort is to ensure that the condition of the people constantly improves and does not deteriorate. In an underdeveloped peasant country socialist revolution can triumph only on two conditions: by receiving timely support from the inore advanced socialist countries; and by winning voluntary support of the peasantry. The interests of the workers and peasants differ and we must not assume that both can be satisfied by the same measures. To satisfy the peasants they must have a certain freedom of exchange; they must obtain commodities and industrial goods.

Scarcity of these is the surest way of losing the confidence not only of the peasants but also of the workers. The proletariat cannot win the confidence of the people by merely telling them what they intend to do however nicely phrased this may be. The people want to see the results of what the proletariat say they can do. Once the confidence of the peasants has been won through concrete results, their enthusiasm for production will be aroused and sustained. This will pave the way for accelerated growth on the basis of planned and proportional development.

These essays are about knowing and changing the world. However much the writers may disagree, they give us an insight into what is happening around us. From this raw material, we can marshal our forces to begin the first steps on our long march towards changing the world. The most hopeful event coming out of Africa today is that young Africans are asking questions.

These young people see their continent to have been turned into an imperialist playground. It is being manipulated, exploited, plundered at the expense of the people. Poverty is taken for granted, with regular interludes of plagues and famine. The three declared scourges of Africa at independence, poverty, ignorance and disease have proved to be unshakable and stubborn; if anything they seem to be flourishing luxuriously on the fertile soil of neo-colonialism. These essays identify the core of our problems and articulate their finding in a scientific way. It is to be hoped that as many Africans as possible will read this book, for only in understanding what is at issue can we hope to move Africa to a truly prosperous future.

Letter to Karim Essack[1]
Amherst, July 9th, 1982

Dear Karim,
Here is my response to your comments.

Re: Our difference with other Marxists

Our difference with non-Marxists and anti-Marxists is essentially antagonistic, whereas that among Marxists of whatever denomination is non-antagonistic. The resolution of the first contradiction is through frontal confrontation and struggle, including if necessary revolution. For the second it is through inner party struggle, i.e. struggle between different "lines", or "tendencies". As a non-antagonistic contradiction its resolution does not entail revolution.

PAIGC government has not declared itself a Marxist-Leninist state but MPLA and FRELIMO however, have. We may disagree with them in their interpretation of Marxism; they may even be revisionists, but as long as they adhere to Marxist principles it is our duty to support them at the same time pointing out their errors; this is critical support.

Countries like Tanzania with broadly populist orientation and with an anti-colonial stance also deserve the support of Marxist-Leninists in the immediate aftermath of independence. Firstly, because Marxist-Leninist parties did not exist under colonial regime and Marxists were not allowed to organise independently. This resulted in Marxists having to work individually only within the nationalist anti-colonial movements. Secondly, given the above constraint, Marxists had to distinguish themselves within these movements by devotion to the masses, honesty in their leadership and style of work, diligence, etc. so that the masses can see through their own experience the distinctive qualities of Marxist leadership in contrast to the petty bourgeoisie. This is an important political "investment" for future Marxist leadership.

In the process, individual Marxists might have been persecuted, humiliated, obstructed in their work, etc., but this was to be expected and there was no point in being discouraged. From a long-term point of view this is positive. (Incidentally, Marxists must always take a long-term point of view in political life, and when the current situation is not favourable for their organized leadership, individual Marxists are obliged to establish the necessary ground work for the future Marxist leadership that will come after them.)

Re: Open letter to Mugabe.

I did not assume for one moment that ZANU was a Marxist-Leninist party. The letter was not concerned with asking Mugabe to establish a communist party or state. It was concerned with the economics of a newly independent state which is also populist. The establishment of the communist party or state will be decided by the Zimbabwe people themselves.

However, as a populist government faced with the menace of white South Africa it is important for Marxists to support the consolidation of modern industry and modern agriculture, even if the social relations are still capitalist. Modern economy helps to undermine old forms and to establish conditions for the urban and rural proletarian development. Trotskyism? No. The Troskyists have elevated these tactics to a principle; to Marxist Leninists it is still tactics, given the concrete conditions in Zimbabwe at the moment. Our greatest setback in Africa is the widespread peasant production which keeps the peasantry backward and condemned to the 'idiocy of rural life'. We should encourage all forms which help the peasants to evolve into proletarians. If the existing industries in Zimbabwe collapse as in Tanzania then even the small number of the working class will be de-proletarised and return to peasantry or remain lumpen-proletariat. This, again from a long-term perspective, will be a retrograde step and a setback for Marxism in Africa.

Marxists must always distinguish between objective and subjective conditions We must encourage the development of objective conditions for socialism even if the subjective factor, i.e. the communist party, has not yet evolved. It is the task of Marxists to struggle for the establishment of the latter without undermining the development of the former. It is not our business to show that, e.g. Mugabe is not a Marxist; that will be negative and a waste of our precious time. Our task is to show what is Marxism and what it is about. What are its objectives and why it is in the interests of the people to support them. If the Mugabes are anti-Marxists and persecute Marxists then we mobilise and wage struggle against them; if they are patriotic and tolerant to Marxists, allowing the proletarians their democratic rights to organise independently then we concentrate our maximum effort in strengthening our organisation for the development of the subjective factor. There is all the difference in the world between Sun Yet-sen and Chaing Kai-shek, although both were nationalists.

Except for the Sudan (up to 1971) no African country would allow independent Marxist organisation, neither during colonialism nor after. S.E.Asian Marxists took advantage of the disarray of colonialism during World War II and the Japanese occupation to organise the masses under their leadership first against fascism and later against colonialism and their local stooges.

No such opportunity occurred anywhere in Africa except in Ethiopia, but even here it was the British and Haile Selassie who took over the leadership of the anti-Italian struggle. Nevertheless, the offshoot of even that limited struggle is the ongoing Eritrean revolution which has created excellent conditions for the evolution of some outstanding Marxist leadership.

Re: The role of Marxists in the absence of independent political organisations

In the absence of their own independent political organisation Marxists in all parts of Africa had either to work within the nationalist governments or to go underground. The first was possible; the second was not. To go underground effectively in the circumstances of our countries you need: (a) fairly large and complex urban centres with some support from the people, (b) wide-scale rural support among the peasants who already have some confidence in proletarian leadership, and (c) a pre-existent party organisation with a minimum urban and rural infrastructure. All these conditions did not exist in Africa, and to go underground without them is to condemn the movement to the negative role of "roving bands".

The alternative was to work within the nationalist governments whenever the opportunity occurred. It is wrong for Marxists to suggest that that move was 'opportunistic'. It was a necessary move from a long-term perspective. Marxists who accepted government positions had no illusion about transforming the Nyereres to Marxism; nor that working with them was plain sailing without risks to their personal safety; or of being used for the consolidation of the petty bourgeois dictatorships. But we must not shy away from taking such risks since this is also a form of struggle under such difficult conditions and limited alternatives. Marxists have never enriched themselves from taking part in such governments nor have they taken that advantage to popularize themselves for their own personal gains. These are the two ingredients of opportunism, the third one being, as Lenin puts it, "impressionists, people who yield to the mood of the moment". Instead they utilized their advantageous position to popularize Marxist and progressive ideas utilizing available state news media, etc. None of them has abandoned principles for petty expediency, even at the risk of their lives. The fact that these governments have not turned out to be Marxist is not a failure of Marxists in government because that was not their objective in the first place. The fact that it has created conditions for the evolution of Karims, Shivjis, and yes, even Shayos of Africa will remain one of their proudest achievements. This is what is meant by leaving judgment to history - from a Marxist long-term perspective.

Secondly, Marxists, in practically every country where they had an opportunity to work with nationalist governments, have earned and continue to earn the respect of the people for their honesty, sincerity and exemplary devotion to the people. This is one of the greatest heritages they have left behind for the future development of the subjective factor.

Thirdly, to take the specific example of Tanzania, Marxist thought spread to Kenya, Uganda and Zambia, and to a lesser extent to Ethiopia and Somalia, thanks largely to the activities and prestige of Marxists in Tanzania. This is no mean achievement if you take into account the dominance of reactionary ideas in all these countries, including Tanganyika itself, in the immediate aftermath of independence. Of course there are setbacks since the road to socialism is not paved with gold nor is it straight. It is uphill and zigzag and it takes years of ups and downs. The Chinese comrades, inspite of their favourable conditions, i.e. the war against Japan, proximity to the Russian revolution, peasants awakening, advanced working class, extensive terrain, etc. took more than thirty years of struggle to achieve victory, and even then the struggle is not over yet.

Re: *The Tanzania that might have been*

Your comment seems to have missed an important point. There is a distinction between a populist state and a socialist one. Tanzania is a populist state and it could have done a better job of it if it had adopted the policies advocated by the Left. Those policies were aimed at the development of conditions for a nationally integrated economy. You don't have to be a Marxist to attempt to do that; you only need to be genuinely patriotic. It was sufficient for the Left to take a patriotic rather than revolutionary position at that moment given the situation described above. Again the example of Sun Yet-sen comes to mind in discussing the distinction between a patriot and a sellout nationalist. The article was trying to show that Nyerere is a sellout nationalist and not the patriot that he claims to be; not only a sellout, but lacking even the minimum of essentials that are required for directing a nation, and therefore he is unfit to lead even a populist government. Furthermore, the article sought to show that in fact he was serving foreign capitalist interests by his policies of so-called self-reliance. Egypt built a fairly healthy economy under Nasser with a strong industrial base with substantial proletarians on populist policies. The masses of the people saw their economic and social well-being daily improving and they supported Nasser to the end. Libya is doing the same under Qaddafi - building modern industries and mechanised agriculture on populist policies. We must support that kind of development if only because it is destroying old forms and introducing modern ones under populist orientation. It is not revolutionary by any means, but progressive. If we criticise the Nyereres for not being communist; it would be silly. We criticise them for not being what they have declared themselves to be, i.e. truly populist.

According to Marxist and revolutionary tradition, there are two levels of discussion: one among Marxists, the other with non-Marxists. Issues of ideological and theoretical dispute among Marxists are best discussed in inner councils and committees (if the Party is in existence), or through "internal correspondence" in the absence of the Party. These discussions are carried out on the Leninist principle of "freedom of discussion, unity of action" in order to promote and strengthen ideological formation of the cadres without benefiting the enemy.

In public discussion with non-Marxists at large we limit the discussion to broad principles that draw all Marxists together in opposition to capitalism. This is the fundamental and primary confrontation, i.e., the antagonistic confrontation between Labour and Capital. Just as there are secondary contradictions among capitalists so there are secondary contradictions within Labour; but when we confront Capital we close our ranks to fight more effectively. We want to attract our youth; to the camp of Labour and once in they can be exposed to inner struggles between lines and tendencies. It is important for them to discuss the world and society within the terms of reference of socialist thought and not that of the bourgeois outlook.

Our disillusion with the Soviet Union, China, Vietnam, etc. should not turn us into their enemy, and our criticism of them should not be of the kind reserved for the enemy.

After all, with all their shortcomings, they are on the side of Labour. Without the Soviet Union, inspite of their revisionism, the world would have been a lot worse for progressive and anti-imperialist forces. It could have been better if they were genuinely revolutionary and we regret the fact that they are not. We struggle against them on that count, but in the final analysis this struggle is not antagonistic. That is why it is important to confine our discussion with the rest of the world to larger philosophical and theoretical issues that distinguish imperialists from the rest of us.

In the 'Introduction'[2] I was arguing against the notion that surplus value is extracted at the point of exchange, I was arguing that exploitation is a result of a specific type of relations of production in which surplus labor is transformed into surplus value; that no new value is created at the point of exchange. In the book,[3] on the other hand, I was trying to expose the false assumption that our salvation can come from some sort of a fairer world order within the confines of the capitalist world order. I made it quite clear in the book that the example was merely a demonstrational model which assumed everything else as being equal. It was only an abstraction which needed a lot more concrete investigation. I see no contradiction between the two. Plunder or loot is the result of a situation in which the capitalist extracts surplus value without even investing in constant capital.

Finally, I want to thank you very much for the trouble you have taken to seriously and critically examine my work and this gives me a lot of encouragement. I know that theoretical competence in Marxism is one of the most challenging tasks that faces us and we must constantly struggle to improve ourselves. Our main obstacle in that direction is the lack of the proletarian Party which would allow us an opportunity to enrich our theoretical understanding through political practice. This I think is the major source of frustrations experienced by many Marxists who have to develop their theoretical formation outside the Party. Marxist creativity comes about only through a union of Marxist theory and workers' movement, and the sooner we resolve this problem the better for the African revolution. Our immediate struggle therefore is for the abolition of the universal one-party petty bourgeois dictatorships which have engulfed the entire continent, and secondly, for the restoration of the proletariat's democratic right to organise themselves politically and independently.

With comradely greetings,

A.M.Babu

Notes

(1) Karim Essack was a well-known Marxist activist and writer from Tanzania
(2) Introduction to University of Dar es Salaam debates on class, state and imperialism (see p..)
(3) African Socialism or Socialist Africa, Zed Press, 1972

Ideologies and the Third World
Third World Review, November 1986

It is quite irritating to discover in this day and age that there are some 'Third World' intellectuals who are still thinking in terms of the false East versus West dichotomy - not in the political sense we have come to accept but in the vague 'cultural' or even geographic sense. It is racism in reverse - it is to put our case from 'this side of racism'. To follow that trend of thinking is to blindly accept archaic notions, perpetuated and perfected over the years, first by colonialism, and then by imperialism that the 'Western world' is the 'home' of great ideas ideals and ideologies. The article under discussion, for instance, is wholly wrong when it declares at the outset that 'Asia is the mother of all great religions and Europe is the mother of all great ideologies', although superficially it may appear to be the case.

It is also wrong to counterpose medieval and feudal thinking and practice with that of the industrial bourgeois epoch, especially at the present level of historical development and then decide to accept the ancient [ones] rather than the more modem [ones] on the ground that the first is purer and the second decadent. It is much better to think in terms of continuity in the form of supersession The old is superseded by the new, although the elements of the former can be traced in the latter. Secondly, it is essential to view the evolution of ideas, of customs and social practice as natural and necessary complements to what is taking place at the economic base.

A feudal economic and social formation creates its own norms, customs, ideas, morality, and culture essential for the system to survive; bourgeois formation similarly evolves its own norms, essential for its own survival. Ideas and practice become 'decadent' only when relations of production become an obstacle for the economy to develop to its historical destination and when its social relations have outlived their usefulness. It will be worse than 'decadence' if at this point you nostalgically begin to eulogise and recreate the past - a past polluted with slave and feudal poison. The solution lies in superseding the present to a higher level of social and economic formation rather than retreating to that past which dictates neither action nor innovation.

It is not even true to say that Asia is 'the home of all great religion' because although the setting is in the Middle East, Judeo-Christian heritage is anything but Middle Eastern. The Christianity that is represented by the Vatican and the Anglican Church is not the same thing as the Christianity of Jesus Christ nearly two thousand years ago. And the ideas and practice (i.e. culture) that influence it today have evolved not from the medieval culture of two thousand years ago but from the culture that was entailed in the evolving industrial civilisation. Although some of the ideas and practices bear traces of the cultural dross of the past it is virtually impossible to pin point what is 'Western' or 'Eastern' in them.

We know, for instance, that Thomas Aquinas, the father of Catholic doctrine, spent all his writing and thinking life not in advancing what Christ had said or thought but to counter the ideas and thoughts of lbn el-Rushd the Berber from North Africa, and it was on these writings that the doctrine is based. The ideas and thoughts of el-Rushd of course were to some extent influenced by the Greek thinkers, but on the whole his thoughts were original and based on the concrete experiences of his own life and the life of the Berbers of North Africa. There is very little 'European' or 'Asiatic' about them and if we are to give them a continental label then they are most definitely 'African'.

But el-Rushd's thinking had far reaching influence and not only on the Catholic Church. His teaching was also the basis of the body of ideas which dominated the Sorbonne right from its inception and later became part of the French 'culture'. The ideas that influenced Voltaire and Rousseau, the founding fathers of bourgeois ideology, were profoundly linked to this cultural background and in the context of the concrete reality of a France in transition from Feudalism to Capitalism. Where does Berber thought end and European thought begin? In the circumstances it is impossible to tell. But we can say most definitely that Berber thought and ideas have influenced French thinking which in turn helped to evoke the bourgeois ideology of Fraternity Equality and Freedom, the very foundation of bourgeois democracy, or of 'Western heritage' to use the language of the article.

The article is also wrong in trying to prove the 'Westernness' of Marxism and to include it among 'other Western fallacies', in the words of Ali Sharf'ati, the so-called 'Rousseau of the Iranian Revolution' (whatever that means). Marx's great contribution to human thought include his labour theory of value, the source of surplus value and the tendency for the rate of profit to fall - his concepts like modes of production and others. His approach to his investigations was dialectical and this formed the basis of his 'law of the unity of the opposites' which led him to the far reaching theoretical formulations that we now know as 'Marxism'.

However, far from being 'Western' these ideas were pioneered by Abdulrahman Ibn Khaldun another Berber, some three hundred years *before* Marx or Feuerbach or Hegel Thanks to his dialectical approach it was Khaldun who first pointed out that value was created at the point of production and not at the point of exchange; hence the theory of surplus value and exploitation later developed by Marx which formed the basis of socialist thought.

Khaldun was probably the earliest philosopher of history who argued that history was not simply chronicling of events but that its task is to identify the patterns of change and to explain them. This theme was developed three hundred years later by Marx in his famous formulation on revolutionary change by observing that philosophers have merely interpreted the world but the real task is to change it.

In his 'six basic principles of social change' Khaldun departed from earlier philosophers' notions of social process which were inspired by 'rationalism' or 'metaphysics' - the foundations of 'Western' philosophy. He introduced, long before Hume and a lot more profoundly than him, the method of observing and analysing concretely the objective realities surrounding a particular society and his thesis was that ultimately the theory of change must be based on the practice of the people. This is not Hume's 'empiricism', it is about observing objective reality in flux. This approach is also utilised abundantly by Marxism in its notions of historical and dialectical materialism. Khaldun emphasised the observation of the laws of social process through the gathering of data and by identifying the relationships among variables. Marx similarly laid stress on studying and understanding the production process, mode of production, social relations of production, the economic base, the superstructure and social formation to understand social processes in order to change the world.

The 'Westernness' of essential Marxism is the 'Easternness' of Khaldun which does not idealise the past but observes it objectively in order to arm itself with the knowledge essential for a revolutionary change. It was Khaldun who pointed out that in order to introduce decisive social change there must be on the one hand a capacity for the creation of social wealth (which Marx called 'development of the productive forces') and on the other, an agent of that change - solidarity among the oppressed to provide its own leadership (which Marx called 'the formation of a revolutionary mass'). There is no end to similarities in the thinking and observations of Khaldun and Marx and whoever suggests that Marxism is irrelevant to the 'Third World' is in for a rude surprise.

As a matter of fact, the article under discussion is itself, if anything, 'Western' to the core in its approach and so are the references it is directing us to. It explains the ideas of the past from the specific 'Western' world outlook - i.e. bourgeois, and criticises the present from the projected consciousness of the feudal past. Marx and Khaldun, on the contrary teach about observing the present as the inevitable product of the past of a specific process of production and the relations of production it has created. Marx and Khaldun would teach that instead of trying to recreate and resuscitate the culture and values of the past, social change of the real world requires the practical overthrow of the actual social relations (which gave rise to the current distorted situation) by creating the two conditions of social change, productive forces and revolutionary mass.

The 'Westerness' of Marx is the 'Easterness' of Khaldun in that although they were separated by vastly different epochs of history they both taught that only a revolution of the oppressed through their solidarity can bring about significant social change that would enable society for the first time to direct its own history. The 'logic' of Marx's theory doesn't lie in the fact that the ideology and consciousness of Marx and Engels were based on the conditions of Western Europe undergoing industrial revolution in the 19th century and therefore 'Western' as the article argues.

The 'logic' of that theory has enabled him to understand the actual, concrete reality of capitalist industrial Europe, but the foundation of his theory was universal and not just European, anymore than Khaldun's discovery of the source of new value was 'African'. The Marxist theory of value is neither 'Western' nor 'Eastern'; it is about commodity production, about selling one's labour power as a commodity to the owners of the means of production, whether that means is machines or land, in Europe or Iran. It is immaterial whether one agrees with the theory or not, the point is that it is about universals and applicable universally wherever society has evolved from producing use values to producing exchange values, or to put it loosely, from subsistence production to production for sale and profit.

Only the worst and most backward type of Black American, the one who shouts 'better dead than red'; would allege that Marx was racist or pro-imperialist. Again it is immaterial. Whether one agrees with his theories or not, intellectual honesty compels one to accept Marx's thought in terms of social and economic formations, of the past the present and of the future - the more relevant and appropriate ones replacing the moribund. The early ones, were 'primitive', and his use of the word was never meant in any disparagement. He talked of primitive accumulation of capital rather than 'primary' because the former was more accurate. He and Engel talked of 'barbaric' rule of Pasha of Tunis in the same sense that we talk of the barbaric rule of our current tyrants whether in Europe, Latin America Asia or Africa.

They both held that from a historical point of view capitalism was a more advanced and therefore a better economic formation than feudalism, just as feudalism was better and more progressive than slavery, and we must judge them from that position and not from the position of 'anti-communism' and the Cold War which blinds sound judgment. They held that human beings were better off as serfs than as slaves and better off as industrial worker than as serfs. From this point of view it was much better for the Tunisian serf to be exposed to a dynamic capitalism than to be condemned to the stagnant feudalism of the Sultan of Tunis. The break up of the past which capitalist production was forcing on the rural communities at home or abroad was actually good for society when capitalism was still historically progressive.

In the middle of the last century when Marx and Engels hailed the impact of Western capitalism on the rest of the world, capitalism was progressive and it played some positive role. It became negative only when it developed to monopoly-capitalism as the last stage of a dynamic system on the way to becoming moribund. Lenin did not rescue Marxism from being an ideology 'which favoured Western imperialism and colonialism', as the article alleges. He wrote about the period when capitalism had lost its steam, had lost its positive role, and was forced to subjugate our economies to the pernicious market forces of a dying system in order to sustain itself; rather like the once powerful but now bankrupt tycoon who is forced to resort to the little wealth of his weaker relatives in order to sustain himself.

A Marxist or dialectical-materialist way of looking at reality will lead us to the view that while colonialism was positive at a certain stage it became negative at the later stage of monopoly capitalism with its notions of racial superiority. For instance when it needed labour for its colonial settlers it fought and banned slavery; but when it became imperialistic and neocolonial it fought to prevent poorer countries from developing independent national economies. To the dialectical-materialist, the first instance was positive and second negative, but the 'empiricist' view will be that if by 'empirical evidence' it is negative now then it must have been negative for all time. That is the significant difference between proletarian world-outlook and bourgeois world-outlook.

There is nothing necessarily 'Marxist' about putting forward a case for de-linking from the so-called 'World market'; it is plain commonsense. You don't need to be a Marxist to know that the economic structure that we have inherited from colonialism and have not changed to this day does siphon off most of our economic surplus to our 'trading partners' in the developed world. And that as long as we do not change this colonial structure surplus will continue to be siphoned off in any economic relation whether with the West or East, and as long as this situation continues there will be nothing left to accumulate in order to reinvest for extended reproduction or development This is not part of Marxist doctrine, although a lot of Marxists support it. Incidentally when the USA delinked from the rest of the 'Western world' during its isolationist policies and renounced its international debts and the 'Monroe Declaration', it was definitely not being influenced by Marxism even by the wildest dreams of MacCarthyism; it was simply safeguarding its 'vital economic interests' by weakening the economic stranglehold of European capital.

It was consolidating its economy in order to re-enter the 'world economy' from the point of its own choice and on its own terms, and not the choice and terms imposed externally. This is what is known generally as entering the world market from 'a position of strength' which is essential whether you are a Marxist or a Jehovah's Witness. The 'Third World' delinkers are advocating precisely this and it does not make any sense to say, as the article does, that 'Economically Marxism helps the process of delinking; but culturally Marxism facilitates the process of re-linking.' This is not meta-dialectic; it is plain balderdash.

Notes

(1) This essay was a response to an article by Ali Mazrui in the same issue of *Third World Book Review*

A Tragedy for Socialism
Africa World Review, May –September 1995

It would have been more appropriate to title this book the "Tragedy of Socialism". Stalin's firing squad that destroyed Nikolai Ivanovich Bukharin (1888-1938) on that fateful day, March 15, 1938, also destroyed the credibility of socialist rule, Soviet style. He had been the editor of the party paper Pravda, Secretary of Communist International (Commintern), a senior member of the Politburo of the Soviet Communist party, and an intellectual of high calibre. Bukharin's show trial began on March 12, he was sentenced on March 13, and shot two days later! This was called "revolutionary justice" by the perpetrators of this tragic travesty of justice. It was easily one of the biggest setbacks in the struggle for socialism world wide.

Bukharin's last words to revolutionaries everywhere on the eve of his murder were: "Know, comrades, that on that banner which you will be carrying in the victorious march to communism, is also my drop of blood". These words will forever haunt all those who blindly supported those sham Soviet trials of the 1930s in the name of proletarian internationalism.

What was Bukharin's 'crime'? There was no crime at all. If anything, the crime was against Bukharin. For the underlying cause which led Stalin to want to 'liquidate' him was simply that Bukharin took a different position on the question of the wherewithal for funding industrial investment. Stalin, and the so-called Left oppositionists led by Trotsky and Evgeny Preobrazhensky had argued in favour of transferring surplus from agriculture (ie, from the peasantry) in order to invest in the industrialisation programme. Bukharin, on the other hand, argued that such a strategy would impoverish the peasantry, would hamper the development of the home market, distort the essential balance between agriculture and industry, it would stifle the growth of light industry - an essential source of rapid accumulation; in short, it would lead to the lopsided development of the entire economy.

It took six decades and a total collapse of the Soviet system to prove him right. Contrary to Western propaganda, what collapsed in the former Soviet Union was not socialism but a distorted and lopsided economy which had the technology to fly to the moon, but lacked the material conditions on ground level to feed, house or adequately cloth its people. It has now at last become clear that in a largely peasant society like that of the Soviet Union, socialism cannot succeed if is not founded on widespread rural prosperity. And this in essence is what Bukharin was advocating.

Donny Gluckstein, author of the book under review, critiques Bukharin from the point of view of Trotsky and of the ultra-left. According to this view, socialism is about strengthening the working-class—first of all by means of rapid industrialisation, the benefits of which would then gradually trickle down to the peasantry by modernising agriculture. It is strategically no different from the current 'supply side' economics adopted by the ultra-rightists in the Anglo-Saxon countries: that is, first enrich the capitalists who will then invest, create jobs, which will then benefit the workers. Just as the capitalists would promote the investor at the expense of the workers in a supply-side capitalist economy, the ultra-leftists would promote the worker at the expense of the peasantry in their version of a socialist economy.

Throughout the book, the author counterposes Bukharin's position with that of Trotsky (as right vs left positions, respectively) and supports the latter's position against the former's. For example like Trotsky he opposes Stalin and his bureaucracy and regards him as the betrayer of socialism and he opposes Bukharin even more. He seems to echo Trotsky's famous line: "With Stalin against Bukharin - yes; with Bukharin against Stalin - never".

In fact Bukharin's interpretation of Marxism was much nearer to Marx's vision of socialism than most of his comrades. His contribution to theoretical and practical Marxism is now - after the collapse of the Soviet Union - acknowledged to be crucial in the struggle to rekindle the ideals of socialism. Lenin himself described him as "Bolshevism's biggest theoretician". Unfortunately, most of his writings and thoughts were either suppressed or ignored after his murder. Communist parties all over the world were instructed by the Soviet party to denounce Bukharin and his works. The author of this book seems to echo some of those blind prejudices of the past quoting some passages from Bukharin's works only to denounce them as erroneous or as based on non-Marxist dialectics. He even describes Bukharin's celebrated Historical Materialism which is an important contribution to Marxism, as a failure.

Bukharin's contribution to the New Economic Policy (NEP) introduced by Lenin in 1921 was most significant. Many unbiased socialist theoreticians now realise that if Stalin had not abolished the NEP in 1929 and if he'd let it take its course as outlined by Bukharin, the Soviet Union today would have been the most prosperous and most powerful socialist economy. The NEP was akin to what China now calls its new policy of Socialist Market Economy. This is based on the principle of "strict planning on major issues; flexibility on minor ones". which is more or less what NEP was about. And the Chinese Communist Party seems to be confidently moving China into the twenty-first century as the fastest growing economy in the world, while Russia's economy socialist-turned-capitalist, is declining at almost the same speed. As China registers a growth rate of 12% in 1994 over the previous year, Russia registers a decline of 25% over the same period.

The driving motive for the introduction of NEP was precisely to boost the Soviet economy into a booming growth economy. It was designed to accelerate the development of the productive forces so as to ensure a constant improvement of the material conditions of the people. It postulated that for socialism to triumph in a backward Russia, it was imperative to win the voluntary support of the peasantry who constituted the vast majority of the population. To achieve this the socialist economy had to ensure that the peasantry obtained commodities and industrial goods to meet their daily needs. Scarcity of such goods was the surest way of losing the confidence not only of the peasantry but also of the working class. Once the people's confidence in socialism as a whole had been won through concrete results, their enthusiasm for production would be aroused and sustained. paving the way for accelerated growth. Socialism would never succeed otherwise. This was the rationale behind NEP which was also Lenin's position throughout his active leadership of the Soviet Union and echoed by Bukharin after Lenin's death. Trotsky and other ultra-leftists however, had a different perspective, a one-sided and non-dialectical class-reductionist perspective. This perspective narrows the dialectical notion of the "struggle and unity of opposites", it singles out only an aspect of the struggle, but not the other side of the dialectic, ie. that of the unity of opposites. A revolutionary is expected to be able to distinguish between historical junctures such as those which entail struggle and those which entail unity. A crucial factor here is the level of the development of the productive forces. In developing countries, for instance, the worker-peasant unity is primary and the necessity for a struggle between them will remain secondary for as long as the peasantry exists. And this unity must not limit itself to sloganeering but by consciously creating the material (economic) basis for it to thrive, the NEP was intended to provide just that.

The ultra-leftists' failure to understand this important revolutionary imperative led them to view NEP with suspicion: they saw it as favouring the peasantry more than the working class. When Bukharin emphasised that the responsibility for developing the productive forces was the responsibility of the socialist state and that of building the national economy became the interest of the state, the ultra-leftists, like the author of the book under review accused Bukharin of making 'national interest' transcend class interest and of assuming economic growth to be equivalent to socialism.

The author devotes a whole chapter (Chapter 8) to a detailed discussion of Bukharin's famous call to the peasantry to 'enrich yourselves'. He in essence accuses Bukharin of subordinating the industrial sector to peasant production. He seems to misunderstand Bukharin's thesis that agriculture is the foundation of any sound and self-sustaining economy, socialist or capitalist. Strong and sustainable industrial development ultimately depends on growth in agriculture. Without sound agriculture there can be no sound and self-sustaining industrialisation.

For instance, the reason why the US is the strongest capitalist economy is primarily because its foundation was built on agriculture—grain and cotton. Cotton provided the basis for the textile revolution in the US economy which led to the expansion of world trade as we know it today. Her heavy industry, developed around light (textile) industry, which thus provided backward and forward linkages between agriculture, light industry and heavy industry which is a key to a balanced and symbiotic development of the three major productive sectors. All this developed spontaneously and unplanned, but because it was based ultimately on agriculture, followed by light industry, it objectively evolved its own momentum which gave heavy industry a sound internal base.

The NEP was to create conditions in a planned way for a flourishing agriculture, light industry and then heavy industry. Instead the Preobrazhensky thesis (see below) advocated the other way round which gave agriculture the lowest priority. It is now clear that the collapse of this Soviet model was precisely due to a backward agriculture and almost non-existent light industry. The lesson from the Soviet tragedy is that without a strong agricultural base the Soviet Union inevitably lagged behind in light industry, and in turn (aggravated it is true, by trade isolation imposed by the West) it did not benefit from modern technology that emanates from light industry.

In spite of the author's biased approach this chapter is very important for understanding some of the major issues involved in the famous Soviet economic debates at that time. He discusses them in great detail, with a Trotskyst bias, of course. Nevertheless, it is a very useful and informative chapter.

The next chapter which is about the Market and Transition to Socialism, is equally important in understanding the socialist political economy. On the issue of the socialist economics of the transition, Bukharin came in direct conflict with Preobrazhensky whose so-called law of Primitive Socialist Accumulation was described by Bukharin as akin to colonialism. This 'law' in effect went against Bukharin's thesis of encouraging the peasants's prosperity; on the contrary, its effect was more likely to impoverish the peasantry, and ultimately starve the country. It was based once again on a narrow-minded and one-sided view of socialism which saw agriculture as at once complementary as well as antagonistic to industry! The argument for this view was that because some of the agricultural commodities were exported to the capitalist world market therefore agriculture was "spontaneous" and in conflict with planned socialist industrialisation.

This debate became complex primarily because of the misinterpretation of Marx's Labour Theory of Value on the part of the ultra-leftists. Without getting into its technicalities, this theory simply means that in a market economy the exchange of commodities is governed objectively by a law which Marx called the "law of value". He showed that what determined the value of a product was the amount of labour time spent on its production, and from this he showed how the capitalist economy operated and how it exploited the workers through appropriation of the surplus value from their labour. All market economies operate on this basis and are therefore exploitative. The ultra-leftists argued that to allow the law of value to operate in some sectors of a socialist planned economy would lead to spontaneity and distortion of the economy.

But this again is a one-sided view. In the socialist economy of the transition like the NEP, commodity production and exchange exist to a significant extent and the law of value must therefore operate. What is important is to ensure that it influences and regulates production in a planned manner, not spontaneously but consciously to achieve the required result. In fact it is now even clearer, as shown by China's current experience, that although the law of value is an objective law its operation can be regulated and it can be used to beneficial results in expanding a socialist planned economy.

This review has dwelt mostly on the economic questions, not because other aspects are less important, but because this question is the most relevant to the urgent need for a socialist solution to current problems, especially in the Third World. Free market economy has no answer to the problems of poverty facing the majority of the human race. Even in the so-called newly industrialising economies of South East Asia, 500 billion people (about the entire population of Africa!) live below poverty level in sub-human conditions. The answer is a planned socialist economy which takes as its primary objective the well-being of the people not the 'well-being' of the market.

This book is timely because although the Soviet system has collapsed, socialism is on the agenda as never before. Notice the ideological campaign which has been launched against socialism even after the disappearanceof the Soviet Union and its European allies. There is nothing which terrifies the capitalists more than socialism because socialism is the only effective weapon in the hands of the workers and the oppressed in the antagonistic confrontation between Capital and Labour. A study of socialism, with all its contradictions and divergent opinions is most important in this era which the so-called neo-liberals claim to be the 'end of history'. The demise of the Soviet Union is not the end of history, but thankfully, the end of a colossal embarrassment to socialism. It is time to renew our efforts in improving our knowledge of socialism and this book is a contribution to that end.

Notes

(1) A review of 'The Tragedy of Bukharin' by Donny Gluckstein, Pluto Press, London, 1995

THE AFRICA WE NEED

The New World Disorder - Which Way Africa?[1]

The 7th Pan African Congress took place at a critical time internationally when the old post-Cold War world system was dead and a new one was/is yet to be born. Old political assumptions and economic certainties are crumbling one by one. Old alliances are rapidly being replaced by new ones. Old contradictions: ideological, north/south, economic, environmental, have not gone away; but new ones: ethnic, religious, territorial, have emerged with a vengeance, threatening global stability. It is an unsettled multi-polar world in which old centres of power and influence are gradually shifting to new, but as yet to be identified, spheres.

African people's situation in the new multi-polar world

In this volatile international scene, we see Africa inevitably embroiled in dramatic changes of her own, reflecting the new situation. New political leaders, of different political persuasions, are emerging everywhere. Mass political consciousness is spreading across the continent with one clear message: 'We want change in this changing world!'

Africans in the Diaspora are equally in a state of flux. They are confronted with new challenges which demand new solutions. The rise of racism and neo-fascism in the US and Europe (both eastern and western) is targeting Africans and people of African origin as scapegoats for economic failures of the racists' own governments.

It is against this background of uncertainty and racism that the historic 7th Pan African Congress was convened. Its primary task was to address these challenges in a realistic way, helped by inputs by African activists from all over the world where Africans and people of African origin live in large and small communities.

To achieve any meaningful understanding of this new situation and to arrive at a realistic 'African position', it is important that we study the phenomenon dispassionately without any preconceived notions. Realism should be our guiding principle, because the issues at stake are not only urgent but too serious to be left to the mercy of demagoguery and confused thinking. Our actions must take into account the concrete reality of Africa as it exists here and now, not an idealized one, and must pay attention to the people's aspirations. We must assess, without any exaggeration, our true capability to influence events at home and abroad. Above all, we must evaluate the material foundation on which our position in the world context must be established. This is also true for the people of African descent in the Diaspora. Needless to say, the continent is in a serious crisis. What needs to be identified are some of the key elements that led to this crisis in order to subject them to serious analysis. There are several political as well as cultural and social issues to be taken into consideration. While such issues should not be ignored, it is ultimately the economic base which must be our starting point. This will then naturally enable us to define appropriately these elements of the superstructure.

The economic foundation

Briefly, the economic weaknesses of Africa can be traced to the following roots:

* We have inherited our economic backwardness from the primitive structure of the colonial economy and aggravated it by our post-colonial involvement in the world economy from a position of extreme weakness.

* We have failed to formulate policies for restructuring these economies soon after independence which would have enabled each of our countries to start on a path to an independent national economy. This failure has condemned our countries to be wholly dependent on, and heavily indebted to, the old imperialist world system.

* A proliferation of weak and self-seeking leaders and coup makers has helped to disrupt the development process which has resulted in putting the continent firmly at the mercy of foreign interests. These come in the form of aid donors, creditors, financial speculators, multilateral agencies

and also in the form of foreign 'experts'. Their primary task is not to help us, but to create the material conditions for multinational corporations (MNCs) to exploit our labour and natural resources, and to perpetuate the colonial structures which facilitate this brutal exploitation.

* As a result of the above inherent weaknesses, the mangled African economies have emerged structurally unfit to take part in profitably, and benefit from, the world market; the continent has thus remained perpetually the loser in this venture.

* Failure to correct the above shortcomings and the ensuing lack of economic complementarity among and between African countries has created conditions for continental disunity. Africa has thus been rendered not only disunited but the majority of our nation-states have remained too small to be economically viable. They are too poor to take advantage of modern technology and unable to benefit from the vast human and natural resources of the continent.

While this condition is now universally known, no appropriate strategy to correct this situation has yet been proposed. Many 'alternative' policies have been recommended by some of the highest 'authorities' on Africa, but results have been disappointingly negative. The reason for the failure of these 'alternatives' seems to lie in the fact that they all start from assumptions and premises set earlier by the very traditional exploiters of the continent. All are based on the simplistic proposition of 'export in order to import' (a shopkeeper's notion of wealth creation!). They make no attempt to look into the structure on which our economies are based, a precondition to working towards a viable solution. This lack of proper diagnosis of our backwardness has had the effect of challenging only the form but not the essence of what has to be changed. This is yet another variation of the strange notion of seeking a solution to the status quo from within the status quo!

Is there a way out of this mess?

Our discussion must, first of all, take into account our food situation which is threatening to be the most serious crisis on the continent for the next decade. We are in a situation where our populations are rising but our food supply is diminishing, owing to a topsy-turvy order of priorities to which Africa has been subjected since independence.

The rapid expansion of deserts which eat up most of our fertile land, from the Sahara southwards, is a serious cause for concern; and this phenomenon too is directly linked to our wrong order of priorities in agriculture and land use. We must devise a sound policy on agriculture which will correct this imbalance and which will determine the whole direction of African economies, and create the essential conditions for continental unity.

The following discussion is a tentative attempt to set the ball rolling. It makes no claim to being the only way out. Rather, its purpose is to provoke critical thinking on the topic. Many of the points raised and solutions recommended are the result of several years of practical experience in the field of development strategy, later refined by contemplation, debates, exchange of views and rethinking which was made possible by a few years in the academic world.

A tentative Pan African alternative

The real meaning of the African crisis is that our countries, collectively and individually, are at a dead end, thanks entirely to the economic and 'development' policies pursued since independence.

The situation is so untenable that no 'reforms', whether inspired by the World Bank or IMF, or whether initiated locally, can get us out of the mess. What is needed is not reforms but a different outlook which calls for a decisive change of direction, a change from the primitive colonial structure of the economy to a national economy; above all, a change in the structure of production. This entails a change from an outward-motivated to an inward-motivated development strategy, whose guiding principle must be one based on the recognition that external causes are only a condition of change and internal causes the basis of change.

This African crisis is reflected in, among other phenomena, the total destruction of our national currencies, thanks to the IMF and the World Bank and their structural adjustment programmes (SAPs). In practically all African countries, there are no national currencies, only fluctuating tokens of the US dollar or of the French franc. All real business is conducted in terms of these two foreign currencies. The reason for this is that, except for the franc zone whose currencies (until 1994) were tied to and backed by the French treasury, the destruction of the national currencies is at once the cause and effect of the 'disunity' between the economy and the financial sector which it is supposed to service.

The disunity of these two most important sectors in the national economy has led to a killing-fields situation for speculative capital and foreign-exchange dealers. And as long as this disunity remains, there can be no reform because the two sectors remain in a perpetual state of disharmony, of one negating the other.

It is the US dollar which takes advantage of the resultant chronic disparity between the official and the so-called parallel exchange rates. All that the IMF and the World Bank can instruct to correct this disparity is to call for a better management of monetary and financial sectors. It is the monetarists' prescription for all kinds of economic ailments. But the result has always been disastrous to the well-being of the 'second liberation of Africa'. As a result, a new theme of Pan Africanism therefore requires us first of all, to ask ourselves: Do we want to continue in that prescribed role? It is clear that Africa's leadership is reconciled to this status, while at the same time calling for a 'new international economic order'. This position is also echoed by United Nations Economic Commission for Africa and the African Development Bank (which has now turned itself into a mini IMF and a spokesman for international financiers) and even by the Organization for African Unity (OAU) itself. But the elusive new world order does not seem to be anywhere near the horizon and the reason for this delay is simple: the existing world economic order is the only possible one under the conditions of the 'free' world market economy. To wish for something else is to indulge in metaphysics. But if we want a 'second liberation' in the real world, we must change our outlook, the direction of our economies and the order of our priorities. The starting point must be the satisfaction of the people's basic needs: food, housing and clothing. We must abandon, as a precondition, the old notion of looking outwards for our survival and instead, orientate the economies to look inward for solutions. External factors - trade, aid, foreign investments and loans - must only complement internal activity, but not the other way round, as is the case in Africa now.

In order to embark on this new path we need to have general, broadly applicable, principles to guide us but which at the same time could be modified to suit local conditions. In an unevenly developed continent like Africa, each region, if not each country, has its own specific characteristics which have to be taken into account before any strategy is formulated. That is why the following will remain essentially general principles to guide us in our analysis and in organizing for radical political and economic action in each specific case and region.

As Africa is undergoing rapid democratic transformation away from the political culture of the one-party states and military dictatorships to multi-partyism, it may be useful for us to have a clear view of what all this means and what our role and responsibility is in providing political leadership.

Although 'free marketeers' want to link free-market objectives as part and parcel of the democratic transformation, we must keep in mind that the two are not necessarily linked. You can have one without the other. The fact still remains that there are two contending social systems, one of which is represented by social democracy, in which the interests of the society as a whole or the community are paramount. The radical tradition stems from this. The reason why the radicals pursue this social system with a bias to society is simply due to the realization that it is the natural condition of the human being. As the clumsiest among all like species, we owe our survival as a distinct species to our social instinct. We always grouped together and invented mechanisms to defend ourselves as a group. Therefore social responsibility is the essential attribute of human nature. For radicals, therefore, democracy must mean social democracy, which promotes and encourages positive aspects of individual initiatives. We may thus categorise this new era of democratic revival as the era of the New Democracy for Africa, by which we mean, if the current democratic upsurge means anything, it must mean a movement for seeking, in Nkrumah's memorable phrase, the 'Kingdom of Self-government' - a movement towards upholding the principle of 'Government by the People'. At any rate, this seems to be the interpretation and expectation of the ordinary people in Africa since the days of the struggle for independence, although the 'born-again democrats' may have a different motive in misinterpreting democracy and confusing it with 'free market'. For a government by the people to be realized and to ensure that it is by the people and for the people, Africa must have a policy and a radical programme necessary to bring about a change, to empower the people in directing and giving meaning to their political, economic and social aspirations, and to chart a new path that will take us out of the post-colonial rut and dilapidation and the current threat of recolonization. In order to do so we should begin by at least recognizing what it is that we are rejecting and what we want to replace it with. Going by our hellish experience of the post-colonial past, we can say that we are rejecting excessive reliance on a political and economic strategy of *outward* orientation, and in its place we need to firmly establish and adhere to a strategy of inward orientation in the political, economic and social direction, as outlined below.

The political direction

The political principles of 'New Democracy'

We must pursue the policy of 'New Democracy' which in essence means putting power in the hands of the people. That is to say, establishing the principle and practice of government by the people.

We must accept the thesis that, while it is absolutely essential for the radical Left to recognize the importance and role of classes in society in its theoretical perspective, we must not, at this economically backward level of our development, follow the line of 'class reductionism'. In this respect, we must accept the dialectical reality that there is 'struggle' as well as 'unity' of opposites That is to say, struggle is only one side of a contradiction and unity is its other side. Each plays its appropriate role in the course of development. Thus, in conditions of economic underdevelopment, the stress must be on unity rather than on class struggle, without of course neglecting the primacy of class relations, especially for the study of the evolution of modes of production.

New Democracy, as government by the people, must be based on a broad-based notion of the 'people', and on institutions that will ensure their democratic representation and control, as well as accountability.

While multi-partyism is essential for parliamentary democracy and for ensuring democratic representation, its establishment as a system does not in itself ensure New Democracy. Nor does it ensure the creation and equitable distribution of the national wealth. A society of mass poverty, on the one hand, and massive wealth in the hands of a few, on the other, cannot develop the necessary conditions for the creation of the national wealth to its fullest potentiality, nor can it be democratic.

To bring about New Democracy, the parliamentary system must be supplemented with and strengthened by other popular institutions and associations like the local governments, cooperative movements, independent workers, women, student and youth organizations, assemblies or organizations for environmental concerns and for minority rights, and so on. These will help unify the people at all social and territorial levels. They will also help devise a sound economic strategy reflecting the people's interests.

To ensure the above is firmly established and sustained as the dominant political culture, with enough flexibility to allow for changes when changes are needed to strengthen and further consolidate that culture, is ultimately the responsibility of Pan African radicals. It is only they, with their commitment to social justice, who must bear the responsibility to remain the 'conscience of their society'.

Radicals must, therefore, play full part in the multi-party system of their country and must ensure the supremacy of their ideas and their aspirations. They should be proud to be 'patriotic' in defence of real 'national' (people's) interests. To ensure leadership, they must have sound policies on all major national issues, and those policies must make sense to the people. They must, above all, project a credible vision of a future which the people can recognize and with which they can identify.

They must take into account what others in the political field are doing, but they must not be influenced by them. They must be influenced by their own perspective, their own world-outlook and remain faithful to their own vision of the future, single-mindedly.

These are the qualities that are needed for leadership in societies mired in poverty, but which have the will and determination to get out of it by sheer effort and reliance on the diligent labour of its people. Their immediate political goal must be the establishment of the 'hegemony of the people'. This objective can be realized only if the following is adhered to strictly: commitment to unify all the popular forces that are for radical change and struggle against all forces that seek to divide them or those who seek to sell the country to external bidders. They must commit themselves to struggle against those who seek to obstruct the democratic process or seek to hamper people's economic aspirations or undermine their well-being through exploitation for individual interests of the more powerful and more privileged.

Radicals must lead the movement to conserve what is positive in the national heritage, and change what is negative; they must commit themselves to direct national assets and natural resources to serve the people and the development of the national economy. The political aim of the radicals must of course be to achieve state power, singly or in alliance with other popular forces, in order to consolidate the New Democracy and prepare the ground for economic revival and reconstruction and the promotion of social wellbeing of the people.

Political organization for New Democracy

In order to reach state power, the radicals must organize themselves in a 'political party' that will lead the people to victory. The party must be guided by its constitution, its rules and codes of discipline. It must have a programme covering the political, economic and social policies it proposes to pursue when in power.

The party must train its cadres for day-to-day political work among the people, take up issues that affect them directly and look for ways to resolve them; learn from the people, and promote direct people's own leadership at all levels of the party organization.

The party of radicals must not be simply a vehicle to state power, but it must also be a means for establishing a culture of political consciousness and political affiliations of people in a community.

In taking over state power the radicals must establish their administration as distinct from the political organization of the party. The administration must serve the entire people within the state without regard to their political affinity or class position. The aim of the administration must be to mobilize all the people in the national effort for reconstruction. The people must always remain the object and subject of national development.

The economic and social direction of New Democracy

Before we can chart a future economic direction, the radicals must first make clear what has so far blocked the way to Africa's prosperity since independence. These obstacles can be summed up as follows:

* dependence on the developed world to help our development;
* excessive use of our socially necessary labour time in the production of useless goods for export, instead of producing useful goods for our own human and development needs;
* continuous deterioration of commodity prices which weakens our capacity for capital formation;
* unproductive use of borrowed money (and the corruption that this entails) and the consequential debt-servicing at very high and unjustified rates;
* poor energy policies that make our countries heavily dependent on oil imports for our needs thus depleting our meagre foreign exchange earnings, and
* an irrational world economic order which we cannot change from a position of weakness.

A radical economic strategy therefore must take into account all the above factors in the course of outlining its corrective policies for laying the foundation for rapid economic and social development.

Creating conditions for an economic strategy necessary for the 'second liberation of Africa'
Unify financial and economic work and stabilize prices

The key problem in most of the mangled African economies is the division between the financial and the economic sectors. Upon gaining state power, the New Democratic government must strive as a precondition to bring about the unity of these two vital sectors. This is primarily a struggle against speculative capital whose strategy and tactics can be worked out in accordance with a given concrete situation. In principle, though, we can generalize by observing that the breakup of the economies in Africa has led to the emergence of a large number of profiteers and speculators as a result of prolonged inflation and currency irregularities. Most of the private funds are therefore used for direct or indirect speculation. A large percentage of private capital is illegally used for what amounts to usury and illegal marketeering, which leads to skyrocketing prices, a tight money market and soaring interest rates. As a result the entire market is dominated by speculators, with a flourishing illegal trade in foreign currencies and precious stones.

As a rule, soaring prices stem from the imbalance between the amount of currency and commodities in circulation. Under these circumstances, speculative activities cannot be effectively checked by mere administrative means. To restore the balance between currency and commodities in circulation depends on a country's approach to economic development. For the neo-liberals and the 'monetarists' who seek all economic solutions from the point of view of money in circulation, their way of restoring balance is via monetary and fiscal policies, no matter what damage this does to the well-being of the population - unemployment, lower incomes for the masses, deteriorating standards of living for the majorities, bankruptcies for small businesses, etc. It is the way of the IMF and World Bank.

But for an economy which is concerned more about the welfare of the people, the way to restore the balance is by increasing commodities in circulation. African countries that have followed the IMF route, like Ghana, Uganda, and others which claim to be 'success stories' may show impressive economic growth figures at the cost of a fall in the living standards for the people. The current plight of the Russians and other Eastern European people shows that the IMF cure is worse than the disease. China, on the other hand, in the wake of its economic reforms, chose the way out by raising production and flooding the markets with commodities and the results are quite impressive. This is the direct method of restoring the balance.

For this kind of solution, that is, the non-administrative

or 'direct' methods or 'frontal onslaught', useful lessons can be learnt from the experiences of the post-war West Germany when Dr Erhard, then Finance Minister, had to deal with runaway inflation and speculative capital. Lessons can also be learnt from the Chinese experience of the same kind after the revolution in 1949. Both these countries, with diametrically opposite social and economic systems, utilized the same direct method to achieve price stabilization.

Expand the economy

This implies moving as rapidly as possible from the primitive mode of production, in other words, the 'simple reproduction' inherited from colonialism and entering the realm of 'expanded reproduction'. 'Simple reproduction' refers to a situation when a society produces its social wealth and then consumes all of it, including the surplus value, so that it is left with only its means of production with which to start the next production cycle. In other words, it is a static society.

'Expanded reproduction', on the other hand, refers to a situation when society conserves or saves some of its surplus in order to invest it so as to start the following production cycle from a higher level and expand its social wealth thus creating a dynamic society. A more dynamic society saves and invests more of its surplus to start the production cycle at a much higher level. In the contemporary experience since the advent of Thatcherism/Reaganism in Britain and the US respectively, and their introduction of dogmatic 'monetarism', the distinction between a more dynamic and less dynamic society is signified by the difference between, on the one hand, the successful German and Japanese economies which conserved and invested a larger proportion of their surplus value; and on the other hand, the Anglo-Saxon economies, starting from the US downwards, which consumed most of their surplus value through money exchange in currency speculation and stock exchange gambling, instead of investing in the production of goods and the creation of new wealth. Making profit out of currency speculation or stock exchange may enrich a few individuals but it does not create new social wealth; only manufacturing and agriculture create new wealth. This movement from simple to expanded reproduction crosses the most critical and decisive threshold essential for moving from a dependent to an independent national economy. Economic expansion needs rapid development of the productive forces directed at producing basic needs, an industrialization fully integrated with agriculture, and a balanced or proportionate relation between heavy industry (i.e., capital goods-producing industries, or 'machines that build machines') and light industry for consumer durables as well as wage goods. In other words, agriculture must serve industry, and industry must serve agriculture.

Learn from historical experiences in economic development

What lessons can we learn from the developed industrial world which now dominates the world economically, diplomatically and militarily? Let us look at each region's experiences.

The European and North American experience

Europe and North America have developed on the basis of industrialization. They achieved this mainly due to specific historical circumstances that obtained at the time. These include excessively cheap (almost free) labour: slavery and colonialism. This led to rapid capital accumulation and a ready 'captured' market abroad and an unprecedented population expansion at home.

In spite of its brutal history of slave labour which accelerated capital accumulation, the US experience has some useful lessons in the logic of its economic foundation which has eventually turned it into the strongest capitalist economy in the world. The US economy was founded on the production of food grains and cotton. In promoting food grains production it made the country self-sufficient in food, which is the most important basic need.

Cotton production on a massive scale, first for export to Britain, later for internal consumption, helped the United States not only to develop and expand the textiles industry, but it also helped to revolutionize that industry by the invention of the cotton gin which transformed the manual separation of seeds from cotton into a mechanical operation and raised productivity several fold.

What is more it made cotton products affordable to poor people world-wide. (In East Africa the Kiswahili word for the printed grey cloth is 'Mrekani', that is, 'American'!) The most important point in the US national economy, however, was that the textile industry provided a key link between heavy industry and agriculture. Agriculture formed the base; textile and other light industries (for example, housing construction, household appliances, consumer durables and many others) evolved around agriculture by supplying its needs and consuming its products. Eventually, heavy industry developed to supply the machines needed to build light industries and the latter in turn became the market for the heavy industry, as well as its supplier of consumer goods for the workers in heavy industry/ light industry/ agriculture, which made the US economy so well integrated internally, with an ever-expanding home-market which provided the stimulus and motive force of the national economy. However, in spite of these advantages, the US economy is still undermined by the weaknesses inherent in the capitalist mode of production with its periodic and very damaging crises.

If the US economy developed on the basis of internal (settler) colonialism and slavery, European economies developed largely on the basis of external colonization and from the income that came from the surplus labour of the slaves in both North and South America. Their economies, however, cannot provide a model for developing Third World countries because, being so dependent on foreign trade, they are extremely vulnerable to external shocks. It is only the weaknesses of the Third World countries as suppliers of cheap raw materials and consumers of imported industrial goods from Europe that keep Europe's economies more or less flourishing.

The Japanese experience

The Japanese bourgeoisie also developed their national economy at about the same time as their Euro-American counterparts. They too helped themselves to some colonial exploitation after the Meiji restoration in 1868. In 1889 Japan emerged as a modern state with ambitions to be an industrial power. After the war with China in 1895, Japan colonized parts of China. In 1905 it won the war against Russia, and in 1910, annexed Korea, and in 1915, presented China with the notorious 'Twenty-one Demands' which sought, among other things, to control China's mineral resources, especially coal deposits in North China. Japan's 'primitive accumulation of capital' was enormously helped by conquest and exploitation of foreign labour and resources. ('Primitive accumulation of capital' refers to the earliest stages of capital accumulation out of the surplus [the value of wealth created by the whole of society and then appropriated by one part of that society for its own use].) The country's development strategy followed the same path as that of Europe, and although now a manufacturing superpower, thanks to the post-war special relationship with the United States, which injected massive capital and technology into the economy, and opened the US market to Japanese goods, Japan is nevertheless extremely vulnerable to external shocks and cannot be a model for Third World development. Although the newly industrializing countries (the NICs) of Southeast Asia are flourishing on the Japanese model, thanks to massive Japanese capital and technology, they too cannot be a model for us because the circumstances and the conditions that gave them a boost - the Cold War, the Korean War, the Vietnam War, the US/Japanese market and technology - no longer exist for the majority of countries, especially in Africa.

The Soviet experience

Before the 1917 socialist revolution, Russia was a colonial power with vast resources, and was beginning to emerge as a capitalist industrial economy, enjoying large investments and loans from the West. After the revolution, foreign loans and investments dried up and the new leaders of the Soviet Union were faced with the problem of finding sources for the 'primitive accumulation of capital'. After some serious disagreements among the policy makers, Stalin (then Secretary General of the Communist Party) and his faction got the upper hand and adopted a policy of transferring massive surplus from the agricultural sector, that is, from the peasantry, in order to invest in the industrialization programme, mostly heavy industry. They called this policy 'the law of primitive socialist accumulation'. (In the socialist theory of accumulation there is only socialist accumulation, and only under capitalism do you have 'capital accumulation', primitive or otherwise.)

Serious socialist economists, led by Bukharin, opposed this proposition, arguing that impoverishing the peasantry would hamper the development of the home market, distort the balance between agriculture and industry and stifle the growth of light industry, which by its nature yields more profits owing to its quick turnover and a very short 'gestation period'. And this trend would inevitably lead to heavy industry as a primary objective (An effect of this focus on heavy industry was ofcourse to enable the Soviet Union to develop a strong armament industry to defend itself from the hostile capitalist countries of Western Europe and the United States). Bukharin and his friends ended in front of the firing squad as 'enemies of the people'!

As predicted, the Soviet policy turned into an economic disaster. Just as Bukharin foresaw, it led to a permanent imbalance between agriculture and industry, mass poverty in rural areas, and seventy years later, the mighty Soviet Union was reduced from a superpower to a humble follower of the United States. Stalin was right in one important respect. As he had predicted, his political decision to favour heavy industry as a top priority helped the Soviet Union survive the Second World War. Moreover, the Soviet Union was instrumental in the defeat of the most powerful and highly technical army of Fascist Germany. Twenty million Soviet people died and saved humanity from the brutalities of Fascism. However the imbalance in the Soviet economy led to a situation in which she was a superpower in military and space technology, but with a Third World economy characterized by mass poverty of the peasantry.

The Soviet experience was unique in that it was the first socialist country in history to challenge the imperialist powers when the Soviet Union was itself still economically and technologically extremely backward. The dilemma of choosing either economic or political priorities that faced the Soviet leadership at the time was exceptionally critical and it may not be fair to judge them purely on economic grounds. However, as those circumstances are not likely to face any African country, it is important for us to learn from the Soviet Union's economic misjudgments so that we do not repeat them in a planned economy.

The Chinese experience

After the revolution of 1949 up to 1956, China followed the Soviet model. But very soon they saw in the model the inherent tendency towards imbalance between the major sectors of the economy and therefore decided to abandon it. In rejecting the Soviet model Mao put forward his famous Ten Major Relationships thesis which were essential for developing a balanced economy. The most important of these relationships was that between heavy industry, on the one hand, and light industry and agriculture, on the other. Mao stressed that the Soviet's lop-sided stress on heavy industry to the neglect of agriculture and light industry results in a shortage of goods on the market and an unstable currency. This conclusion was not due to an inspired prophetic vision, but rather due to a full grasp of the laws of economic development. In any case, 35 years after that observation, events have proved the Maoist thesis to be realistic and correct, confirmed by the tragic collapse of the

Soviet model in Europe. China, in the meantime, is making great strides and by mid-1992, it had become the fastest growing country in the world with an annual growth rate of 12 per cent, and a trade surplus with the US alone of some 20 billion dollars, which is second only to Japan's!

What can we learn from the Chinese miracle? The one thing that is most outstanding is that while the US has achieved its balanced development, as noted above, by unique historical circumstances (slave labour, settler manpower from Europe, etc.) in a haphazard and unplanned manner, China is reaching her balanced development through:

* efficient deployment of the nation's socially necessary labour time and
* through a sensible and realistic planning mechanism of observing the cardinal principle of proportionate and balanced development of the national economy.

At her rate of current growth, China will be a medium industrial power at par with, say, Italy, by about the year 2020. As the only fastest developing (ex-semi-colonial) country without external conquest or colonization, China is probably the perfect model for all African countries to emulate.

Ideal conditions for industrialization and development

A combination of several factors as noted above, including Anglo-Saxon settler economies in America, Australia, Canada and New Zealand, created ideal conditions for advanced agriculture, industrialization and development; which followed more or less the same pattern:

* Agriculture expanded in order to feed the growing domestic populations. But that agriculture was not based on the production of coffee or tea or cocoa, the standard Third World crops, but largely on food grains, cotton, oil seeds and other industrial crops as raw materials for domestic industry.
* Influx of labour from the rural to the urban industrial areas resulted in labour scarcity in agriculture and created

conditions for innovations and capital-intensive farming, labour-saving techniques and raised productivity.

The growing demand for labour-saving techniques in agriculture-induced industries to go for the production of producer goods and created conditions for capital-goods production.

* Population growth created demand not only for more food, but also for more clothing and housing, which promoted textile industrialization and the housing and construction industry, which constituted the foundation of national economies by creating massive employment opportunities and raising living standards. Expanding industrial capacity needed wider markets beyond the home market for the finished products. Expanded industrial activity in turn demanded more raw materials from abroad.

* The ensuing competition among the industrializing countries for external markets and for sources of raw materials stepped up colonization, 'settler-ization' abroad, further technological expansion and naval superiority which facilitated further colonization. All this gave Europe, the United States and Japan the power to dominate the world economy which they exploit to this day.

What can Africa learn from these various experiences?

The above experiences of the developed countries in Europe, the United States and Japan and with the exception of China, were exceptional historical circumstances which no longer exist for the developing Third World.

There is no going back to the 'birth throes' of capitalism (slavery and colonialism) which helped Europe and the US to develop, although not for want of trying in Africa by the International Monetary Fund and the international bankers it serves. People are everywhere resisting any attempt to reintroduce the humiliating conditions of subjugation familiar under slavery and colonialism.

In other words 'primitive accumulation of capital' in our case cannot take place in the same fashion as was the case in Europe, the US and Japan, through slavery or through the savagery inflicted on the native Americans and through colonialism. But the fact still remains that we must have the wherewithal for our own 'primitive accumulation of capital' if we are to develop the productive forces and move on to expanded reproduction without which there can be no development.

Again, if in Europe and the US the massive expansion of urban centres was indicative of economic growth and has created the necessary conditions for industrialization, in Africa the expansion of urban population, on the contrary, is only indicative of the condition of rural stagnation and under-development, which in itself obstructs national development.

Nor can the mass poverty in towns and cities that we are now experiencing in Africa provide a stimulus to modern agricultural farming, as it did in Europe and in other developed countries. Nor can it be a source for accumulation as in the above cases; on the contrary, it has the effect of obstructing development and of worsening rural impoverishment, for the simple reason that our economies hardly respond to internal conditions. We only respond to 'external shocks'!

This situation in which the majority of African countries find themselves today is what is referred to as 'contracted reproduction'. In this case, a society goes through several production cycles without allowing social wealth to maintain itself and instead allows it to shrink and become less and less. Then, as in the days of 'easy money' in the mid-1970s and 1980s, society goes out to borrow money from the international money markets, not to enhance its production cycle, but on the contrary, in order just to keep it in the vicious cycle. Apparently, these economies are not even *static*; they are declining!

Can Africa emulate the past?

What can an African country do in order to develop a self-sustaining, independent national economy? We cannot of course re-create the above 'favourable' historical circumstances that have helped advanced countries to develop; nor will the latter help us develop and become their competitors. On the contrary, ever since the beginning of the 1980s, Europe and the United States have been doing everything to destabilize our economies through the IMF and the World Bank. The Bretton Woods system itself, since its inception in 1945, has been the main source of Western prosperity by ensuring a steady flow of wealth from poor countries to the rich (the net outflow, which includes the effects of debt-servicing, brain-drain and resource transfer, is currently estimated to be around 200 billion dollars a year, or about 23 million dollars per hour!). We have, therefore, no alternative except to find our own way of starting the capital accumulation process, which includes putting a stop to this massive outflow of wealth. For Africa alone the net outflow of value from the continent to the Western world is estimated at 200 million dollars per day! This amount, if retained in the continent, can be an important starting point for our 'primitive accumulation of capital'.

This means that we must be realistic and discard any illusion that anybody else can help us develop except ourselves. If we cannot recreate historical circumstances, it is within our means to at least create 'artificial' conditions which can and will induce development.

If the West achieved its primitive accumulation of capital at the expense of Africa and other colonies, and the Soviet Union achieved hers at the expense of her peasantry and her Asiatic colonies, who will Africa exploit for our primitive accumulation of capital?

Our experience since independence has shown that we cannot hope to start our accumulation via the export of primary commodities to the world market. The world market, on the contrary, has been and is the main contributing factor to our poverty and under-development for two reasons. First, we waste almost all our socially necessary labour time in the production of useless agricultural commodities primarily for export, yet we earn hardly anything to set our accumulation in motion. Thus we put more into the world market than we get out of it, which means a net loss. Any waste of socially necessary labour time has its penalty, and in our case we pay the penalty by being condemned to absolute poverty and mass starvation.

A strategy for initial capital accumulation

If we seriously want to set in motion the process of accumulation for productive investment, it is essential to first of all adopt a different world outlook in our approach to development. In other words, we must start with a different frame of mind This outlook must be based on accepting the fact that *external* causes are only a condition of change, while *internal* causes are the basis of change.

We must learn to utilize our socially necessary labour time more efficiently, concentrating more on the production of what we actually need for our own development rather than on what we hope to gain from exports. If a society wastes a large proportion of its social labour time mostly in the production of agricultural commodities for export, and gets less and less in return, as is the case in many African countries, then that society is bound to head for serious economic and social problems.

This is the state in which many African countries find themselves. We are paying the penalty for wasting our socially necessary labour time in the production of commodities which we can only sell, but which we cannot ourselves use. If there is no demand for them, or if we are offered an unacceptable price which will not enable us to buy goods needed by the society in compensation for the social labour time so wasted we face financial crisis. We cannot eat coffee or tea if no one wants to buy them! In other words, we produce what we do not consume, and consume what we do not produce. The penalty for this kind of dysfunctional national economy is, in some extreme cases, to expose the people to famine and starvation on a mass scale. Gains from exports can begin to be economically useful only when the economy is soundly based internally and the needs of the people are regularly met.

To start the accumulation process we must rely entirely on the diligent labour and skills of our own people (now wholly exploited by external forces), and on our own resources and on an expanding internal market. To achieve this we must have a people's own leadership at the helm instead of the wasteful and corrupt petty-bourgeois ones we have so far experienced. We cannot, realistically, immediately abandon production of 'cash crops' as a source of foreign exchange earning. We must have a long-term plan to minimize our dependence on such crops, the production of which takes so much of our labour time without commensurate income; and at the same time means neglecting to produce what we need for our own development. We should strengthen our economic base by importing new technology and capital goods as needed for that objective. After setting in motion the process of real national development, we will then be able to fully enter the world market on our own terms, and from a position of relative strength, like any other developed country.

We must learn to be frugal; to be, collectively, a nation of savers and not of waste-makers and vulgar consumerism that we are at the moment. This requires exceptional discipline because we cannot afford to be anything less at the start of our long journey to national prosperity.

As we are so heavily indebted, thanks to the sins of the previous governments, there are two ways of resolving or minimizing the pain of the problem. We may either renounce the debts on the 'odious debt' principle, which is a perfectly legitimate ground in international law because the people were not consulted when the debts were contracted, and the governments that contracted the debts were mostly illegal either because they were military regimes who came to power through coups, or one-party dictatorships which did not enjoy the mandate of the people. Finally, we do not have anything to show for it on the ground. Indeed most of the debts are held in Western bank accounts of our corrupt leaders.

It is obvious that most of these loans were corruptly contracted and therefore the people are not obliged to honour them. The bankers must suffer the consequences of their wrong decisions, as in any business that runs at a loss. Or they and the corrupt leaders must settle accounts between themselves, either via the Swiss banks or through courts.

The second way out is, if we accept to bear the debt burden, then Africa can collectively start to negotiate with our creditors for a twenty-year moratorium on debt-servicing and immediate freeze on interest, both of which are a major source of capital outflow. Smart bankers would naturally accept this second option.

The meagre foreign exchange that we are currently earning from our exports must be spent most frugally by carefully choosing between importing either absolutely essential consumer goods, that is, on social consumption like health service, education and transport, on the one hand, or on goods to advance our technology and on producer goods, especially machine-tool industries, that is, machines that build machines, on the other.

We must gradually change the composition of our exports and imports to conform with our reorientation strategy. Stepped-up export of manufactured or processed goods will increase our foreign exchange earnings and enable us to import advanced technology and equipment. That is to say, by gradually minimizing the production of cash crops for export and instead diverting our efforts to the development of food, housing and textile and garment industries, to begin with, in order to expand the home market and raise people's incomes. By doing so, we will be creating favourable conditions for utilizing our socially necessary labour time more efficiently and productively for people's needs. The foundation of our economy, as that of any developed economies, must be home-based

As 90 per cent of our populations are engaged in agriculture, then initially the modernization of agriculture must be our top priority, and the raising of rural incomes the motive force of our economies. By improving rural skills through production and construction -irrigation work, water conservation, fish farming, flooding control, soil improvement through intensive use of natural manure, afforestation, proper training in the introduction of technical know-how and modernization of agriculture - we will help promote rural industrialization and promote economic complementarity between the urban and rural sectors of the economy, thus solving one of the most disabling contradictions in under-developed economies, namely the urban/rural dichotomy. It will also help stem the rush to the cities by rural youths. As the Chinese slogan aptly puts it in its campaign to keep the youth in the rural areas: 'Leaving the farmland, but not the village: entering the factory, but not the city'

Our industrial development, therefore, must initially be geared towards serving agriculture, which in turn must serve industry. This strategy will help set in motion the process to a self-sustaining, independent national economy, gradually put a stop to capital outflow, and will accelerate the process of accumulation, of the development of the productive forces and thus enter the realm of expanded reproduction.

Identify areas where savings can be affected

To start with we must drastically reduce spending on the military and cut down official foreign travel, now widely abused and a big drain on our foreign exchange. Overseas embassies must be cut to an absolute minimum; limit these to five or six essential areas of significance for promoting real 'national interest', for example, the UN, Washington (IMF and the World Bank), London (British Commonwealth), or Paris (for the Francophones), Brussels (EEC), and at the OAU. Embassies are notorious for squandering foreign exchange resources, legally and illegally.

We have to learn to utilize every potential internal resource first before resorting to imports. This is most essential in the early stages of capital formation, for example, the use of natural manure instead of (imported) chemical fertilizers. For instance, one cow produces one tonne of manure annually. Tame and train some of the wildlife for production work. Wildlife is potentially a great source of energy which in many cases can be used to replace (imported) oil-driven machines. In Burma, the entire timber industry is based on elephants; in Zanzibar, the entire clove and coconut transport was based on animal-driven carts which brought much prosperity to the nation; oil milling was based on camel energy, and so on. We can resort to modern machinery only when we have a sound and prosperous basis at home. Japan utilizes the most ancient and most modern technologies side-by-side, and as a result they have achieved what we now call the 'Japanese miracle'.

We must strive to establish a most efficient public transport system which will make large-scale importation of private cars unnecessary and the foreign exchange thus saved could be diverted to importing productive inputs in the form of new technology and machines essential for increased production of consumer goods needed by the people, creating more employment and raising people's standards of living. There are several other areas for saving our limited foreign exchange resource, which can be investigated. For instance, Cuba, after being abandoned by the Soviet Union and embargoed by the US, has embarked on ingenious methods of saving their meagre foreign exchange earnings in order to continue to maintain their socialist system. There is a lot that can be learnt from the Cuban experience, both as a warning and as an economic necessity.

Above all, special attention must be paid to developing a scientific economic management capability which is essential for rapid economic transformation. So far our experience with the leadership in Africa is that it tends to be excessively 'political'. The civilian leadership pool (that is to say, where the Idi Amins of this world have not taken over state power) ranges from university graduates of one kind or another to semi-literate rabble-rousers, depending on the needs of the top man in authority at any given time, that is, to increase his popularity, to step up his security or secret police; to isolate a certain section he thinks dangerous; to step up political thuggery and intimidate the population and so on.

National economy is normally given lowest priority. An economist would be appointed as a minister of finance or economic affairs or agriculture or industry, without the faintest idea of economic management or the intended direction of the economy. Managing the national economy and knowledge of economics are two separate fields and they must be distinguished as such, otherwise the economist will make a mess at managing the economy and the trained manager will make a mess at forecasting economic trends. Economic management entails formulating policies like, for example, who is responsible for decision making? How many kinds of ownership - state-ownership, private ownership, cooperative ownership, planned or market economy or a combination of both, in which case which is to be primary? What are the intrinsic relations within the economy? How to coordinate production with marketing? How and where to invest the accrued surplus funds, for what? national, regional or district objective? What are the principles guiding the national economy and how best to attain them within a specific time frame? How to balance the two major departments of social production, that is, means of production and means of consumption? What and how to set priorities and for what specific or general purposes? Are all these to be left to the 'market forces' to determine or to a national plan or a judicious combination of the two? And so on and so forth. All these need special orientation which a university graduate or a mob-rouser may not share or be aware of. Scientific management of the economy needs training and orientation in all these aspects before launching the economic transformation exercise.

Three basic approaches to development

Within the two main social systems mentioned above, that is, the *neo-classical* and the *social democratic*, there are three methods usually adopted as a strategy for development:

* the ideological, that is, either capitalist or socialist or 'mixed';
* the economy, that is, responding only to the 'economic imperative', for better or worse, and
* serving the people, that is, the economics of the New

Democracy, which is a scientifically-based common-sense approach to development, giving priority to the long and short-term needs of the people and then organizing the economy accordingly for the attainment of that objective.

Experience has shown that the first approach has many dangers because going exclusively by the dictates of one's ideology, unchecked by the scientific method of verification, one very often tends to lose sight of the concrete realities of a given situation. Ideology must remain only as a guide to action, but never turned into a dogma. Serious mistakes have been made by both capitalist and socialist 'fundamentalists' who have refused to alter their course even when danger signals indicated disaster ahead. This shortcoming has become obvious by the catastrophic results of the ideology of 'monetarism' in the Anglo-Saxon countries in the 1980s and by the rigid Soviet model which distorted the very essence of socialism and socialist planning.

The second approach too has many shortcomings. For one thing, economics on its own has no foresight; it can forecast figures, but it cannot predict their social outcome. It can probably work for 'good economic results' but these are not always in conformity with the social or people's needs and their welfare. It is rather like the proverbial doctor who performs a technically 'successful surgical operation' although the patient dies. That is why it is said that 'national economy is too important to be left to the economists'.

The last approach is more pertinent because it is guided constantly by what society or the people need. That is why we should call it a common-sense approach. Of course, if you are dealing with developing a national economy you must have economists, but only as technicians and not as initiators of policy. The common-sense approach uses economics to justify or to subject to critical analysis what has been ordained by the 'authority of the people', to give 'indicative figures' of what might happen to the growth of the economy in the abstract if action A or B were to be taken, but not to decide whether to take A or B. That is a political decision.

The key factor contributing to the current African crisis is that ever since independence, African countries have been run on the principles of the economics-driven approach. Where you had 'five-year plans', it was the economists, mostly foreign and not the political representatives of the people who laid down 'national objectives'. This has been the root cause which has led Africa down blind alleys to virtual economic ruin. The crisis is made worse by once again following the dictates of the same foreign economists in the hope of bailing us out! In every case these economists tend to be steeped in capitalist ideologies, which have no relevance to our conditions. And they always 'get it wrong'. On the other hand, their radical opponents, mostly with socialist orientation, often tend to challenge them on the same grounds, but from a different direction. The result is a 'dialogue of the deaf' which does not reach the people because they cannot follow what the fuss is all about.

Where national economies were not planned, no specific economic objectives were set; it was only hoped economic prosperity would be achieved by encouraging full play of individual greed operating in the 'market place'. Countries like Kenya or the Ivory Coast operated on this basis and they were hailed as success stories, but actually only a handful, again mostly foreigners, benefited at the expense of the majority of the impoverished masses. There has indeed been a lot of 'economic activity', impressive office tower-blocks and so on, which gave the impression of 'growth', but in real terms the people at large have become worse off. In both these 'success' models, there are currently intense political and economic upheavals.

That is why we should stick to the common-sense approach as the guiding line of the economics of New Democracy. Whereas the traditional development theories have treated the question of poverty and deprivation as an outcome of some amoral international arrangement, and that the situation can be alleviated by means of changing the world economic system and stepped-up exports, the common-sense approach treats the situation more seriously. The causes of our poverty are not external but internal, although the external causes help to aggravate the already rotten situation. And to correct it we must seek internal solutions and then and only then, external factors may be resorted to in order to stimulate the corrective or transformatory process. But at the same time the common-sense approach must thoroughly understand the situation in the external world, that is, the world economy, because only in understanding who controls it, its history, its mechanism, its motive force and our position and role in it, can we best use it to our advantage and not allow ourselves to be used by it.

The International perspective: the slide to the status quo

As part of the world economy Africa cannot help but play her part in it and seek answers and solutions to her problems by taking into account what is affecting the continent in the context of the political economy of the world.

But there is an important distinction between trying to understand the world political economy and seeking our role in it, on the one hand and, on the other, simply being subservient to it and only reacting to it as if we are helplessly reacting to the forces of nature. In the latter category we should put the new African elites, the decision makers, who are inordinately influenced by the multilateral agencies, like the old elites before them who were brainwashed by the colonialists. They do not seem to be able to take the initiative on any major issue affecting their countries. They simply sing the tune of the prevailing refrain orchestrated by the imperialist powers. They are propagating the notion of the 'global management of an interdependent world', which really means managing the status quo for the benefit of the imperial powers and at the expense of the poor countries. This is not the way of looking for solutions to our problems within the context of the world economy. This is a futile pretext of seeking solutions to the status quo from within the status quo!

It is an attempt at seeking adjustments within the same old economic world order without attempting to change our own role in it, beginning with changing our own economies as a precondition to a new order. It is a negative way of seeking to establish the 'new international economic order' while we remain in the same economic status of commodity producers. That kind of 'globalism' is meaningless; it is only a way of intoxicating the poor with hope.

The real world economy, in fact, is not interdependent; it is an exploitative arrangement whereby one section of the world benefits from the weakness and backwardness of the other. And it is in the interest of the former to maintain the situation as it is. Africa has no power to change it, shout as we may. We can only change what is in our power to change and that is our own economies first, their structure and direction.

We made a fatal mistake right at independence. We had a choice then between siding with the emerging world socialist movement and (mercifully) being cut off from the capitalist 'world economy', or remaining junior partners in an economy dominated by the US and the ex-colonial powers from whose colonialism we had just emerged.

In Asia, only China, North Korea, Laos and Vietnam chose to join the world socialist movement which sought to bring about a completely new world order, a socialist world. In Africa none went that way, although we invented various forms of socalism ("African socialism" in Tanzania, "Workers"or People's republics in Guinea, Ethiopia, Angola, Mozambique, Somalia, etc.) to fool the masses while we were putting them more firmly under the grip of Western domination.

In a comparatively short time, China and North Korea became medium-sized industrial powers, largely self-sustaining, while the rest of us became more and more maldeveloped, with millions of new social problems emerging by the day. But in the case of China, by mid-1956, with extraordinary foresight she had abandoned the Soviet planning model which had the fatal weakness of emphasising the development of heavy industry at the expense of light industry and agriculture; instead, China decided to put in practice the Maoist strategy which came to be known as the Ten

Major Relationships. In rejecting the Soviet and East European model, the Maoist thesis pointed out that: "the lop-sided stress on heavy industry to the neglect of agriculture and light industry results in a shortage of goods on the market and an unstable currency". Thirty-five years later, this observation has proved to be remarkably correct with the tragic collapse of the Soviet system in Europe, while China continues to make great strides in her economic performance and modernization.

In spite of the inherent weakness in the Soviet model, however, the West could see in it the potential for becoming a serious challenge to the West's strategy of world domination, or hegemony. The West, therefore, decided to fight it to the finish, with all its enormous advantage over the young emerging socialist system. When Africa began to gain its independence, this war against socialism was at its peak. Africa, consciously or unconsciously, decided to side with the West against socialism, at the same time declaring ourselves to be non-aligned between East and West! It was never explained how anyone can honestly be non-aligned between a just and an unjust system. In any case, we decided of our own free will to place our countries under the sphere of influence of the West as junior partners and we were condemned never to see any serious development of the continent, collectively or individually. As long as we remained in this demonstrably unjust world economic system from a position of weakness, with circumstances so heavily weighted against us, there was no way we could attain any form of development beneficial to ourselves.

What, therefore, are the causes, both external and internal, of the African crisis?

External causes of the African crisis

The 'modern' world economic order was created soon after the anti-Fascist war in 1945. It was designed to continue with the war by other means; this time against the socialist order which was then emerging as a system that could provide an alternative to the status quo, especially to the poor countries. Thus, the first Conference to reestablish the old system in a new guise was held at Bretton Woods in the United States, and the system became known as the Bretton Woods System. Its declared objective was to stabilize international monetary and financial regimes which were disrupted in the pre-war period of the 1930s, to help the Western world's economic recovery and to combat socialism in the post-war era. The main institutions created for the job were the World Bank, the IMF and GATT (the General Agreement on Tariffs and Trade), all of which were at the same time designed, in addition to recovery, to strengthen the Western grip on the world economy. We became members of all of these institutions soon after independence Thirty years on, we have already been demoted from the status of independent and honourable members of these institutions to that of their 'obedient servants'.

It will be useful for those who urge us to deepen our involvement in this economic arrangement in the spirit of 'interdependence' to remember that at no time has the system ever worked in our interest and there is no evidence to show that it might do so in the future. The alleged 'interdependence' can only be of the kind in which we are permanently dependent on the West's massive exploitation of our human and material resources. The system itself has a long history starting from the dark epoch of the slave trade, to colonialism and imperialism, and in all of these phases Africa has remained its constant victim. An interdependent world indeed! But we need not go too far into the past. Our immediate purpose is to have a full grasp of the current international economic order in order to find the way out of our problem.

The nature of the contemporary global economy

To come to the nitty-gritty of this modern world economy, it is of primary importance to first of all understand the role of international finance as a major force that lubricates it. Very briefly, there have been three significant areas of international finance. The first was between 1870 to 1914 which was dominated by Britain. The second was between 1920 to 1929 when the centre of international finance shifted from London to New York, but it collapsed in 1930 with the Great Depression followed by the Second World War. The third era - the era of US hegemony, the Bretton Woods era - started in 1947 until 1985 when the US itself was reduced from a creditor to debtor country as Japan replaced it as the world's foremost creditor nation.

The decline of US hegemony, which inevitably cost Africa a lot owing to her dependence on the dollar (for example, for every 1 per cent rise in interest rate, the debtor countries have to pay four to five billion dollars in interest!), was brought about by excessive irresponsibility of US policies: the over-printing of the paper dollar (more than 600 billion dollars!), mismanagement of the international monetary and financial systems, adventurist wars of aggression (Korea, Vietnam and others), the advent of Reaganomics and its monetarist orthodoxies and so on. In other words, the US used the system to its own advantage and became the root cause of the global economic problems of the 1980s, the debt problem being the most significant one for Africa.

The debt burden made debtor countries even weaker while correspondingly the creditor countries, under the IMF leadership, gained strength through its insistence on conditionality and reliance on the old imperial policy of divide and rule over debtor countries so that they would not form a united front of debtor countries and negotiate from the strength that this unity would bring. Although the debt crisis, like the crisis in the monetary and financial systems, was brought about by the actions of creditor countries themselves, the responsibility is placed on the debtor countries: the developed countries dumped loans and capital into the Third World, seeking a large return in interest. Unequal trade terms cut into Third World export income, weakening their ability to service their debts on time. And of course, the rise in interest rates has compounded the African crisis.

Furthermore, the failure of the misdirected struggle launched by the Third World for the so-called New International Economic Order which had sought to bring the multilateral financial agencies, the IMF and World Bank, under the jurisdiction of the UN General Assembly, has helped to absolve creditor countries from any responsibility for the debt crisis. That failure has actually strengthened the position of the IMF vis-a'-vis Third World countries. From then on, it has continued to impose its own 'conditionality' on African countries with impunity, resulting in massive unemployment, a steady decline in the living standards of the people and spreading domestic political instability, with all its devastating consequences. Ironically, one of the original purposes for which the IMF was created, in addition to facilitating world trade, was to promote employment and general well-being!

Under the existing conditions of this 'interdependent' world, there is no way that Africa can repay its external debt, estimated conservatively at 300 billion dollars, while the net outflow of wealth from Africa to the West continues to mount, leaving nothing for domestic capital formation and investments. Conservative estimate puts that outflow at nearly 200 million dollars per day, and mounting!

The declared principles of the multilateral agencies and their relationship with the new countries, as they were emerging from colonialism and joining the institutions, were defined as providing aid to assist developing countries to reach a point where they could 'participate fully in an open, market-oriented international economy' and that aid policies were to be subordinate to the norms of the market system. But even in those early days it was clear that, as far as the emerging countries were concerned, this objective contradicted the principle of national sovereignty because it frustrated the right to development of these young countries by forcing them into a world market system which was itself not open, not free and extremely imperfect, favouring only the strong against the weak.

Comparative advantage and free trade

For their part, the dominant nations always insist that 'all's fair in trade and war'. But this is acceptable only as long as you are in a dominant position! Their interpretation of 'fairness' was elevated, long ago, to a principle known as the 'comparative advantage' principle. Its history, as we know, goes far back to the philosophy of the British philosopher, David Hume, and was later expounded in the economic theories of Adam Smith and David Ricardo in post-Industrial Revolution Britain when it dominated world trade. To this day, this 'law' has remained the basis of liberal 'free trade' theory. Our elites who are now blindly advocating the notion of an interdependent world use arguments stemming from theories based on this 'law', ignoring the fact that it was conceived and applied by Britain at a time when it had all the advantages over other nations.

But even then weaker nations had a different approach and were very critical of the comparative advantage thesis. They saw in it a serious threat to their own national security, domestic welfare and industrial development. This must be even more so today for countries whose economies and foreign trade are largely based on primary commodities. Can there really be any comparative advantage between the peasant producer of, say, coffee or tea and the industrial producer of the tractor from whom the former has to buy his inputs? The only advantage is the absolute advantage to the industrial producer. As a matter of fact, our present experience proves to us, again and again, that the industrial producer countries find this system of 'free trade' so advantageous to them that they are prepared to use force, via the IMF and the World Bank, (or even in a bilateral form as in the case of Cuba versus the US), against any poor country that tries to embark on an independent route to development or which dares to resist their dictation or challenge their hegemony.

Historically, even the mighty Germany of the last century found it necessary to protect its economy, dignity and sovereignty against what they dubbed the 'imperialism of free trade'. This was at a time when Germany was already becoming an industrial power in its own right, it realized that it would not be to its advantage to abide by the thesis of comparative advantage and free trade when it was still weak compared to Britain, which then had only a decade or so head-start over Germany. Similarly, for the poor and weak countries of Africa today, like the then poor and weak countries of the last century, the primary preoccupation must not be a blind adherence to the international trade norms or belief in the 'law' of comparative advantage which is really the law of the strong over the weak, but to produce for their own needs, that is, the need to strengthen their state systems so that they do not become vulnerable to the dictates of other interests. Secondly, they must struggle for the attainment of unity of state and nation in a continent so mangled and fragmented by slavery and colonialism. Thirdly, it is vital to reorient the economy so as to achieve a unity between industry and agriculture, a precondition for integrating the economy internally and evolving an independent national economy in place of the present colonial economy. You may call this 'economic nationalism', but all countries that started late on the road to development (Germany, the US, Japan, the Soviet Union, China, etc.) had to resort to this development strategy and history has proved them right. Why should Africa be the exception?

Internal causes

In the wake of the economic crisis and the debt problem which have put Africa in its most serious socio-political plight, various 'alternative' strategies are being offered from different perspectives. As noted above, there are three main approaches to development, the ideological, the economistic and the common-sense approach. So far the alternatives that have been outlined for Africa are either of the first or second type, but none from the point of view of the 'common-sense' approach.

The Lagos Plan of Action was designed to be operative from 1980 to the end of the century. Its objectives are the achievement of:

- regional food self-sufficiency,
- the provision of shelter, health care, housing,
- sustained growth and development and
- national and collective self-reliance.

There is also the African Priority Programme for Economic Recovery during 1986-90, adopted by the United Nations. This was followed by the African Alternative Framework to Structural Adjustment Programme, by the UN Economic Commission for Africa (UNECA). All these ambitious programmes were motivated by honourable intentions, no doubt, but so far none of them has produced any hopeful signals. On the contrary, we are more than halfway through the Lagos Plan of Action, and indications are that Africa is worse off now than it was in 1980 when the programme was launched.

We have already gone beyond the target of the UN Priority Programme for Economic Recovery and we have seen no recovery at all, anywhere. The African Alternative Framework sounds more like a theoretical debate between UNECA and the World Bank rather than a serious strategy for Africa's alternative policy. That is why it has failed to be anywhere near achieving its stated objectives. The reason why all of these so-called alternative programmes have failed is because they all start from the same premise, namely that Africa has no alternative except to go for an export-led development strategy. That is to say, Africa must rely on the export of its primary commodities to earn foreign exchange to enable it to import its domestic needs. That is why, on the basis of this rationale, we see Africa's cities and towns jammed with all types of foreign cars when we cannot even produce spare parts locally to service them! The concrete reality is that this strategy is inapplicable to Africa's current level of development based on its present production structure. Its acceptance as the linchpin of policy goes counter to the basic law of development which, as we saw, asserts that internal causes are the basis of change, while external causes remain only as conditions of change and not the other way round. Any country that tries to alter this reality is doomed to failure.

The internal causes of the crisis aggravated by the debt burden may be summarized as follows. In addition to the topsy-turvy structure of our economies which gravitated outwards rather than inwards, a new phenomenon entered the world economy. The oil crisis of 1973, the transfer of massive surplus 'unwanted' dollars to the oil-producing countries and their recycling them back to the Western banks created a crisis of surplus of unusable funds (unusable because no developed country wanted to take responsibility for the overprinted 600 billion US dollars). As foreign banks were thus eager to dump their 'petro-dollars' and other surplus funds in the mid-1970s, African countries recklessly borrowed and fell into the debt trap. They failed to draw up comprehensive repayment timetables, taking into account the total amount of the debt incurred, the investments absorbed, interest due for payment, their foreign exchange reserves, development of the productive forces, exports, the foreign exchange to be earned, the growth rate and target of their national economies. The resultant imbalance between the debt incurred and income forced them to incur new debts to pay for the old ones.

Secondly, inappropriate use of foreign loans resulted in poor economic performance and low foreign exchange earnings. Loans largely went into financing consumption (for example, building brand new capital cities, ultra-modern airports, and so on) and hardly any went into the development of the productive forces, which in turn weakened economic efficiency and earned no surplus.

A realistic alternative strategy for development

Africa won its independence on the strength of its 'political' nationalism. Unlike European nationalism, which has mostly expressed itself in jingoistic terms, African nationalism is anti-imperialist, anti-predatory and anti-jingoism - it is a nationalism of resistance and therefore, progressive in essence. But we must not limit it only to political aspiration, it must extend to the economic struggle. While we remain internationalist in outlook, we must base our internationalism firmly on our nationalism - this time it is the nationalism of survival!

what then is the scientifically-based commonsense approach? Our primary purpose is to change the economic structure from its present colonial orientation. The new structure must seek to increase the production of goods needed by the people. To achieve this objective the national economy must establish sound relations between its different branches, within each branch, and between all the links in production. The human resources, and material and financial resources of society must be utilized rationally.

Lastly, the improvement of the people's livelihood must be directly linked with the development of production and construction in such a way that they promote each other. This structure will ensure a continuous growth of the national income.

The strategy for this objective in principle, with each country devising its own detailed strategy taking into account specific national conditions, can then be summarized as follows:

1   Discard any illusion about export-led development for economies with extremely backward agriculture and no industry to speak of. We must, as a cardinal principle, look internally for our progress.
2   Recognize that neither the Western model of relying on the 'invisible hand' of the market, nor the Soviet model of lopsided development of heavy industry and indiscriminate nationalization, is any good to us. What we need is to make use of both the invisible hand' of the market and the visible hand of central planning and long-term programmes.
3   Move as quickly as possible, as a matter of top priority, from the primitive mode of production inherited from colonialism and enter the realm of expanded reproduction. It is the most decisive threshold on the way to an independent national economy.

4   Develop the production base in agriculture and industry, initially for the purpose of fulfilling the basic human needs - food, clothing and shelter; in the course of producing these basics the rest will follow: employment, expansion of the domestic market, increased output and surplus funds for investment, social welfare, etc. This will arouse mass enthusiasm for production and social harmony.
5   Raise standards of living of the people by improving the quality of life.
6   Understand fully the laws of economic development and seriously study our own national conditions. On the basis of this knowledge, devise a sound policy (in addition to agriculture and industry) on energy, environment, communications and transport; promote small and medium enterprises to serve the growing home market with emphasis on labour-intensive industries to provide employment opportunities, promotion of skilled labour and the expansion of the cash economy; raise educational and modern technological standards and culture; constantly improve medical care, and develop a sound policy on foreign investment in order to make effective use of foreign capital without losing national economic independence. We must also develop a sound foreign trade policy in order to put foreign earnings to full and productive usage. All these objectives must be guided by a policy of prudence and frugality in both the public and private sectors.
7   On the debt question: short of declaring 'odious debt' we must negotiate urgently for a twenty-year moratorium on debt-servicing and interest-freeze to allow the national economy to pick up reconstruction momentum. To be effective, this can best be done maximally, on a continental or at the minimum, regional basis in collaboration with other African countries.
8   All this requires a dedicated leadership, honest and incorruptible.

It can and must be done if Africa is not to be recolonized!

Notes

(1) This paper presented at the 7th Pan African Congress in Kampala 1994 appeared in 'Pan Africanism - Politics, Economy and Social Change in the Twenty-first Century' ,(Ed) Tajudeen Abdul-Raheem, Pluto Press 1996

Some key dates in the life of A.M.Babu

22 September 1924 — 5 August 1996

1924   Babu was born in Zanzibar on 22 September to parents whose ancestry went back to South Yemen, Comoro Islands, and Pate on the Kenya coast.

1944   Started work as a weighing clerk at the Clove Growers' Association in Zanzibar

1951   Went to Britain for further studies — initially he studied accountancy but soon changed to philosophy and politics.

1953   Became Secretary of the East and Central Africa Committee of the Movement for Colonial Freedom; was on the editorial board of the Paris based revolutionary magazine Afro Asian Latin American Revolution

1957   Returned to Zanzibar to reorganise the Zanzibar Nationalist Party into the largest mass party in East Africa

1958   Attended the All African People's Congress in Accra, Ghana and was among those who set up the Pan African Movement for East and Central Africa PAFMECA

1959   Visited China for the first time and met the leaders of the Communist Party of China

1962   Was imprisoned by the British on charges of sedition and detained for nearly two years

1963   Babu left the Zanzibar Nationalist Party with many others in the left-wing of the party and launched the Umma Party which drew in a cross-section of Zanzibari youth across class and ethnic divisions

1964   Sultan of Zanzibar — a British puppet overthrown by the Zanzibar Revolution on 12 January, People's Republic of Zanzibar established, Babu became Foreign Minister in the new government

22   April Union of Zanzibar and Tanganyika was signed by respective Heads of State and Tanzania was formed, Babu was not consulted and was in

fact out of the country.
May, Babu was offered and accepted a post in the Tanzanian cabinet. Attended UN session as leader of Tanzanian delegation
In December 1964 addressed mass rally in Harlem with Malcolm X

1965 Babu and Nyerere on state visit to China

1972 February dismissed from the Cabinet by Nyerere. In April arrested with 40 other members of the Umma Party and detained in prison in mainland Tanzania

1975 Tried in absentia for treason and sentenced to death by firing squad

1978 April releaseded from prison along with other Umma Party members after a prolonged international campaign

1979 Took up academic post at San Francisco State University and University of California, Berkley

1981 Moved to Amherst College Massachusetts

1984 Moved to Britain and based himself in London.. In October, Babu visited Zanzibar for a brief visit

1985 Visited Eritrea then at the height of its struggle for liberation and on his return wrote the first articles about the struggle from an African perspective

1985 - 1996 established close links with a number of other liberation struggles fighting neo-colonial regimes most significantly in Uganda and Ethiopia and was effectively a mentor to the leadership of these movements

1992 Took up academic post at Birkbeck College, London University , teaching international relations

1995 Returned to Tanzania to contest the first multi-party election as Vice Presidential candidate for the opposition NCCR Maguezi but was prevented from standing by legal hurdles set up by the ruling CCM party.

Sources other than books from which Babu's articles have been reproduced

African Concord, London and Lagos
Africa Contemporary Record, New York
Africa Events, London.
Africa Now, London.
Africa World Review — journal of the Africa Research and
   Information Centre, London
East Africa and the Horn, London
Inqilab — magazine of South Asia Solidarity Group, London
New African, London
Pacific News Service, San Francisco
Red Pepper, London
South, London
Southern Africa Political and Economic Monthly, Harare.
Third World Book Review, London

INDEX

AAPC, 95-96, 99, 101
Accra, 63-64, 95-96, 101-102, 133-134, 159, 344
Addis, 45, 59, 72, 74, 111, 143, 160, 233, 241
Afewerki, Isaias, 101, 106
African Socialism, 220-221, 283, 332
aid, 6, 11-12, 18, 22, 27, 37, 39, 41, 47, 51-55, 91, 104, 109, 127, 136, 160-161, 170-171, 183, 185-186, 193-194, 224, 240, 258, 302, 306, 336
Algeria, 37, 48, 65, 91, 102, 110, 137, 154, 160, 167
Angola, 70, 75-76, 92, 103, 141-142, 150-151, 157, 180-182, 186, 196, 244, 269-270, 332
Arusha, 16-18, 21, 70, 76, 112, 154, 156-157

Banda, Hastings, 144-145, 152
basis of change, 39, 223, 305, 323, 339
Ben Bella, Ahmed, 102
Berlin Conference, 24, 28, 89
Botha, 144, 162, 181
Brandt, Willy, 36, 120-121, 156
Bukharin, Nikolai, 291

Camp David, 161, 166
Casablanca, 179, 189, 233
China, 29-34, 40-41, 45, 49, 65, 86, 116, 123-124, 135, 154-155, 166-167, 169, 171-174, 189, 194, 206, 226, 259, 269, 281, 293, 296, 312, 316, 318-320, 332-333, 338, 344-345
Chinese revolution, 166, 169, 318
Chou-en-lai, 166-168
colonialism, 4-5, 24-27, 63, 65, 73, 75, 79, 86, 89-91, 96, 101-102, 105, 175-176, 190, 201, 205, 212-213, 237, 264, 278, 284, 289-290, 269, 314-316, 320-321, 332, 334, 336, 338, 341
Cuba, 181-182, 227, 327, 337
Cultural revolution, 30-31, 33

Dar es Salaam, 9, 74, 255, 283
debt, 12, 14, 24, 40, 71-72, 82, 105, 131, 133-134, 173, 188, 225, 324-325, 335-336, 338, 340, 342
democracy, 12, 29, 31-33, 54, 128, 156, 184-185, 190, 197, 201, 203, 205-207, 209, 211, 213, 215, 217-228, 247, 265, 273-274, 286, 306-308, 310-311, 329-330
Deng Xiaoping, 31
DuBois, W.E.B., 95, 101
Dumont, Rene, 15, 23

East Africa, 25, 62-64, 75, 89, 96, 101, 105, 140, 142, 159, 164, 168, 177, 255, 258, 315, 344, 346
East African Community, 68-70, 112
ECOWAS, 68, 93
Egypt, 40-41, 45, 78-80, 91, 108-110, 134, 137, 142, 159-162, 189, 192, 208, 234, 247, 281
Engels, 9, 256, 288-289
Eritrea, 80, 89-90, 93, 103, 105-

106, 109, 111, 167, 182, 210, 231-234, 236, 238-242, 345
Essack, Karim, 283
Ethiopia, 40-42, 52, 78, 80, 90, 103, 105-106, 108-109, 111, 160, 162, 164, 182, 187, 189-190, 210, 232-235, 278, 280, 332, 345

Fanon, Frantz, 102
FRELIMO, 150, 276

Gadaffi, 139, 142, 211-212
Garvey, 95, 101, 159
GATT, 19, 117, 132, 334
Ghana, 63-64, 90, 92, 95-96, 101, 133, 159, 162, 189, 193, 220, 312, 344
Gorbachev, 86, 187-188
Great Leap Forward, 29, 171
Gromyko, Andrei, 191-192
Group of 77, 51, 213
Guinea Bissau, 75
Gulf War, 127, 132-133, 136

Ibn Khaldun, 286
IGAD, 107-112
IMF, 19, 48, 87, 98, 117, 121, 130, 132, 169-170, 180, 186, 226-227, 250, 269, 271, 304-305, 312, 322, 326, 334-337
Israel, 79, 85, 109, 111, 129, 134, 159-165, 234-235, 239

Kagame, Paul, 103, 106
Kampala, 69, 103, 154, 157, 247, 343
Kaunda, Kenneth, 159
Kenya, 11, 48, 61, 64, 68-71, 101, 108, 112, 140, 142, 157, 162, 168, 177, 184-185, 190-191, 202, 280, 330, 344

Kenyatta, Jomo, 101
Khomeini, 85, 109, 244
Kinshasa, 63, 141
Krushchev, 33

Lagos Plan of Action, 36, 41, 72, 82, 338-339
Liberia, 160, 162, 177, 189, 199, 208, 242
Libya, 54, 80, 108, 141, 143, 162, 189, 281
Lome, 87, 98, 189, 271
Lubumbashi, 74
Lumumba, 8, 63-66, 101, 196

Malcolm X, 84, 86, 97, 345
Mamdani, Mahmood, 272
Mandela, 144-145, 181, 244-245, 251
Mao, 8, 31, 33, 85, 173-174, 266-267, 269-271, 318
Marx, 256, 286-289, 292, 296
Marxist, 126, 157-158, 179, 253, 255-259, 261, 263-265, 267, 269-273, 275-283, 285, 287-291, 293, 295, 297
Marshall Plan, 148, 175
Mauritania, 67, 189
Mboya, Tom, 159, 177
Mengistu, Haile Mariam, 234, 239
Mitterand, Francois, 156
Mobutu, 101, 160, 162, 211, 225, 270
Monrovia, 179, 189, 233
Mozambique, 70, 75, 92, 103, 150, 152, 157, 182, 186, 190, 210, 233, 244, 332
MPLA, 74, 76, 146, 150, 276
Mubarak, Hosni, 109, 111
Mugabe, 10, 145-146, 277-278
Multinational corporations (MNCs), 303
Museveni, 81, 103, 106
Mwanza, 59

Nabudere, Dan, 272
Namibia, 71, 92, 141-142, 157, 181-182, 186, 232, 244
Nasser, 91, 109, 115-116, 160, 189, 191-192, 208-209, 281
Neto, Agostinho, 73
New Democracy, 12, 29, 31-33, 128, 220, 224, 265, 273-274, 307-308, 310-311, 328, 330
New International Economic Order, 39-41, 174, 181, 231, 305, 332, 335
NGOs, 53, 55, 112
Nkrumah, 8, 60, 64, 90-91, 101, 115-116, 159, 189, 191, 193, 220, 233, 307
Non-alignment, 115-117, 123-124, 126, 133, 189
Nyerere, 8, 17-18, 74, 76, 86, 90-91, 144, 159-160, 168, 173, 222, 280, 345

OAU, 24, 28, 36-37, 40, 42, 67, 72, 74, 78-83, 89-93, 105-106, 111-112, 138, 140-143, 151-152, 159-161, 164, 168, 212-213, 232, 234, 238, 305, 326
Obote, Milton, 177
OPEC, 129-130, 161

PAFMECA, 59, 61, 63, 96, 344
Patrice Lumumba, 63-64, 101
Pearson Commission, 6
Perestroika, 179, 183-189
productive forces, 12-13, 31, 132, 148, 170, 265, 274, 287, 293-294, 314, 321, 326, 340
proportional relations, 20, 43-44

Rapid Deployment Force, 141-142, 195
Rodney, Walter, 4, 9

Rwanda, 52-53, 103, 105-107, 112, 246

SADCC, 70-72, 75, 157
Salim, Ahmed Salim, 79, 81, 83
Sankara, Thomas, 208-210, 214
Shivji, Issa, 272
Somalia, 52, 67, 93, 105, 107-108, 112, 135-136, 142, 189-190, 280, 332
South Africa, 10, 48, 67, 70-72, 75-76, 85-86, 92, 101-102, 138-139, 144-145, 148, 150-152, 154-155, 157, 159, 161-164, 167, 180-181, 186-187, 202, 210, 212-213, 219, 232, 243-245, 247, 249-251, 277, 346
structural adjustment, 82, 98, 105, 227, 305, 339
Sudan, 80, 105, 107-111, 136, 142, 187, 190-191, 205, 242, 247, 278
SWAPO, 141-142, 244

Tajudeen Abdul-Raheem, 99, 343
Tanzania, 16-23, 48, 69-70, 74, 76, 86-87, 90, 103, 112, 144, 154, 156, 158, 160, 168-169, 172, 232, 239, 247, 272, 276-277, 280, 283, 332, 344-345
TAZARA, 33
trade, 17, 19, 32, 51-52, 55, 67-70, 72, 86, 91, 100, 123, 149, 151, 159, 162, 177, 180, 183, 187, 195, 210, 227, 235, 267, 271, 295, 306, 312, 315, 319, 334-338, 342
Truman Doctrine, 175, 193

Uganda, 59, 68-70, 81, 103, 105-106, 108-109, 111-112,

144, 154, 160, 168, 177,
190, 219-220, 222, 247,
272, 280, 312, 345
United Nations (UN), 3, 35-37,
39, 65, 68, 82, 100, 105, 107,
112, 117, 123, 127-128, 136,
143, 157, 180, 182-183, 190,
192, 213, 232-234, 246, 271,
326, 336, 339, 345
UNCTAD, 51, 121, 214
UNITA, 74, 76, 146

Vietnam, 33, 65, 129, 237, 259,
270, 281, 316, 332, 335

World Bank, 11, 19-20, 27, 35,
37, 48, 82, 87, 98, 104,
117, 130, 132, 169-170,
180, 186, 226-227, 258,
269, 271, 304-305, 312,
322, 326, 334, 336-337,
339

youth, 84, 157, 188, 210, 219,
281, 308, 326, 344

Zambia, 70, 74, 76, 144, 184,
232, 280
Zanzibar, 59, 61, 101, 166-168,
327, 344-345
Zimbabwe, 10-11, 14, 37, 70-71,
92, 190, 212, 214, 244,
277